Building Soils Naturally

INNOVATIVE METHODS
FOR ORGANIC GARDENERS

Phil Nauta

Building Soils Naturally

INNOVATIVE METHODS FOR ORGANIC GARDENERS

Phil Nauta

ACRES U.S.A.
GREELEY, COLORADO

Building Soils Naturally

Acres U.S.A.
P.O. Box 1690
Greeley, Colorado 80632-1690 U.S.A.
970-392-4464 • 800-355-5313
info@acresusa.com • *www.acresusa.com*

Printed in the United States of America

Publisher's Cataloging-in-Publication

Phil Nauta, 1981-
Building soils naturally / Phil Nauta. Greeley, CO, ACRES U.S.A., 2018
xvi, 306 pp., 23 cm.
Includes index and bibliography
ISBN 978-1-60173-033-6 (trade)

Text from the "Weeds" chapter is excerpted from *Weeds, Control Without Poisons* by Charles Walters, © 1999, Acres U.S.A. Illustrations were created by Regina Hughes, originally published in *Selected Weeds of the United States* and *Weeds in Kansas*.

Effective Microorganisms™ and EM© are registered trademarks of EM Research Organization (EMRO). EMRO's products are distributed in the U.S. and Canada exclusively by TeraGanix Inc.

While the words "organic" and "natural" do have very specific legal definitions under various governing bodies around the world, in *Building Soils Naturally*, these words are used to define practices and products that are beneficial to plants, soils, animals, people and the planet.

1. Gardening — soil — improvement. 2. Gardening — organic. 3. Gardening — techniques.
I. Nauta, Phil, 1981- II. Title.

S593.N38 2012   631.4

Dedication

To Heide Hermary,
the co-founder of Gaia College and author of
Working With Nature — Shifting Paradigms, who taught
me many of the lessons in this book and helped give me
the framework to fill in the blanks.

Acknowledgements

Most of the lessons in this book came to me from people who have spent many years experimenting, researching, testing and teaching what they've learned. I owe this book to all of them, especially Heide and Michael Hermary of Gaia College, the folks at Acres U.S.A., and the authors in the bibliography. Big thanks as well to Tamara Schwartzentruber and my ex-wife Heather for their excellent editing skills and support in writing this book.

About the Author

Phil Nauta grew up working for his parents in their garden center. He maintained the nursery stock in the yard and did some of the landscaping. He was also in charge of maintaining their 9-hole, par-3 golf course. He continued to do this through university while he obtained his business degree and commercial pilot's license. Not content with flying, he went on to complete a certificate in Organic Landscape Management from Gaia College.

Since then, he has played many roles in the organic gardening world. He started a gardening business called Only Organic, later taken over by his sister. He received his Permaculture Design Certificate and completed a certificate in Sustainable Building and Design from Yestermorrow Design Build School. He became a Certified Organic Land Care Professional through SOUL, The Society For Organic Urban Land Care. He later served as SOUL Treasurer for three years and continues to maintain their website. He started The Organic Gardener's Pantry to sell high quality organic fertilizers. He has taught courses for Gaia College and helped put together their cutting edge online learning environment.

When he's not in the garden, he's in front of the computer trying to get the word out, or at the piano, pretending he's Duke Ellington.

Phil's Gift to Readers

Visit *www.BuildingSoilsNaturally.com* to get free bonuses for readers of this book.

Contents

Garden Action Strategies

Introduction

One of the most exciting gardening topics I've taught in a classroom setting is on the microbial inoculants called Effective Microorganisms (EM) and compost tea. The best part is when the students each take a taste from a bottle of food-grade microorganisms. EM was initially concocted for agriculture, but of course it wasn't long before some people had to try drinking it themselves. It's a liquid with many of the same microbes that are in yogurt, wine and bread, although not quite as tasty.

Actually, some people love the taste and some don't, but what's fascinating is how it can drastically improve your health. There were often a few students who weren't feeling up to par in class, and usually at least one of them would start to feel better just a few minutes or even seconds after drinking only a tablespoon of probiotic microorganisms. Sometimes the improvement would be so great that they were visibly cured. That's the power of microbes, which also have many beneficial roles in the garden. You'll be reading a lot about them in the pages that follow.

The lessons in this book apply to both ornamental and food gardens. Many of us are becoming more and more interested in growing food, so my examples often center around that. We know that most produce from the grocery store doesn't have the nutrition it used to, and we're excited to grow our own nutrient-dense fruits, vegetables, grains, nuts and seeds — even mushrooms, which are fungi.

The Romans reportedly used to salt the land of their enemies in order to create soil that couldn't grow healthy crops. Now, many farmers and gardeners do something similar to their own soil with chemical salt fertilizers and pesticides. In the last half of the 20th century, pesticide use increased by 1,000%, yet the percentage of crop loss due to insects nearly doubled. Growing food has become a war against nature. Nature is seen as flawed, and our goal is total domination.

During this same period, the majority of our topsoil has been lost. We know that the destiny of civilizations in the past that destroyed their soil has been collapse. That's why Roosevelt said "The Nation that destroys its soil destroys itself." The majority of our groundwater, lakes and streams are also polluted, along with our air.

Fortunately, the earth will eventually repair itself, and we can take action right now in our own backyards. We can vastly improve our own soil and grow high-quality food. We need to, because although agriculture has drastically increased the amount of food it can grow during the last 60 years, that food has less nutrition. Some research shows that the nutrients in our food are down 60 to 70% on average.

Our grains, for example, such as alfalfa, wheat, oats and spelt, are supposed to have solid stems. Tell this to the farmers in your area and they will probably look at you rather suspiciously. All of their grains have hollow stems. They've never seen grain with a solid stem, so they don't know that's how it's supposed to be. I'm not picking on farmers — it's just an indication of how long our food has been deficient. Most people don't remember how food really should look and taste.

You simply can't learn how to grow healthy plants in most horticulture and agriculture universities and colleges. You can learn how to grow plants that *look* good and how to kill "pests" with chemicals, but you can't learn to grow healthy plants because we've forgotten what that means. We've forgotten that healthy plants don't get attacked by predators in the first place, that nutrient-dense foods don't rot even when left on the counter for months, and that weeds can't possibly take over a lawn that's healthy. We've come to think of large crop losses to plant predators as being natural, but this is simply not natural at the scale in which we're seeing it happen today.

Despite the admittedly grim state of current growing practices, this book is an uplifting look at how we can grow food that looks like it's supposed to look and tastes like it's supposed to taste. Food that's so nutrient-dense it slowly dehydrates on the counter over several months instead of rotting in a week. We can grow food that has many, many times more nutrients than the food in the grocery store — even the food from the organic section. For this, we need healthy soil, and it doesn't happen by itself. It's crafted like a work of art. It doesn't happen just by composting, fertilizing or companion planting. It happens through a holistic approach that integrates many disciplines.

The organic movement is a positive one. The fact that it's growing so much has advantages and disadvantages. Of course, we want more organic food available to us, but now that it's big business, huge companies are coming in for the profits. The main downside of this from my point of view is that some organic food, while containing fewer toxic chemicals, isn't necessarily more nutritious than conventional food because it's grown with industrial farming methods that don't focus on creating healthy plants. There is also increasing pressure from some of these large groups to weaken the organic certification standards, resulting in food that ultimately has less nutrition and more toxins.

That's not to put down the thousands of organic producers who are trying to grow more nutritious food. Many of them are succeeding and we should definitely buy from them. The point of this book, however, is that we can do even better in our own backyards. We can grow more nutritious food than can be found in the store and market, and more healthy, pest-resistant flowers and ornamental plants than can be achieved through the use of chemicals.

This book covers how to do that, starting from the basics and getting into more advanced topics. I have a few important caveats:

My purpose isn't to propose new theories, but rather to pull together what's been proven to work already, from the research and experiences of some of the most influential experts across many disciplines, as well as my experiences putting their ideas to practice. Much of this information comes from the organic and biological farming community, as that is where most research takes place. Some of this knowledge is over one hundred years old, and some is from the last decade. I hope to take this amazing body of knowledge, which is mostly only read by a very small part of the agriculture community, and make it available to home gardeners.

This is not "the lazy gardener's guide," although I could see that being a fun and useful book which could include topics such as which vegetables are the easiest to grow and which weeds can be used in salads. It's also not "the penny pinching gardener's guide" either, although that would be an extremely important book if done well. We need strategies for growing food in our own communities and in developing countries that work with low budgets and lack of access to external inputs. It's a goal of mine to learn how to do this effectively and see if I can help out somehow.

That's not to say that I will be promoting the spending of big dollars on your garden, just that a small investment in the health of your soil is worthwhile. You also won't need to toil in the garden for hours every day in order to achieve the desired results, but a little work up front pays big in the long run.

The reason this book is not about how to garden without doing any work or spending any money is because it's about growing exceptionally nutrient-dense plants and food. If you want simple, check out *Square Foot Gardening* by Mel Bartholomew. I'm not impressed with its potential for producing optimally healthy food, but the book has done a good job of encouraging millions of people to start growing their own food because the methods outlined are inexpensive and relatively easy.

From my point of view, growing healthy food often requires work and spending a bit of money on a few external inputs, mostly in the short term to get the ecosystem working. I've included costs for the main fertilizers I use (2012 U.S. dollars) to show how inexpensive many of them are. This approach is much less expensive than the chemical programs brought about by the green revolution that have bankrupted farmers around the world. In the long run, organic can be very low cost.

The organic movement has helped us learn to build soil naturally and affordably through methods such as composting. The permaculture movement is addressing some of the cost and sustainability issues through intelligent design and use of local materials. In my mind, neither of these movements have gone far enough in providing proper mineralization and nutrient balance in the soil, but they have definitely brought tremendous wisdom to the table. The methods outlined in this book are a combination of these and other disciplines that hopefully come together to form a complete picture of healthy soil building.

I concede that I might have waited another 10 years to write this. While I've been in the gardening world practically my whole life, I've only been doing this organic thing since 2005. I still have more to learn, but I have enough knowledge and experience working with soil and plants to be blown away by the possibilities, and I just don't want to wait any longer to share them with you. I don't want to wait any longer to give you the knowledge to be able to take action on something so important — creating healthy soil for growing healthy plants. We need to start this now.

I also don't want you to rely on me as your only source of information. Seek out the books I discuss in the text and bibliography, and other books that interest you. There are some brilliant people out there who have been doing it longer than I have. Acres U.S.A. carries many of the best books.

One downside of writing a book is the feeling I have that everything has to be perfect. There's some pressure to take a stance on certain issues that is the correct stance. The thing about gardening — and life — is that there is no one right way.

I advocate an above-ground compost pile and I think some manure can help, but some people have success burying compost in a trench, and others have good reasons for not wanting to use animal products. I say you shouldn't till sand into clay because I've seen it turn into concrete, but others have done it with no apparent ill effects. I strongly support bringing a few outside inputs into the garden to get it more quickly and optimally producing, but some prefer to be more self-sustaining from the get go. In this book, I sometimes try to present both sides of issues like these and other times go with what I feel is best.

I apologize to readers who like all facts to be backed up by footnotes. I'm a gardener before I'm an author, so I didn't want to set about writing a textbook. As such, I didn't use footnotes. You can check the bibliography for additional information about any of the topics I discuss. I also have a warning — this book is loaded with information. Don't worry if you don't get all of the details the first time through. You can read it again and use it as a reference. This information has proven successful for many years, so it will stay relevant for a long time. Our knowledge is always evolving, but the overall concepts are "evergreen."

I like to look at gardening as managing a whole ecosystem instead of just separating it into parts. We are in the age of scientific reductionism, breaking things into smaller and smaller parts. This has its uses, but we often forget to step back and look at the whole system, at how the constituent parts interact. In this book, you'll learn how to address the whole system that is your garden.

The first part of this book covers the soil food web: bacteria, archaea, fungi, protists, animals and plants. Included also is how to analyze your soil both qualitatively and quantitatively in order to make garden management decisions. The biggest section follows with six strategies for creating health and abundance in your organic garden. The last section brings it all together into a garden health management action plan.

Hope you enjoy!

Phil

The Soil
& Its Inhabitants

It was night and a bacterium was sitting down to dinner in the soil. It froze as a nematode went whizzing by in search of food, fortunately in a hurry or the bacterium would have been eaten alive.

The fungi next door had been there for three minutes, but had not attacked, so the bacterium figured it was friendly. It seemed to be having fun anyway, trapping nematodes and eating them, so our bacterium considered it an ally tonight.

The bacterium had spent the day consuming bits of organic matter to help build the soil village. There are many like it, with new ones being born all the time — a good thing, since the lifespan of the bacterium is less than an hour.

And so it goes. The bacteria, the fungi, the protists, the nematodes, the earthworms and other small animals, and plants working to build the village.

Conventional soil science teaches that soil is a relatively inert medium, an anchor for plants made of sand, silt and clay and a handful of nutrients for plant growth. If soil has enough nutrients, gardener's will be okay.

Traditionally, not much has been mentioned about organic matter and next to nothing on the soil food web. In many soil textbooks, you would likely find multiple chapters on fertilizing with nitrogen, phosphorus and potassium (NPK) and next to nothing on organic matter and botany. Fertilization is seen as the number one soil management strategy in many textbooks.

Chapter 1

Plants

Plants are brilliant. Their brilliance is so often underestimated or even ignored, but let's take a closer look. They photosynthesize: they take carbon, water and nutrients from the soil and air, lounge out in the sun all day, say some kind of magic spell or something and tada — they get a bit bigger.

And then we eat them. Pretty much everyone and everything eats them. They give us energy and medicine. It's proven a successful life strategy for them and they will be around long after the last mega mall crumbles to the ground and the last humans have all moved to Mars or something.

Plants make it rain — it turns out that when you cut or burn down a rainforest, it often stops raining in that area. Plants make oxygen. They help make soil and then they help protect it. They are alchemists, the original pharmacists making all of our drugs. If you follow the steps outlined in this book and grow exceptionally nutritious food, you will be getting natural doses of plenty of compounds that end up in our most common pharmaceuticals, but without the harmful side effects that come from isolating and concentrating these compounds into drugs.

Plants are an integral part of the soil food web. Their roots work through the soil, create fresh organic matter as they constantly grow and die back, and actually dissolve rock to form soil. Their bodies turn into organic matter every autumn when the leaves fall, and also at the end of their lives.

Plants know when a storm is coming and experience electromagnetic "nightmares" when it arrives. They have musical preferences. They know how you feel about them. They know when a spider is climbing up the fence beside them. They share nutrients with each other, through the mycorrhizal fungi that not only attach to their roots, but attach to the roots of most of the other plants nearby, even miles away.

Most of us can't communicate with them very well anymore, but that doesn't mean they aren't good communicators. They certainly communicate with animals, bacteria, fungi and each other.

They invite so-called "pests" and "diseases" to eat them when the time is right. At the same time, they warn each other when they are being eaten so others can fortify. They communicate with bacteria to help them build homes right on their roots in order to facilitate nitrogen fixation, and with mycorrhizal fungi when the fungi are entering their root cells.

Plants Love Music

Plants love music. The right sounds can produce tremendous improvements in growth, while the wrong notes can do just the opposite. They are more aware of their surroundings than we think, in some ways more so than us.

If they had a choice between Gershwin's "Rhapsody In Blue" and Elvis Presley's "Blue Suede Shoes," they would probably choose the former. In fact, an experiment in Illinois where Rhapsody In Blue was played 24 hours a day under controlled conditions yielded thicker, greener plants with an increase of 40% in the weight of corn plants and 24% in soy plants.

The book *The Secret Life Of Plants*, by Peter Tompkins and Christopher Bird, details many such experiments. Another experiment showed that after two weeks, plants physically leaned 15-20 degrees towards a radio playing classical and jazz music, while they scrambled to grow away from rock music and became sick. Marigolds "listening" to rock music died within two weeks, whereas those in the classical music room six feet away were flowering.

By far the most noticeable positive reactions have been to classical Indian music. T.C. Singh, head of the department of botany at Annamalai University, did many experiments with Indian music and plants, getting amazing results. Eventually, he stimulated rice harvests that were from 25-60% higher than average, and nearly 50% higher for peanuts and tobacco. Experiments were done on many other plants and have "proven beyond any shadow of doubt that harmonic sound waves affect the growth, flowering, fruiting, and seed yields of plants".

Of course, many people think this is absurd, especially when it comes to plants responding to music. Scientists often think it may be possible, but that it must all be happening purely because of physics and not because plants prefer Debussy to Deep Purple.

It's romantic to think of plants having a taste more for the "intellectual" music, and I strongly believe this relationship between music and plants is possible after all of my studies into the amazing world of plants. In terms of music, I don't know enough to argue one way or the other. Still, I'm always more apt to listen to a sitar or string quartet over a Stratocaster electric guitar when I'm out pulling weeds in my garden.

How Plants Eat and Breathe

Plants "eat" primarily by photosynthesis. They break down carbon dioxide and water and turn them into various carbon-based molecules. They need the energy from the sun, along with proteins and minerals to make this happen. Oxygen is released during this process, which allows us to hang around this planet.

So they need carbon dioxide, water, proteins, minerals and Mr. Golden Sun. Interestingly, plants are composed of about 95% carbon, oxygen and hydrogen, so the proteins and minerals are only a small, but vital part. This photosynthesis takes places in the leaves and other green plant parts. While plants get carbon dioxide from the air, they are actually very happy to get as much of their carbon as possible from the soil through their roots. And while the roots are the major water and mineral harvesters, the leaves perform these functions, too.

The most evident part of our job as gardeners with respect to photosynthesis is just to make sure we put plants in the right sun exposure in the garden and make sure they have enough water available. Then they can then get the right amount of sun, carbon dioxide and water — all of which is 95% of what they need. This is easy enough with a little bit of plant knowledge and a water source.

As I said earlier, even though the minerals make up only 5% of the plant, they are crucial. Gardeners also have a role in making sure our soil has the right mineral balance because we are planting many things that probably wouldn't be growing there if they had the choice. Almost any soil will support some kind of plant life, but if we are particular about what plants we want to see, and if we want these plants to be healthy, there is usually some work to do.

Like us, plants breathe oxygen. While only the green parts photosynthesize, all cells breathe. The main purpose of breathing is turning those carbon-based molecules from photosynthesis into more useful forms of energy. The roots need to breathe, too, so they need air in the soil. The organisms in the soil help make big pore spaces for this air. We cannot sustainably create this through tilling or aerating — in fact, these ultimately do the opposite if done too often, and we end up with compacted soil. All we can do is make sure the soil dwellers have the tools they need to do a good job, which is what this book is about.

How Plants Survive

Plants are exceptionally good at surviving. Some have thorns to ward off animals. Some have thick bark, or thick hair, or wax on their leaves. They build themselves with ingredients that are difficult for microbes to digest.

When their branches get injured, they just discard them and grow a new one. Before they drop them, they make sure to build a strong scar, often with toxic chemicals, so predators can't get in. This is one reason why we don't necessarily want to prune all damaged plant parts or the leaves and flowers of our perennials after flowering that are turning brown. The plant will drop them when it's ready.

Plants produce chemicals for defense. Some of them are kept in a special storage area of the plant to be moved and used only when needed. Others chemicals are in the leaves all the time. Some are produced as more of a general feeding deterrent and some are quick-acting poisons. Hydrogen peroxide is used to counteract enzymes secreted by certain pathogenic fungi, while other chemicals just kill the fungi directly.

Some of these chemicals become our pharmaceuticals and pesticides. Salicylic acid is abundant in many fruits and vegetables when they are grown on healthy soil. Aspirin uses a synthetic alternative, acetylsalicylic acid, that causes all kinds of horrible side effects. I can follow my doctor's advice and take aspirin every day if I want to experience some of these side effects, or I can eat fruits and vegetables grown on healthy soil.

Some plants employ others to help defend them — bacteria, fungi, and even insects. One of the most famous insect/plant examples is the ant/acacia relationship. Certain species of acacia trees provide homes and food for ants, who in turn protect the plant from insects and even herbivores. They even prune away other plants that are getting too close. More common to all plants, bacteria and fungi colonize them from head to toe, protecting them in exchange for food.

Different kinds of plants have different survival strategies. Some plants, especially annuals, survive by simply growing really fast to get above plant-feeding animals and by producing tens of thousands of seeds from each flower. Longer-lived plants spend more time building strong root systems, difficult-to-digest plant parts and bark, and toxins.

The reason it's good for us to learn about all of these things is because in order to produce strong bark, build strong leaf scars, produce toxins, cooperate with other species, and produce many seeds, plants need healthy soil. Plants are exceptionally good at surviving, if they have the raw materials they need.

Soil, Water, Air, Temperature and Light

These are the non-living, environmental factors in the garden. This book is mostly about soil and water, but I'd like to outline briefly some interesting information about air and temperature.

I should also mention light. Plants need light of course, some more than others. Put a shade plant into full sun and it will probably get sick. The same goes for a sun-loving plant placed in the shade. Some microbes like light, too, even those in the soil. Light is guided down to the root zone along the roots. Interestingly, light intensity in much of North America has decreased at least 10% in the last 50 years from pollution.

Air

Plants are over 50% air. They're over 40% carbon, most of which comes directly from the air, and over 40% oxygen, which comes from the air and from water. They're 1-4% nitrogen, which originates in the air. While some plants are pollinated by birds, insects and other animals, all conifers and grasses and many deciduous trees rely on wind for pollination. That's how they mate. Many plants also use the wind to spread seed.

The air in most North American gardens contains pollutants that have traveled across the ocean from Asia. Pesticide spray can come into your garden from 50 miles away. Acid rain — caused largely by us through our vehicles, factories, electricity generation plants, and meat production — is causing environmental problems around the world.

As organic gardeners, air is important to us, but we admittedly don't think much about it because we don't have control over it. Sure, we can drive less, fly less, and use less power in general. We can eat less meat and not burn toxic things. But is there anything we can do in the garden? To start, it makes sense to think about air circulation across your property when you're designing your garden, and place plants and structures in a manner that allows for air movement.

Our friends in the soil need air, too. Most of the helpful bacteria and fungi are aerobic. They need air just like us. So do plant roots. A healthy soil is made up of approximately 25% air. This is not achieved long-term by rototilling or aerating the soil. In fact, that can destroy the soil structure if you do it too often without incorporating organic matter. Proper air in the soil is achieved not by us, but by the hard work of the microorganisms, insects and earthworms building themselves cities. Our only job is giving them the tools they need to do this.

The Top Five Inches of Soil

A good soil is alive with microbial life. There are the protozoa, which are the smallest forms of animal life. And there are the nematodes, little eel-like animals that are more commonly thought of as parasites. The top few inches of a soil system also hold bacteria, yeasts, fungi, actinomycetes and algae. Researchers have calculated that a doublehandful of biologically active soil will contain more units of life than there are people on the face of the earth. Aerobic life must have its air. Anaerobic life — below the top few inches — has to have an air-free environment. That is one reason eco-farmers do not like the moldboard plow. That instrument is unkind to the farmer's unpaid labor force. It puts aerobic life in airless chambers, and moves anaerobic life up to where there is air.

The top five inches of almost any soil system contains 95% of the soil's aerobic life. These bacteria, together with crop residue and organic matter, need oxygen. Humus, as the end-line result of decayed organic matter, is concentrated in the top two to five inches of soil. And humus is the life of the soil, so to speak. Its tag reads physical, but it is really the bridge between the biological and the chemical. Since most nutrient systems are prolific in the top five to seven inches of surface soil, and quite the opposite in the subsoil, field samples of soil for laboratory analysis must be taken at a uniform core depth. A separate subsoil sample directly below the surface sample will reveal numerous differences.

— Charles Walters, in *Eco-Farm*

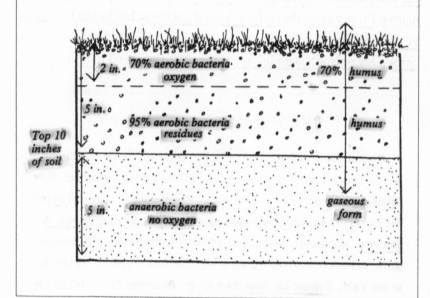

Temperature

Plants grow in a certain temperature range, which varies depending on where the plant evolved. When it gets too hot, they manufacture proteins to protect themselves, and start breathing more quickly, which means they're releasing more water, which in turn cools them. We simulate this when we spray a little bit of water on the leaves during a very hot afternoon. We used to think the water drops magnified the sun and burned the plants, but more recent research shows this isn't the case.

Before it gets too cold in the fall, annual plants have produced seed and died, perennials and other deciduous plants have stored their nutrients back in their stems and roots before discarding their leaves, and other chemical changes have occurred.

But what about the soil? In the soil, most microbes don't get to work until it's warm enough for them. The overall metabolic activity of the soil food web doubles for every 18 degree Fahrenheit (10 degree Celsius) increase in temperature. This means nutrients in the soil become available to plants in the spring just when they need them, although there may be a temporary deficiency in certain nutrients until certain microbes get moving. Phosphorus is the most important example of this. Mycorrhizal fungi are major suppliers of phosphorus to most plants and they need relatively warm temperatures to get to work. Foliar fertilizers can be useful during these times because they're quickly taken up by plants.

We also want to have enough air in our soil so that it warms up quickly in the spring. A compacted, wet soil stays cooler much longer. Traditionally, some farmers would throw rocks or other substances such as charcoal on their fields to melt the snow more quickly. In our garden, we may temporarily rake the mulch layer aside so the air and sun can more quickly warm the soil. We also want to promote a dark, organic soil that absorbs more heat, and we want a mulch layer in the winter to protect the soil from freezing temperatures, and in the summer to protect the soil from the heat. Organic matter — a crucial component of soil health — may even disappear too quickly in the summer if the soil becomes too hot.

Which Nutrients Do Plants Need?

You'll see that I will use the words mineral and nutrient, so let's clarify the difference. A mineral is solid in its natural state and can always be identified by a specific chemical composition. Many elements are minerals, such as calcium and magnesium, as are combinations of elements (molecules) such as quartz. A nutrient is a broader term that includes minerals, vitamins and any other chemical or compound that an organism needs to live.

For a long time, we thought plants needed only 16 elements from the periodic table. We know better now, although most horticulture schools and gardening books still teach this. Of course, plants need those elements and they may be the most important, but many plants also need a majority of the 80+ elements in the soil, if only in tiny amounts. We don't really know exactly what they need, but we know it's more complicated than just involving 16 elements.

I've always found it difficult to make sense of what all the nutrients actually do in plants, perhaps because it is very complex, or perhaps because I never thought it was the most important thing to remember. Yes, nutrients are important, but as to what happens when they get into the plant, I leave that up to the plant. It's still good to know a few of the basics and I'll get into this when we look at supplementing nutrients.

What we need to know for now is that plants need access to many nutrients in specific amounts and ratios in the soil, and we may need to help balance those proportions because our soils are generally out of balance for what we want to grow. Minerals make up only about 5% of a plant, but they are involved in every process that goes on in the plant. Plant tissue tests can show us how much of each mineral is in a given leaf, but that doesn't necessarily translate to how much they take up, or how much is in the soil, or how much we need to supply as fertilizer.

It's important to remember there are three elements we don't often think about because we don't generally try to supply them as fertilizers: carbon, oxygen and hydrogen. We *should* think of them because they comprise more than 90% of a plant, with the rest being other nutrients. They are present in all plant parts and involved in probably all processes that take place in plants.

Different plants evolved under different conditions, and therefore have different mineral compositions. Beans are said to be high in nitrogen and spinach high in iron. Perhaps more importantly, it appears they can sometimes take elements and change them into other elements through a process called biological transmutation. If they have an abundance of manganese, for example, they may be able to change it into iron. More on that later.

Nutrient Access Versus Nutrient Quantity

There has been some research, such as that done by Brazilian soil scientist Ana Primavesi and put to the test by Roland Bunch, showing that it's important for plants and microbes to have consistent access to a small amount of many different nutrients. In fact, that is much more important than sporadic access to a large amount of nutrients — as is the case when we pile on chemical fertilizers, or even mineral fertilizers, at one time.

Ana Primavesi did an interesting experiment. This was done with hydroponics, and it's just one experiment, but the principles still apply. She had four test plots. A regular solution was given to plot 1 every four days. Twice as much was given to plot 2 every four days. $1/50^{th}$ of the regular solution was given to plot 3 every four days, and $1/50^{th}$ of the solution was given to plot 4 every *two* days. So the first 3 plots were fertilized every four days, while the 4th plot was fertilized every two days.

Plot 2, with twice the nutrients, did not grow as well, indicating more is not always better. Plot 3 also did not grow as well, so less is not always better. Where it gets very interesting is in plot 4, which grew slightly better than plot 1, presumably because plants had more consistent access to the nutrients, even though it was at $\frac{1}{50}$th the amount.

So consistent access to a small amount of nutrients was more important than access to a large amount of nutrients all at once. This is also what organic matter does for us in soil. It holds onto nutrients and is composed of nutrients. Through the breakdown process, these nutrients slowly and consistently become available to plants, frequently and a little at a time.

Ana Primavesi, Elaine Ingham and thousands of people around the world have confirmed that plant health is improved when the soil food web is improved, one of the main reasons being that microbes make nutrients more available to plants. One simple experiment from Elaine Ingham illustrates this. Grasses grown in sterile media didn't do as well as grasses grown with one species of bacteria, which in turn didn't do as well as the plots where one species of bacterial-feeding nematodes were added with the bacteria. When the nematodes eat the bacteria, nutrients are available that can be used by the plants.

Summary

- Plant health can potentially be improved by playing music, especially Indian, classical and jazz.
- Plants have multiple means of protecting themselves, provided they can get what they need from their environment.
- Most plants need dozens and dozens of elements, not just the nitrogen, phosphorus and potassium found in many fertilizers, and not just the 16 promoted by some sources.
- It's more important for plants and microbes to have consistent access to all of these nutrients in the correct proportions, rather than a big influx less frequently.

Chapter 2

The Soil Dwellers

The "soil food web" refers to the inhabitants of the soil village. They are an army of tireless workers — 20,000 to 30,000 different species of organisms found in a teaspoon of healthy soil. We call it a web to focus on not only the different creatures living in and on the soil, but — more importantly — on how they relate and interact with each other. If you cut one silk strand out of a spider web, the whole web is affected. Each strand is necessary, and each member of the soil food web has a role to play, too.

While a few of us might enjoy getting to know what they look like, how they eat and how they move, more important to us as gardeners are the miraculous ways their interactions influence our garden, and what we need to do to encourage the interactions that support healthy plants.

We've looked at plants, and now I will briefly introduce the five other kingdoms of life in this chapter — bacteria, archaea, fungi, protists and animals — and my focus will be as much on what they do as on what they look like. You may wonder why it's so important to learn about all of these guys when you're reading a book about gardening. They're as important to the garden as the sand, silt, clay, fertilizer, water and everything else. They make the soil and maintain it. They build villages and delegate tasks based on their individual strengths.

Many are extremely small, but despite their size they rule the world — and they rule our gardens. They transform the minerals and organic matter in the soil into something that can support an abundance of life. Many nutrients won't be taken up by plants until microorganisms have converted them to the right form. Some of them pull nitrogen out of the air and change it into a form that they, and plants, can use. Some bring nutrients directly to plants in exchange for food from those same plants.

Without a vast array of soil food web players, we wouldn't have soil. They also work to protect plants from plant-feeding predators, both in the soil and above ground. Some of them eat dead things and some of them eat living things and eventually they die themselves. All of this contributes to the organic matter and mineral content of our world. Yes, a few of them also eat plants, but the vast majority are friends of plants — just like the vast majority of bacteria in our body are our friends.

If we use toxic chemical fertilizers or pesticides, or withhold water from the landscape (such as by using drip irrigation), or do a lot of deep rototilling or other soil disturbance, many of these soil workers probably won't be around for very long. Even if we do something seemingly benign, like use any of the horticultural soap products, we destroy many of them. We really, really want them to be around. Without them, our garden becomes a desert.

So rather than thinking about taking care of our plants, it might be more appropriate to think about taking care of our soil food web, including our bacteria, fungi and protists — our microorganisms, or microbes for short.

Getting familiar with them is the first step towards creating a healthy garden. Some of our most important gardening tasks involve making sure we have enough microbes. Most of our other tasks involve making sure they have what they need.

What They Need

Some microbes breathe air, just like us. They're called aerobic microbes. Other microbes die in the presence of gaseous oxygen, so they live in places where there is none, such as deeper in the soil. They're called anaerobic microbes, or anaerobes. Yet another group of microbes called facultative anaerobes can actually switch their respiration depending on whether or not there is sufficient oxygen present. The human pathogen *E. coli* belongs to this last group, but so do many beneficial microbes, such as the yeast that makes bread.

In general, we want to promote the aerobic microbes in our soil because they tend to be the beneficial ones. Anaerobic microbes are not bad in themselves, but the by-products of their respiration and metabolism include hydrogen sulfide and other ingredients toxic to plants and other soil life.

Microbes need water, some more than others. Bacteria in particular need a moist environment, whereas fungi can handle it a little bit drier. Some microbes need light. In fact, some of them photosynthesize like plants. They all function best in their own specific temperature range. They slow down when the soil freezes, some of them going right to sleep, but many of them working right through the winter. As it warms up in the spring, more and more of them wake up and get to work, just as the plants are waking up and need the services of these tiny friends.

Bacteria

Bacteria are the tiniest members of the soil food web. They are single-celled organisms — they each have just one cell. There are hundreds of millions of them in a gram of healthy compost, even a billion. Pick up a handful of good compost and you have more bacteria in your hand than there are people in the world.

How is it possible that anything is that small? I can't even fathom it, just like I can't understand how there are at least 100 trillion stars in one galaxy and 100 trillion galaxies in the universe. The astronomers have lost me here, and the biologists have lost me when I try to imagine the tens or hundreds of billions of bacteria in and on my body, 10 times as many as there are cells that make up my body.

Bacteria consume minerals by taking them in right through their cell wall. They can swap DNA and other body parts with each other, so a colony can learn extremely quickly. This could be the basis for a good horror movie. Actually, it's a real phenomenon that not only bacteria, but insects and weeds are becoming more and more resistant to our antibiotics and pesticides.

Bacteria occupy the majority of the leaf and root surfaces of a plant. They break down simple substances and toxins and aggregate the basic building blocks of the soil. Some common bacteria are Lactobacillus, Rhizobia and Pseudomonas. Bacteria are dominant in aquatic systems and the soil of grasslands, whereas fungi become more dominant in the soil of shrublands and forests.

There is another single-celled group called archaea that I lump in with bacteria, but don't tell any microbiologists that because they probably wouldn't be happy with me. Apparently archaea mostly look kind of similar to bacteria, but have genes that are more similar to plants and animals than bacteria. There are many more differences that have caused some biologists to classify them in their own kingdom. For our purposes, bacteria and archaea are classified together because their cells don't have a nucleus, whereas everyone else's do — fungi, protists, animals and plants.

Fungi

In some forests, the total mass of fungi outweighs the trees! Fungi provide many of the same services for plants as bacteria. They may be single-celled (such as the yeast that makes your bread, yogurt, wine and beer), or they may have billions of cells (like in a mushroom).

A mushroom is the fruit of certain types of fungi, but the majority of mushroom biomass is actually underground, winding through the soil kind of like a microscopic root. They form string-like hyphae, many of which join together and form a mycelium. In one minute, some fungi can grow five times further than a bacterium will travel in its whole life, though that's still too small for us to see with our naked eye.

Fungi generally eat by excreting digestive enzymes that dissolve their food, which they then absorb through their cell wall like bacteria. They eat complex organic materials that most other living things can't easily digest (such as lignin), and they harvest minerals from rocks that are virtually inaccessible to other organisms until released by the fungi (such as phosphorus). It's a good thing because plants need this phosphorus, and often can't get it themselves.

Some fungi form a special relationship with plants and actually attach to the plant root. Some of them go right inside the root, and even inside the cells of the plant. They are called mycorrhizal fungi ("myco" means fungus and "rhiza" means root). These fungi are especially good at harvesting and bringing minerals up to the plant, but they also bring nitrogen and even water.

Like bacteria, fungi get food in the form of carbohydrates from the plants in exchange for their services. Sure, some of them such as powdery mildew also eat plants, but in the big picture this is a good thing. Someone has to eat the unhealthy plants in our garden, and we sure don't want to. I haven't gone into detail yet about how microorganisms don't like to eat healthy plants. I'm saving that for later.

Some fungi also eat bacteria, and others eat the microscopic worm-like animals called nematodes. Some bacteria and some nematodes turn the tables and eat fungi, too. Everyone has to eat right?

Fungi dominate forest soils. In a grassland, the total biomass of bacteria is more than that of fungi, or is occasionally even at a 1:1 ratio. In a deciduous forest, by contrast, the fungi to bacteria ratio may be 10:1 or more, and in a coniferous forest, 100:1 or even 1,000:1.

Knowing that grassland soil is dominated by bacteria and forest soil is dominated by fungi helps us understand why it isn't always true that a field will eventually become a forest. Until the soil community changes, the plant community won't change. Where these two systems come together at the edge of the forest, a drastic change in the soil food web can occur in as little as a six inch distance. If you have a field that can't seem to grow anything other than short grass, it probably needs to be inoculated with the right microbes to support longer grass, or to eventually support a forest. There is little point in planting any trees until the correct soil food web has been established.

When we put our mulch on the soil surface, particularly a wood-based mulch, we are promoting more fungal growth. When we incorporate it into the soil, we promote more bacterial growth. Also, if we till our gardens, we cut the fungi hyphae all to pieces, resulting in a bacterial-dominated soil. Trees, shrubs, perennials and strawberries prefer fungal-dominated soil, so if we're trying to establish a shrub garden or grow trees, it makes sense to leave the mulch on the surface. Annuals and vegetables prefer a bacterial-dominated soil, so we may turn the organic matter into the top couple of inches.

Fungi only occupy 5-20% of the leaf surface, but it's important for them to be there to compete with certain disease-causing organisms. They're also very good at breaking down more complex substances in the soil, and scavenging for and holding onto minerals, especially calcium. They are the kings when it comes to building soil structure with their miles of mycelium.

Fungi have an energy to them that you can almost feel. I gained a deeper appreciation for them when I started growing mushrooms and eating them. Yes, many of us eat fungi, and some fungi eat us. It's the cycle of life.

Protists

Protists are the outcasts in the microbe world, their main distinguishing feature seems to be what they aren't — they're neither bacteria nor fungi nor animals nor plants. You may be familiar with some such as the amoeba and the paramecium.

Many of them are single-celled, but not all. Sometimes they join up to form wonderfully gooey slime molds that can actually work together as one, navigating a maze in order to get to the food hiding at the finish line. The kelp you may have seen washing up on ocean beaches (an algae now manufactured into one of the most popular organic fertilizers) is actually a protist, not a plant. Algae produce the majority of the oxygen in this world, so it's good for us that they are around.

There are also some protists that have given us some problems. Phytophthora causes blight in potatoes and was a major contributor to the great Irish famine that caused over 1 million people to starve to death in the middle of the 19th century. Another Plasmodium causes malaria in humans.

Despite the unpopular ones, protists are mostly beneficial, and — like us and all other forms of life — they're just trying to get by. A protozoan can eat 10,000 bacteria in a day. With 10,000 amoebae per teaspoon of soil, they can eat 100 million bacteria each day. During this process, nitrogen is converted to ammonium, upon which many of your plants will happily dine. We say that bacteria and fungi *immobilize* nutrients by storing them in their bodies, and then protists (along with other microbes, plants and animals) *mineralize* these nutrients — meaning they make them available again, by eating the bacteria and fungi.

Protists also form many symbiotic relationships with bacteria, where each benefits the other. Protists live in a liquid environment, mostly in the water, but some of them live in wet soil and have some similar roles to bacteria and fungi. We don't specifically talk about them all that much in gardening, but when we talk about bacteria and fungi, they're often implied.

Animals

Humans, dogs and birds are all animals, and worms and insects are classified as animals too. So are the microscopic nematodes that eat the grubs in your lawn. Some nematodes cause problems for gardeners, but most are beneficial. Many animals live in the soil as part of the soil food web, and most animals influence it with their manure. Some animals eat only plants. Some eat only other animals, but often those animals ate plants, so ultimately all animals rely on plants for food. All animals also rely on microbes.

Animals have a big part to play in the garden. Their manure is organic matter and fertilizer for the soil, and it often contains seeds transported from somewhere else that will germinate and grow into plants. Plants have been very clever to buddy up with animals for this purpose. Sure, they have to manufacture some fruit for this process to take place, but their species will live on, so it's worth it.

Plants are pollinated by animals, especially birds, bees and butterflies. The colony collapse disorder that is plaguing the bee world is a problem not only because we won't have honey, but because we're losing one of our main pollinators — and therefore our food.

Insects (such as mites) and microscopic animals (such as nematodes) are largely responsible for making minerals available to plants as a result of eating microbes, just like the protists mentioned above. They also transport microbes around the soil just by moving around. Otherwise, many of the microbes wouldn't get very far.

Just these animals being there, eating plants, walking around, howling at the moon — as we'll discover, it's all important for a healthy garden.

Cooperation and Competition

All of these members of the soil food web exist in the same space. They work together and they also compete. They fight wars for land and food and water, and they join together to produce these same things. There is competition, but there is also cooperation. None of this is bad — it's just nature. It's all good. As gardeners, we are thrilled by this cooperation because it allows us to garden, to grow healthy food and beautiful flowers.

The cooperation between plants and microorganisms is fascinating. The microbes bring food and water to plants in exchange for other food that is made by the plants. This is the original bartering system. Plants can send well over 50% of the carbohydrates and thousands of other substances they make during photosynthesis into the soil as exudates (food) for microbes. The microbes give plants the food they need in return, as well as protection from predators. These exudates are one important method plants use to build soil.

Perhaps the most popular example of cooperation is between plants and pollinators — mainly insects and birds. Plants custom-make food specifically for their pollinators, who come and get the food. In the process of moving from flower to flower, they pollinate the plants.

One of the most interesting examples of cooperation in the soil is nitrogen-fixing bacteria, many of which live in little homes right on the roots of certain plants, mostly legumes like clover and peas. These bacteria take the nitrogen out of the air and change it into a form the plants can use. Plants can't do this, but they can get carbon out of the air — something the bacteria need. Thus begins the trading that allows all other life on earth to exist.

Certain species of microbes colonize the leaf surface, contracted to defend the leaves against predators and pollution. If they aren't there, the plants won't last long. Many other species set up shop in the rhizosphere, the area right around roots where much bartering takes place. Plants send out certain foods to attract the specific microbes they need at any given time.

There are endless relationships like this. It's important for us to realize that we need all of these players in our garden in abundance. We need a lot of them and we need a diverse group. Just like we don't want to plant monocultures, we don't want bacterial monocultures, or fungal or animal monocultures, either.

In fact, if we only have a few of the 30 or so functional groups of microorganisms (groups that have similar functions, such as nitrogen fixing, decomposing, or photosynthesizing), then our garden will gravitate toward becoming a desert. We can artificially keep it alive for quite a while, but we will also see the system get more and more sick

— as we are seeing right now all over the planet. We will have more and more plant predator problems, and eventually nothing grows. We need to promote diversity in the soil food web. More important than how many species we have is how many functional groups we have.

In nature, this cooperation and competition produces environmental prosperity, and it can do the same in our gardens. When it does we start having other issues we have to deal with, but these are good problems to have. It's a good problem to have so much food coming out of your garden every day that you can't possibly eat it alone. It's a good problem when you have to be careful where you throw an apple core because there's a good chance a tree will form. It's a good problem to have an orchestra of birds waking you up in the morning and bees buzzing around your back door.

The reason it's helpful to learn about the members of the soil food web is because our main goal is to support them in order to have a healthy garden. Knowing what they need helps us achieve that goal. The rest of this book is about not only caring for plants, but for all inhabitants of our gardens — especially the soil.

Summary

- Healthy soil depends on the web of relationships between many different kinds of organisms.
- Microorganisms, animals and plants scavenge the soil, water and air for nutrition.
- Through competition and cooperation, microorganisms, animals and plants recycle and trade nutrients, create healthy soil, provide each other with defense and other services that keep the system balanced.
- These all have important roles to play in creating a healthy garden, and our job is to tweak the system to provide all of them optimal living conditions so they can do their work.

Chapter 3

All About Soil

Before we can improve our soil, we need to know a little more about what makes it tick.

Soil Formation

Soil gets started when rock is broken down by mechanical, chemical and biological means. This process can take thousands of years.

The mechanical aspect of breakdown is brought about by water, wind and temperature fluctuations. The chemical aspect consists of various reactions often caused by interactions between oxygen, water, carbon dioxide and rock. The biological breakdown process depends on the soil food web — microbes and plants working directly on the rock creating their own organic acids. This process speeds up drastically as more organic matter is produced. They also make some of the chemicals mentioned above.

There's a very good chance that your soil did not come directly from the underlying rock. Often, the parent materials or even the soil itself has been blown in by wind or brought in by glaciers, volcanoes or historic waterways, but the soil formed somewhere as virgin soil. Virgin soils don't have organic matter. Lichens — organisms made up of a symbiotic partnership between algae and fungi — are often first to arrive on the scene along with pioneering nitrogen-fixing plants like alder, broom and black locust.

Nitrogen is needed for plants to grow. Alder, broom and black locust don't actually fix nitrogen, but they partner with bacteria that do. These bacteria take nitrogen out of the air and convert it into a biologically usable form. The plants can then grow bigger and this is the start of making organic matter. Other plants will eventually come in when the soil is ready and the nitrogen-fixers will gradually be phased out. This all takes time.

Our soils are often in poor shape, and while we should definitely bring in some compost, I also like to take a cue from nature and plant some nitrogen-fixing plants. Actually, in a new ornamental garden on poor soil, I often use a lot of nitrogen-fixing plants — at least 25% of my total. I use clover and vetch as a groundcover, beans and peas in my vegetable garden, goumi, birch and many others in perennial plantings.

Another implication is that we can learn a lot about our soil by looking at the plants that are naturally growing in it. If we're getting a lot of clover, we may have a lack of organic matter and nitrogen in the soil. If we're getting a lot of dandelions, we have a calcium deficiency or imbalance. We can actually learn to make some fertility decisions with a bit of knowledge about weeds.

During the soil formation process, the quartz in the parent rock becomes sand and silt. Most sand and silt are composed of this quartz, which is silicon dioxide. The clay, on the other hand, is formed when oxides of silicon and aluminum come together into a molecule and then many of these molecules join together. Sometimes it's silicon and iron. The other minerals in the parent rock just float around as minerals. Some are leached and some attach to the clay.

So sand and silt are both mostly quartz rock made small, whereas clay is formed from a chemical reaction between certain minerals. The significance of this difference is next.

Soil Texture

There are three sizes of soil particles. From biggest to smallest, they are sand, silt and clay. Sand is gritty and it doesn't stick together.

You've seen it on it's own on the beach or in a sand box. Silt is smaller and more powdery, but is still separate grains. Clay particles are much, much smaller and they join together to form a sticky substance kind of like play dough.

So *soil texture*, a bit of a misleading term, is actually a specific way of describing the relative particle sizes in your soil. It refers to the percentages of sand, silt and clay that are present. Note that even if you have a clay soil or sandy soil, you probably have all three soil particles to some degree.

The quickest way to learn what kind of soil texture you might have is to take ⅓ cup of loose soil, remove any debris, and slightly moisten it uniformly throughout the sample. Then roll it into a ball. If you have a hard time doing this or if it breaks easily under pressure, the predominant soil is sand. It will also feel a bit gritty. The more it stays together, the more silt or clay you have.

Try to roll it out into a cylinder. The longer the cylinder you get, the less sand you have. It can be tricky to differentiate between silt and clay, but silt is smoother with more individual grains and clay is stickier with no discernible grains. Clay can also stain the hands.

There is another test to determine texture that I prefer called a sedimentation test, but it is a little more involved. Take a clear one-quart jar with a lid and fairly straight sides — a major curve at the bottom of the jar will distort the results. Go to your garden and dig down 6-8 inches, taking enough soil to fill the jar about ⅓ full. Be careful to remove any large stones, gravel and organic matter, since this test is only meant to determine the mineral particle size of the soil. Next, add a few tablespoons of liquid dish detergent, which helps separate the soil aggregates, and fill the jar up with water to one inch below the top rim.

Cover and shake it for a minimum of 10 minutes. Set it down where it won't be disturbed, being careful not to slosh it sideways as you set it down. When you come back, after at least 24 hours, you should end up with a sand layer on the bottom, then a silt layer, then clay, and perhaps a bit of dark organic matter. The sand will have settled out right away and the silt within an hour, but the clay takes longer.

It's usually fairly easy to see the three distinct layers. Measure the height of each layer and divide by the total height to determine your percentage of sand, silt and clay. To be accurate, there is actually one more step. Your results are in volume, but the soil texture triangle uses weight for units. To fix this, multiply the percentage of sand by 1.19, the percentage of silt by 0.87 and the percentage of clay by 0.94.

If you have 70% sand, 20% silt and 10% clay soil, you have a sandy loam. If you have 50% sand, 20% silt and 30% clay soil, you have a clay loam. There is no need to remember these percentages, since some time ago a smart person put together a little chart that makes it easy to figure out. It's called the soil texture triangle.

Soil Texture Triangle

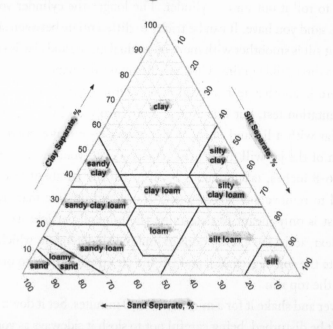

Modified from S.J. Thien. 1979. A flow diagram for teaching texture by feel analysis, Journal of Agronomic Education. 8:54-55. United States Department of Agriculture, Natural Resources Conservation Service. *http://soils.usda.gov/education/resources/lessons/texture/*

When you've done your sedimentation test and know your percentages, you can use this triangle to determine your soil texture. Follow your clay, sand and silt percentages into the triangle, where all three intersect. This is your soil texture type. You may want to do this test in a few places around your garden and average out the results. Knowing our soil's texture influences a lot of our soil management decisions, which we will see as we continue on.

Soil Structure

While soil texture refers to the percentage of sand, silt and clay in your soil and is ultimately summarized with words such as sandy loam or silty clay, soil structure looks at how these individual soil granules clump together into various shapes and sizes and what that means for factors such as water and air movement, compaction, biological activity and root growth.

This soil aggregation is performed mostly by microbes, plants and small animals. Bacteria excrete gluey carbohydrates that allow them to cling to soil, and help soil particles stick to each other. Fungi send a latticework of mycelia throughout the soil, binding particles together. Certain fungi create a sticky protein called glomalin that excels at binding soil together. All of these microbes need the nutrients to be in balance in order to make a nice soil structure, along with water and organic matter. Even worms aggregate soil by constantly eating and excreting soil particles. As do other critters that live in the soil. Organic matter is broken down into humus, which bonds electrically with clay to form aggregates, called the clay-humus complex.

In a perfect world, your soil would be approximately 45% mineral soil, 5% organic matter, 25% air and 25% water. So that's 50% solid and 50% pore spaces. It rarely works out exactly like this, but that's kind of a loose goal. The big pore spaces hold more air and the small pore spaces hold more water. This provides just enough water and air for the plant roots, microbes and insects — not too much and not too little. Some gardeners even strive for higher organic matter content in relation to soil, but you don't want to add too much, too quickly.

The reason small pore spaces hold water is because water molecules stick to each other through cohesion, and to solid surfaces through adhesion. A small space has just enough solid surfaces in close proximity for a water drop to stick. When water goes into a big space, it just keeps going through, so air ultimately ends up occupying that space.

If your soil is dominated by sand, the resulting structure will likely allow for excellent water infiltration and drainage. Infiltration is how water enters the soil from above, while drainage is how it leaves the soil due to gravity. In a sandy soil, the water will more easily get into the soil and even get down deep into the soil, but not that much of it will stay around. This is because the relatively large size of the sand grains creates many big pore spaces for air, but not as many small spaces for water.

While the water-holding capacity of a sandy soil isn't great, there is a lot of air and not a lot of compaction in a sandier soil, like at the beach. That has its benefits, which is why sand is used so much as the base for golf course greens. Golf greens get a lot of foot and machine traffic, so the sand helps resist compaction. Roots and microbes can breathe and extend their reach quite far in sandy soil.

At the other extreme, if your soil is dominated by clay, the resulting structure will likely result in less than ideal infiltration and drainage. Water will puddle on the surface and won't go down as deep and it will not drain as well because there are so many small pore spaces near the top of the soil to hold it. Of course, that means it holds onto more water and needs to be irrigated less often. The water-holding capacity is excellent, but some of the water is held so tightly that plants and microbes can't get it. Also, with fewer big pore spaces, there's less air in the soil and less resistance to compaction.

Silt falls somewhere in the middle. Water infiltrates and drains better in silt than clay and this texture has an even better water-holding capacity because more of the water is actually available and accessible to plants. There are also more big pore spaces for air in the soil.

What about organic matter? It turns out that it does everything right in terms of soil structure. It infiltrates brilliantly and drains freely, but not before holding onto a tremendous amount of water. It still allows for plenty of air in the soil, but it resists compaction. Also, it plays a huge part in actually binding your sand, silt and clay into the aggregates that give the soil structure.

So the amount of sand, silt, and clay in your soil is your soil texture. Soil texture along with organic matter, the soil food web and the nutritional makeup of the soil influences your soil structure, which is how it all clumps together. This in turn determines how much water will infiltrate, drain and stay around, and how much air will be in there. It also determines the potential fertility of the soil.

Fertility

The inherent fertility of your soil is dictated by the rock from which it originated. If we look at a rock like limestone, it's going to be mostly calcium with a bit of magnesium and not much of anything else — certainly not a well-balanced soil. On the other hand, many of our soils were brought to us from the movement of the glaciers in the last ice age and so we may have a soil from a mix of parent materials, which is consequently more balanced.

One of the reasons we want to know about our soil texture is because sand, silt and clay bring different fertility potentials. Sand and silt come from the same parent materials, and so have basically the same implications for soil fertility. While there are many different parent materials, the most common is quartz.

Quartz is mostly silicon dioxide. It generally has a limited amount of minerals in its composition that will become available to plants, and it can't hold onto other nutrients in the soil. Soils that are high in sand and silt, therefore, are inherently less fertile than soils high in clay, not taking into account organic matter. Farmers know they'll get lower yields on sandy soil because of this lower fertility, which is one reason why adding organic matter is so important, as we'll see.

While sand and silt are the same other than their particle size, clay is totally different. Clay is made of many different elements, and the outside of most clay particles are covered in negative charges because of how the minerals, mainly silicon and aluminum, are chemically bound together.

Many other minerals in the soil such as calcium, magnesium and potassium are positively charged, so they attach to the negatively-charged clay, but not to the sand and silt. The clay also attaches to organic matter molecules in the soil. The fact that clay has these negative charges is one reason why having some clay in your soil is truly a wonderful thing.

Cation Exchange Capacity (CEC)

A positively charged mineral in the soil is called a cation, pronounced "cat-eye-on" with the emphasis on the cat. Years ago when I read about cations from a book for the first time, I spent a year walking around praising cations (as if it rhymed with passions), before I figured out how it was supposed to be pronounced.

The cation exchange capacity of the soil basically refers to the ability of the soil to hold onto these positively charged nutrients like calcium, magnesium and potassium so they don't leach out. Since a majority of minerals in the soil are cations, this is important.

The use of the word "exchange" actually advances the definition a little bit because it refers to the ability of the soil to attract, hold and release these nutrients. The people who name things put that in there to show that it's an ever-changing, dynamic process, which is important to note. Nutrients are always getting bumped off the soil molecule. Some are taken up by plants, some are leached further down, and some attach somewhere else. I guess if the soil held onto the minerals, the plants would get rather grumpy.

In fact, while hydrogen isn't considered a plant nutrient, microbes and plant roots use hydrogen cations to trade for other cations sitting on a cation exchange site. Roots do this by excreting carbon dioxide, which combines with water to form carbonic acid and hydrogen. Some of the hydrogen knocks other cations off the exchange sites, which the plant can then take up. Brilliant. I prefer just to think of CEC as how good my soil is at retaining positively charged nutrients. Note that CEC doesn't tell me how many nutrients I have, just how good it is at retaining and exchanging what is there. More on that soon.

As we discussed in the last section, the sand and silt don't help at all with CEC because they don't have a charge. It's all about the clay, and specifically what kind of clay you have. Some clays are better at holding onto cations than other clays. Gardeners have no way of knowing what kind of clay you have other than researching the local soil reports or asking local soil labs, but a soil test tells our CEC — an important number.

Pure clay can have a CEC anywhere between 0 and 150, with most non-tropical clays, such as those in North America and Europe, falling in the 25-100 range. Interestingly, humus which is organic matter broken down into its most stable form, has a CEC of 100-300. That's great news because we can therefore immensely improve the ability of our soil to hold onto cations by building up the humus in our soil, which will be beneficial to almost all soils — but most notably for low-clay soils.

By the way, if you're a math or science buff, you might like to know that the unit of measurement for CEC is milliequivalents per 100 grams of soil (mEq/100g), but it's not really important for our purposes.

Nutrient-Holding Capacity

While the CEC is one of our main indicators of fertility potential, there are minerals in the soil that aren't cations. Most notably, phosphorus, sulfur and some forms of nitrogen are often in the soil as negatively charged minerals called anions (pronounced "ann-eye-on" with the emphasis on the "ann"). Anions are not held on sand, silt or clay, but they are held by organic matter. Not only does humus have a spectacular CEC, but it holds onto anions, too. More good news.

Organic matter not only holds onto cations and anions, but it's full of minerals that will eventually become available when the organic matter decomposes. Leaves, grass, animals, trees — it's all organic matter that will eventually be broken down. And let's not forget the microbes. They consume minerals, too, which become available when they die. All of these, the cation exchange sites, the anion exchange sites, the organic matter, and the microbes, contribute to the soil's overall nutrient-holding capacity.

It can be seen that while clay is the only rock-derived soil particle that can hold onto cations, organic matter can hold onto cations and anions, and is actually composed partially of minerals itself. Organic matter is already looking pretty important and we're only talking about fertility. That being said, some clay is very helpful because it actually helps keep organic matter in the soil and stops it from leaching. So we are happy with some clay.

pH

Soil pH is talked about a lot in the gardening world, but most people don't understand it and the number garnered from a pH test is generally misused. After this short section, you'll know how to use pH data better than most garden experts. Now, pH can get very technical, but I'm going to stick to what is relevant to us in the garden, yet try not to oversimplify too much for the scientists out there.

For our purposes, pH is basically a measurement comparing how many positively charged hydrogen ions we have in our soil versus the other cations — calcium, magnesium, potassium, sodium and aluminum. The more hydrogen ions we have, the lower our pH is and the more acidic it is. The more of the other cations we have, the higher our pH is and the more alkaline it is. The scale goes from 0 to 14, with 7 being neutral, but most soils are between 4 and 9. At 4, all cation exchange sites are occupied by hydrogen, so there's not much in the way of nutrition for plants.

At just under pH 7, all cation exchange sites have cations other than hydrogen, which doesn't necessarily mean the soil is highly fertile because we still don't know which cations are there. In theory, it could be all magnesium, which would not be a very balanced soil. Also, what if you're gardening on a soil with 98% sand and silt, both of which have no CEC? In this example, even if all of your clay and organic matter exchange sites are occupied by cations, your soil is probably very low in cations because you don't have many exchange sites. A pH below 4 involves additional organic acids and above 7 or 8 involves additional carbonates. Usually the pH is somewhere in between, which means we have some hydrogen and some of the other cations.

Most nutrients, particularly the most essential nutrients, are most readily available to plants somewhere in the 6-7 pH range, gradually decreasing as the pH gets further up or down the scale. Some micronutrients become more available outside this range, especially in low pH soil, potentially to toxic quantities. So it's not that the acidity of a 4.5 pH soil is harmful to the soil, it's that most nutrients aren't as available to plants, and a few may be too available. Further, many microbes can't live at an extreme pH, so the soil food web will be lacking.

So we can see it's best to have a pH somewhere in the middle. Actually, between 6 and 7 is generally considered ideal, which may be true, but this is where a mistake is often made. Let's say we take a soil sample and determine the pH is 5.5. We will be told to add lime to raise the pH of our 5.5 soil, usually this is dolomite lime.

The reason we are told to do this is because, as discussed earlier, cations can knock each other off exchange sites. All things being equal, the hydrogen ion is the most attracted to a cation exchange site. If we look at the major cations in decreasing order of their affinity for cation exchange sites — that is, how strongly attracted they are to the cation exchange sites — it goes hydrogen (H^+), calcium (Ca^{2+}), magnesium (Mg^{2+}), potassium (K^+) and sodium (Na^+). There are many other micronutrients in the full list, but these are the major ones.

Hydrogen has the greatest affinity for a cation exchange site, but there's one other factor that influences which cations will bind to exchange sites. If there's an abundance of some other cation, such as calcium (Ca^{2+}), some of it can knock off some of the hydrogen. This is called the "mass effect."

Back to our example of adding dolomite lime to raise pH. Dolomite is calcium carbonate and magnesium carbonate. The calcium and magnesium in the lime will knock some of the hydrogen off the cation exchange sites. Some of that hydrogen will combine with the carbonate, and some of it will go elsewhere. That will give us less hydrogen and more cations, therefore raising the pH. This may happen in the short term, and even in the long term if done annually for a number of years, although the soil will tend to move back towards its starting pH. Still, it works for now.

So the problem is not that dolomite lime won't raise the pH, but that our pH test did not tell us if we actually needed calcium and magnesium. Perhaps we already have too much magnesium, or too much calcium. It's almost certain that we don't need both in the ratio that dolomite lime gives us. On the other hand, some *high* pH soils are due mostly to sodium and potassium, and they actually still need calcium and perhaps magnesium. We wouldn't know that if we just used the pH number as our basis for liming. Adding more of the wrong nutrient is just going to make things worse, as we'll see later.

It is the pH that gives us a clue that we may have a nutritional and microbial imbalance in our soil, but this gives us no information as to why that may be so. As such, it's of very little use to us. If we do regular pH testing over a number of years, making sure we always take our soil sample from the same place, at the same time of day and year, in the same conditions, the one thing it can help tell us is if our soil management practices are working, since pH will move towards neutral when we balance the nutrients in our soil and increase the organic matter content. Besides, plants seem to grow well in soils of various pH levels given plenty of organic matter.

It's not that pH isn't important to plants and microbes. For the most part, we're happy to have it be between 6 and 7 to have the healthiest plants. Remember, hydrogen is used in cation exchange and for mining certain minerals from the soil, so a slightly acidic pH is ideal. It can be difficult for plants to get phosphorus out of an alkaline soil. Knowing the pH value, however, doesn't help us much with soil management decisions, and it certainly shouldn't be used to determine how much lime to add to the soil. pH is the result of the elements in our soil, not the cause. From Charles Walters' *Eco-Farm: An Acres U.S.A. Primer*, "excess acidity is nothing more than the reciprocal of fertility depletion."

Plants that are considered "acid-loving" may just need certain trace minerals in abundance, and those trace minerals are more available in acidic soil. Rhododendrons, for example, are often thought of as acid-loving. In reality, they love magnesium, which is sometimes more available at a low pH, and they aren't particularly fond of calcium. They'll grow just fine in a high pH soil if they have sufficient magnesium. Other acid-loving plants may just need a fungal-dominated soil. Fungi decrease soil pH, so it may be that these plants don't care at all about the pH, and they just want their fungi.

Trying to make your soil acidic by applying peat moss or chemicals doesn't give the plants the nutrients they need or the biology they need. What we need to do is focus on all of the soil management practices we will be looking at, such as creating high quality compost and using things like rock dust and seaweed in order to give the plants the chelated minerals they need. When all of these factors are brought in line, the pH will follow.

Even if we have a perfect pH, we don't actually know which nutrients we have and how available they are to plants. This is where soil testing comes in, which is coming up later in this book.

Organic Matter

We have seen that while organic matter makes up a relatively small part of the soil, it is critical. It's kind of like how you can make bread without yeast, but it won't work very well. You just need that teaspoon of yeast in there. Organic matter is as important in the soil as yeast is to bread. You just need perhaps 3% to get you started.

Organic matter is anything that is living or was once alive. When looking at the soil, we're mostly referring to fallen leaves or needles and twigs, dead and live plant roots, and dead and live microbes. All of these can be fresh and whole, or in the process of being broken down, or already broken down into its most stable form — humus. Compost is organic matter, too.

We've seen that organic matter takes center stage when it comes to water-holding capacity and drainage, promotion of air in the soil and resistance to compaction, holding onto cations and anions, and providing fertility because it is made of nutrients and other substances. It's said to be a particularly important source of nitrogen, phosphorus and sulfur, but has many micronutrients, too. Not only is it a source of nitrogen, but nitrogen-fixing bacteria actually need it for energy so they can do their job.

Organic matter is the source of many compounds in the soil, such as certain phenolic acids and auxins. These enhance plant growth and help protect plants from predators. More high-quality organic matter in the soil generally means more beneficial organisms and fewer non-beneficial organisms.

Humus is organic matter that has been broken down so much by microbes that it resists being broken down any further. The microbes will work away at it if there is no other food available, but they'd prefer something else. By the time organic matter has been transformed into humus, many of the elements have already been released.

In the soil, humic acids are important chelators, which means they combine minerals into organic compounds that are more available to plants. They also tie up toxins, making them less available to plants. Humic acids will already be present in good soils with a lot of organic matter. Otherwise, they'll be lacking and it will be beneficial to bring them in as a supplement (called humates), while also focusing on increasing the organic matter content of the soil.

Humic acids greatly improve the soil, increase plant root growth and metabolism, enhance seed germination, and help plants deal with environmental stresses. They remove odors in slurry and compost piles, and keep irrigation lines clean. We also use humates in liquid applications of organic fertilizers onto plant leaves, because they help the plant take up and utilize the nutrients in the solution many times more effectively.

Summary

- Soil texture is simply the proportion of sand, silt and clay in the soil, while soil structure is what results when the soil is manipulated by microbes, plants and animals.
- The soil texture, structure and organic matter content give us clues as to the soil's ability to infiltrate, drain and hold water and provide sufficient air, as well as to the soil's inherent fertility, CEC and nutrient-holding capacity.
- This is all important, but we still don't know the quantity and balance of nutrients in the soil, how available these nutrients are, or the quality and quantity of the soil food web, which is why we need to do some detective work — coming up next.

Why is Humus Important?

Most people think they would like to have high humus in the soil, but Albrecht's work in this area revealed that even humus cannot completely annihilate all the problems. With soils that are high in humus always expect copper deficiency problems. Peat and muck-type soils generally mean production problems because of copper deficiency.

The term humus is not used on most soil audits, but there is the designation, organic matter percent. Humus and organic matter are often used interchangeably. Humus is made up of decomposed residues which have been completely broken down in the soil by microorganisms. The organic matter or humus terms notwithstanding, when talking about a long-term reservoir for nitrogen, phosphorus, sulfur, boron and zinc, I am not talking about undecomposed residues. This is referring to the humus (that is, completely decomposed organic residues) — without it, the reservoir function wouldn't happen.

Why does humus hold nitrogen, phosphorus, sulfur and boron while clay does not? Because humus is "stronger" than clay. If you could take a handful of clay in one hand and a handful of humus in the other hand, and measure the nutrients, humus has three times the nutrient-holding ability of the clay.

Humus improves the physical properties of soil. It helps hold water better. It certainly adds to the tilth and friability of soil.

Next, it aids in micronutrient nutrition of plants through chelation reactions. It encourages microorganisms in the soil because it serves as a good source of food for microbes.

Humus aids in solubilization of plant nutrients from insoluble minerals. This means that it helps break down fertilizers that are on-scene in the wrong form and tied up or complexed.

— Neal Kinsey and Charles Walters in *Hands-On Agronomy*

Chapter 4
Soil & Plant Testing

Soil testing isn't particularly complicated, but there are some things you need to know to do it right. Some of the simple tests we can do on our own, and the more difficult nutrient testing we should leave to a soil lab that can do a much better job. The goal of the next two chapters is to outline a simple process for soil and plant testing, so simple that many of the steps can be done annually, as the real benefit of testing comes from comparing results from year to year to see if what you're doing is working.

What exactly should we test? Ideally, we would like to have some information about the texture and structure of our soil, the mineral content, and the health of the soil food web. We record this in a simple garden diary. This is one of the hardest things to get gardeners to do, but please, please, please start a garden diary. Not only can you keep track of what you plant every year, but you can takes notes on your soil testing process and results.

Look at the Soil

The easiest test, and arguably the most important, is to spend just a little bit of time getting acquainted with your soil firsthand. If you're like many people, reading about this kind of stuff is more fun than doing it. It's easier for some of us to learn this than to put it into practice. It took me a while to get into this because I'm a mathematical person who likes to look at the numbers in a soil test, but playing in the dirt is a vital step I've come to cherish. You need to actually go outside and do this to get any benefit from it. Find some kids to help you. They love digging around in the soil for earthworms.

Dig a hole approximately 12 inches long, wide and deep. Try to take the soil out in big chunks if possible and place it in a wheelbarrow or on a tarp. First of all, how easy is it to dig? It should get easier every year as your organic matter content increases, your soil food web grows and your nutrients get more balanced. Take note of how easy it is to dig, or rate it on a scale of 1 to 10. That way, when you can stick your arm down into the soil up to your elbow after 10 years, you'll remember where you started.

Look at the color of the soil. Dark brown is good. Pale beige, gray or blue is generally not as good. Smell it, too. Soil should smell pretty nice. It definitely shouldn't smell bad, like rotten eggs. Does it look like something you'd want to grow plants in?

You can use half a cup of soil to determine your soil texture — the relative amount of sand, silt and clay in your soil. The sedimentation test from the previous chapter is my favorite, although you can judge just by manipulating some soil in your hand, as in the ribbon test, also from the previous chapter. This information gives you a clue about the water and air conditions in your soil. It also gives you a hint as to its ability to hold onto cations.

Look at the soil you've taken out and make some notes about its structure. It takes some experience to do this, but it's really just a subjective, qualitative assessment of how your soil looks. A good sign is if the soil particles are aggregating together in some way, rather than staying separate like sand on the beach. You also don't want huge compacted clumps of clay.

Another method of looking at structure comes from Graham Shepherd's *Visual Soil Assessment*, a very good free guide for looking at your soil that you should download at *www.carbonfarming.org* because it has amazing photos to help you analyze your soil. Try to dig an eight inch cube of topsoil and drop it a maximum of three times from waist height into a bucket with a firm base, even with a piece of wood inside to help break up the cube. Put the broken soil pieces and all of the fine soil from the bucket on a large plastic bag. Some of the big clods will be cracked and you can break those apart at the cracks. Then organize your soil from big clods to small clods. The more fine soil and fewer clods you have, the better. A good soil is mostly broken down into fines, whereas a poor soil stays mostly big clods. It's okay if yours is mostly in big clods, because you're going to improve it over the next few years.

Break up the remaining soil and count the earthworms. There are a few geographic areas that don't have earthworms, and very sandy soils are often low, but most garden soils should have some. Earthworms are sensitive to their environment and chemicals, so if you have them it's a good sign. If you have 10 in that square foot of soil you've pulled out, you're doing okay. More is even better. I'm thrilled when I can find 25 of them in an eight-inch square soil cube.

You can also look down at your soil for other insects. If you have a mulch layer, peel it back and see what's living there. A magnifying glass helps with this. You may even be able to see fungal mycelium, especially around plant roots, and if you have nitrogen-fixing plants like peas and beans, you should be able to dig up a plant and find the tiny spherical nodules that house the bacteria on their roots.

Look into your hole. Do you have a defined topsoil level that is darker than the soil below? The darker it is, the more organic matter content. Measure that darker layer. Unlike in conventional agriculture, where the topsoil and organic matter have rapidly decreased over the last 50 years, we're going to increase yours over the next few years, so it's nice to know where we're starting.

Did you dig in an area where there were some roots? The deeper they go, the better. If they're stopping at a certain depth and growing sideways, there may be a hardpan there that we will slowly break up when we plant strong, tap-rooted plants and when we increase the organic matter content of the soil. A lack of fine root hairs in your soil profile will indicate a lack of oxygen.

pH

We've already seen how knowing the pH of our soil isn't all that useful, other than as one of the indicators that shows if our practices are moving our soil in the right direction, often toward a balance point somewhere between 6 and 7. I wouldn't even worry too much about that.

Actually, one of the main reasons I wouldn't worry is because soil pH fluctuates substantially over time — not only throughout the seasons, but over the course of a matter of days. Temperature, moisture, biological activity — all of these have an effect. Often pH tests give wild swings of up to 2 points over a 24-hour period. You'll get a pH number on a professional soil test, and that's where I leave it.

Soil Biology

If you're a market food grower, you may want to know how many microbes you have in your soil and how diverse they are. You can get a microscope and learn to do some of this yourself, but for most people it's best to have a lab such as Soil Foodweb do it. At the time of this writing, it's about $60 for a basic test that covers bacteria and fungi, which is a good start. You can pay over $200 to include protozoa, nematodes and mycorrhizal fungi. Prices are currently double in their Canadian labs.

The only reason to do this kind of testing is if you're prepared to act on the results, and that means balancing out your soil food web. That involves learning how to make specific composts and compost teas that select for specific kind of microbes, which I touch on later in the compost tea chapter. This is a lot of fun, but I understand that most home gardeners won't want to jump into it. It's worthwhile mainly for landscapers and people who grow a lot of food.

I may do biology testing on a new garden if I know I'll be gardening there for a while. Otherwise, I just go ahead and make the best compost and compost tea I possibly can, albeit not as specifically suited to the soil as it might be based on testing. For now, I think soil mineral testing is more important. The reason I include biology testing here is because I feel there's a good chance that many of us who currently test our soil minerals will one day be testing our soil biology too.

Plant Testing

There are a couple of methods of directly measuring the health of your plants with instruments. Just as with soil, before you get to these more technical tests, it's very important to simply look at your plants and take some notes.

You can look for insect predators and diseases as indicators of plant sickness. A little more advanced, you can look for leaf discoloration that indicates certain deficiencies. I don't use this is my only means of determining deficiencies, because I think it's more complicated than that, but it's useful to compare these indicators with other plant and soil tests. Here are some examples of visual deficiency indicators.

A calcium deficiency can produce many symptoms, including thick, woody stems and cell death at the base of the leaves. A nitrogen deficiency often causes the leaves to be a pale yellow-green color. A sulfur deficiency does this, too. A phosphorus deficiency can show up as a purplish color on the lower leaves and as overall stunted growth. A potassium deficiency often shows up as yellowing and cell death around the edges of the leaves, or in between the veins. A magnesium deficiency often looks like this, too. You can see that it's not always easy to pinpoint specific deficiencies since they often look the same, but it's a useful start when you'll be comparing with other tests.

The two main instrument tests for plants are plant brix and plant sap pH. It's also possible to test the minerals in plant tissue. I don't have any experience with this, so I can't comment much on it. The tests are becoming more accurate and the good soil consultants are learning how to do a better job interpreting the data. It used to be they would supplement what was deficient in the plant tissue, but they're learning it's not that easy. They may find a certain micronutrient is low, for example, but supplementing with that nutrient may not be the answer.

Brix, however, is one of the most exciting tests in our toolkit. It measures the dissolved solids in plant juice, which includes sucrose and fructose, vitamins and minerals, protein and amino acids, and many others. We like to know the brix of our fruits and vegetables for a couple of reasons.

The first reason is that brix is a rather nice summary of how well we're doing with our soil management practices. When we balance the soil nutrient ratios, increase organic matter content, build our soil food web and so on, plants get healthier and brix goes up.

As your brix rises, your food tastes better — I mean way better, and your taste buds won't lie. Food stores longer and is more nutritious — way longer, and way more nutritious. Very high-brix foods don't rot. Other than tomatoes, most fruits and vegetables will slowly dehydrate, but stay nutritious and highly edible. They can stay good for years! Seeds germinate more quickly, and plants get bigger and produce more food. They resist heat and frost damage and are healthy overall.

Once you get the brix above a certain number, which varies for different plants but is often around 12, plant predators will diminish or go away completely. In general, they won't be able to eat or even sense the plant as food. It's too healthy for them. At this point, your food is a powerhouse of nutrition. We call it nutrient-dense. Imagine eating an apple that has many times more nutrients than an apple you buy at a store.

Dr. Carey Reams is credited with doing much of the original research in discovering that high brix means high quality, and he also determined necessary brix levels for many different foods. He is reported to have entered the same watermelon in a contest three years in a row to show how long food can stay good if it has a high brix reading.

We measure brix with a refractometer, a decent model costing about $100. Some say it's the most important tool of the serious food grower. I get all of my instruments like this from Pike Agri-Labs, and there are other good merchants around too. You don't have to rush out and buy one now, but as you get more into growing, it's worthwhile.

I have even taken my refractometer to the local market to test food before I buy it. Rex Harrill on his brix website points out that If you do this, be respectful of the vendors and offer to buy a sample before you test it.

Gardeners can use brix to see if the food we are growing is getting healthier over time. Like a soil pH test, it doesn't tell us much more than that.

The second reason we may want to test brix is more practical and useful. We can measure the brix in a leaf or especially a fruit from one of our plants, for example a tomato. Note that a "fruit" is just the reproductive part of a plant, so botanically speaking, many foods we call vegetables are fruits, such as tomatoes, pumpkins and avocados. So we test the brix, then foliar feed that tomato plant, wait 30-60 minutes, and measure the brix again. If the brix has gone up at least a couple of points relative to a control plant that we also test, the tomato liked that fertilizer and we should spray the whole crop. If it stayed the same or even went down, the tomato might not want that fertilizer today. Even good organic fertilizers are sometimes not wanted by our plants.

This is an advanced technique that takes some practice. It isn't as useful for home gardeners growing many different kinds of vegetables in their garden with just a few of plants of each variety because it might not be worth the time to test, say, one tomato plant in order to spray the other three. Or maybe it would. If you're trying to grow the best tomatoes and you want to get many dozens of tomatoes from each plant, it could be worth it. If you have a huge bed of something like potatoes, go for it.

For many plants, you need a reading of 12 brix in all parts of the plant, so if you're still getting plant predator damage above 12 brix in the fruit, test the leaves. They may be the weak link. Other plants need even higher brix. You also need to make sure you measure from the same place on both the test and control plants. A series of cloudy days will bring down the brix. Too much nitrogen or potassium will bring down the brix. A hot, dry, windy day may bring up the brix, giving you the impression that you're doing better than you really are.

Other unknown factors seem to cause the brix to increase and decrease throughout the year. The way to get brix up long term is through improving the health of the soil. Phosphate is especially correlated to brix, so if you get your phosphate availability consistently up, your brix will go up.

I'm not going to get into the details of using a refractometer, as those instructions come with the device, but it's really simple. Use a pair of pliers or a blender to get a little bit of juice out of the fruit or leaves and place it on the glass plate. Look through the hole like you would look through a kaleidoscope and you have your brix reading.

A refractometer can also tell you if you have enough calcium. A blurry line where the upper and lower part of the scale join tells you calcium is sufficient. A sharp line indicates deficiency. Not everyone agrees with this seemingly strange methodology, but I've found it to hold true much of the time when compared to a soil test.

The second test to do is a plant sap pH. This isn't something I recommend most home gardeners need to worry about, but it's interesting enough that I'll mention it here. For some reason, the closer the pH of a plant's sap is to 6.4, the healthier that plant will be, regardless of the species of plant.

If the sap pH is above 6.4, there's a good chance there is a shortage of the anions nitrogen, phosphate and/or sulfur. The plant is also likely to be found as food by insects. The higher the pH, the worse the problem. At a sap pH of 8, you will definitely have insect trouble.

If sap pH is below 6.4, there's a good chance you have a shortage or imbalance of the cations: calcium, magnesium, potassium and/or sodium. The plant is likely to be found as food by diseases. At a pH of 4.5, you will definitely have disease trouble. As we'll see, baking soda can help curb fungal diseases, perhaps simply by raising the leaf surface pH. Also, the further the sap gets from 6.4 in either direction, the poorer the quality, taste and storage life food will have. I have read that our urine and saliva should be close to 6.4, too.

The reason I don't suggest home gardeners do the sap pH test is because you need to spend a couple hundred dollars on a special pH meter, and when you've determined your plant sap pH, you're not really much closer to knowing which nutrients are deficient. As such, this test is mostly used to see if your management practices are moving your plants towards better health.

Summary

- A valuable test is to simply dig a hole and note the ease of digging, color, smell, texture, structure, earthworms and insects, topsoil layer, and root growth.
- Soil biology testing will be making its way into the mainstream and is helpful in giving guidance on what kind of compost and compost tea you should be making.
- Brix testing is both extremely fascinating and useful to determine which foliar sprays to apply.

Chapter 5
Soil Nutrient Testing

In 2006, I started an organic gardening service, one of the few in my city at the time that were truly organic. This was my first chance to apply what I had learned from intensively studying organic gardening to other people's gardens instead of just my own. I was mostly quite successful, but had some problems dealing with weeds in some lawns, and the occasional other pest. It took me a while to figure out that it was because I was neglecting to do what is outlined in this chapter, and in later chapters on supplementing nutrients to balance the nutrient ratios in the soil.

Most of my students and consulting clients have skipped this step, too, to the point where I now say, "I know you're probably going to skip this step the first year, so all I ask is that if things don't work for you like they should, you'll go ahead and get your soil tested and then start to apply the appropriate fertilizers to balance the nutrients." I understand the hesitancy to go pay $50-$75 for a soil test, and then more money on the fertilizers. I know many people don't want to do it, and the good news is it's possible to grow food with just compost, so don't worry if you don't want to jump into this right away.

That being said, this is a book on growing the most nutrient-dense food and plants possible, so it's definitely necessary to know. To me, this is crucial and it's what's missing in most organic gardening books that often focus more on organic matter and perhaps applying a few organic fertilizers, often fertilizers that can make things worse.

While talking to local farmers and soil experts can garner some useful information about the most common soil deficiencies and excesses in your neighborhood, this information is often not as useful in an urban setting. Many of our practices, or those of people who previously gardened our soil, can make the fertility in our back yard much different than our neighbors. The soil may change when compost or topsoil has been brought in, pesticides sprayed, chemical or mineral fertilizers applied. If you or someone else has applied dolomite lime for 10 years in a row, that may have drastically changed the nutrient balance from its original state.

To get better information about the soil, we need to do tests. The qualitative tests from the last chapter are part of this, as is the brix test. We also do a couple of quantitative soil tests. We want to do these different tests because if we make decisions based on only one, there is a good chance we'll make the wrong choices. It is much better to have data from multiple sources in order to make more a informed decision. While the numbers you get from the tests in this chapter are useful, it's important to also remember to look at your soil, weeds and plants to see what they're telling you, and to bring all of this data together. A soil test alone doesn't always give accurate enough information to make big fertility decisions. Looking at your garden is just as important.

Most home soil test kits that you can buy are pretty much useless. In fact, even professional soil labs give widely different results from each other based on the methods they use, even though they have good equipment. Still, these are many times better than the average home kit, although a decent home kit is manufactured by LaMotte and sells for $600-$700.

Soil tests measure a moment in time, but the soil changes throughout the year, even over the course of a few days. Temperature, moisture, and biological activity each have an effect. To be honest, the results coming back aren't even close to 100% accurate. There are too many factors to take into account. In fact, some people argue that professional soil tests are a waste of time. It's true that they are rough estimates, but their usefulness has been proven by thousands of soil consultants who have successfully used them to improve soils and crops. It's important to always use the same lab, because at least it will be using the same methods from year to year if it's a good lab that has been around for a while. That way you can more accurately compare numbers between tests you do over the years.

Still, you will come across some well-known organic gardening adherents who don't like soil tests. In *The Organic Method Primer*, a wonderful book by the way, Dr. Bargyla Rateaver says they're basically useless because they're based on the incorrect idea that plants take up most of their nutrients in ionic form. Some of the tests I recommend try to take this into account, especially the Reams test that we'll be looking at soon. Still, while the results we get back aren't 100% accurate, we know they're helpful because soil management decisions based on them have been used for decades with great success.

There are also some things we can do to improve accuracy. We can take a good soil sample, choose a good soil lab and get the right tests done.

When to Test

It's worthwhile to sample your garden soil once a year in order to track long-term changes and continually work to move your soil towards an ideal level. The goal isn't necessarily to get all the way to the ideal, but just to move in that direction. I sample once each year on big food gardens — in early spring or fall.

If you just want to do it once in the first year and then forget about it, that's fine. Just make sure you don't skip doing it once. I would suggest sampling one more time, a year after the first one, to see what effect your inputs have had and to see where you need to go from there. You'll probably see that you're better off than the previous year, which may cause you to want to sample again the following year. That's great, but if not, that's just fine. At least go for one sample.

It's very important to sample at around the same time each year, under the same environmental conditions. After harvest is a good time to sample, although some people like to test their soil in spring. Spring or fall is what I say, and the sooner the better. You don't want to sample during a drought or if you've applied fertilizers in the last month that supply high doses of specific nutrients. Liquid kelp and fish wouldn't affect the test much, but mineral and chemical fertilizers would. Take a quick note of when you sample, including the date, temperature and a qualitative indication of the moisture level.

How to Take a Soil Sample for a Lab

Farmers will separately test different parts of their field, but this gets too costly for most home gardeners, so you need only do one test, but you do want to combine at least three samples from different parts of your garden. If you're primarily interested in growing food, take three or more samples from your vegetable gardens and combine them. Skip the areas in your yard that have obviously different soil conditions, or test them separately.

Most labs suggest your shovel should go down 6 or so inches to get a soil sample. Market gardeners looking for a complete analysis often go down as far as 3-4 feet, being careful to take different samples perhaps every 12 inches in depth, in order to evaluate what's going on in the various subsoil layers.

Home gardeners will want to get soil from the surface down to at least 6 inches. The easiest way to do this is to dig a hole first and then you can use your shovel to take a nice vertical slice of soil from the side of that hole that will include all depths. What I mean is, you don't want all of the sample to come from 6 inches down, and you don't want it all to come from near the surface. You want soil right from the surface, excluding coarse mulch but including any soil crust, down to your testing depth.

When you're taking these samples, be sure to keep everything very clean. The shovel should not be rusty. The pail needs to be sparkling clean and cannot previously have contained fertilizers. After the samples have been thoroughly combined in a pail, usually 2 cups are placed in a new, clean bag or container to be shipped to the lab. Some labs are happy with 1 cup. Most labs don't care if the sample is wet or dry.

The results are only as accurate as the sample you send, so be sure to combine samples from several different places in the garden, to the correct depth. Don't include much organic debris, and keep the whole process uncontaminated. Sample from the exact same spots each year. Mark them in your journal or with scarecrows, birdhouses or pet rocks on site.

Choosing a Soil Lab

While it may be tempting to drive a sample over to your local soil lab, this may not be the best option. Right now, most soil labs aren't doing a great job. They're still stuck in the same chemical mindset of soil management that many of the colleges are teaching. While local soil labs do often have valuable knowledge and data on local soils, if they aren't focused on organic or biological soil management, I don't use them. We just don't speak the same language.

Also many soil labs that are evolving their thinking to more holistic soil management methods are making some of the same old mistakes. If you find a lab that suggests liming based on pH or total base saturation without considering what nutrients you specifically need, look elsewhere. If you find a lab that offers organic recommendations as being secondary to chemicals, you may want to look elsewhere. You can figure these things out by reading their website or giving them a call. Some of the ecological soil scientists do advocate small amounts of certain chemicals, but the focus should still be on organic inputs.

I have two favorite soil labs. There are many others out there. For me, I ship to these instead of using my local lab. I would even recommend shipping to them if you live in Canada. You just have to fill out a couple of extra forms for customs requirements. If we're going to go through the trouble of doing a soil test, let's do it right so we can feel confident about the results. These labs are doing the kind of tests that I believe are most useful, based on the research of Albrecht, Reams, Callahan and Andersen, to name just a few. See the Resource list in the back of this book for their full contact information. Current prices are $50-$75. You can use another soil lab, just make sure they do Albrecht testing and/or Reams/LaMotte testing or a similar test:

Crop Services International

Based in Grand Rapids, Michigan and led by Dr. Phil Wheeler and Ron Ward, authors of *The Non-Toxic Farming Handbook*.

www.cropservicesintl.com

Not only are they doing base saturation and Reams testing, but they work with biodynamic farmers and other energetic systems such as electronic scanning that we will look at in a later chapter. I highly recommend them. You can get both the base saturation and Reams tests plus recommendations, see their website for details.

International Ag Labs

Based in Fairmont, Minnesota and led by Dan Skow, co-author of *Mainline Farming for Century 21*.

www.aglabs.com

These guys do great work, too. They rely on Reams testing for their recommendations, but they will do a base saturation test for you, too, see their website for details.

Cation Exchange Capacity (CEC)

A soil test will include a value for CEC. The more clay and organic matter, the higher this number will be. Here are some recommended numbers, although they will vary depending on who you ask. Sandy soils low in organic matter will have a CEC between 1-10. They have very little ability to hold onto cations. The 20-25 range is getting to be decent, but 25-40 is ideal and would probably mean you have good organic matter and a decent amount of clay. Above 40 is high clay and/or organic soil that may include a lot of material such as peat. Pure organic soils, such as a peat bog, go as high as 100 CEC.

The CEC value on a soil test isn't always particularly accurate. A better indicator of CEC may even be the simple ribbon test. Take half a cup or so of your soil, make sure it's moist, and squeeze it into a ball. Form it into a ribbon. If you can't do that, your CEC is low (sandy soil). If you can form it into a long ribbon, your CEC is high (clay). A simple test, but potentially more effective.

A lower CEC soil that has a lot of sand needs to be fertilized and probably watered more often, because it can't hold onto either for very long. On the up side, it's easier to balance the nutrient ratios since a smaller amount of fertilizers added can make a big difference to the small amount of nutrients already there. A higher CEC soil that has a lot of clay and/or organic matter doesn't need much fertilizer or water, but if the nutrient ratios are out of balance, it can take a lot of fertilizer to correct them.

Base Saturation

The first main test we probably want to get done is called a base saturation test. It gives us an indication of the percentage of base cations, or positively charged ions — calcium, magnesium, potassium and sodium, possibly aluminum and importantly, hydrogen — in our soil. The significance of the base saturation test is that it includes hydrogen, which makes things easier for us. If you can't get a base saturation test, another test is called an exchangeable cation test and it doesn't include hydrogen. This makes it rather time-consuming and difficult to interpret properly.

Much of the initial research that produced the numbers that follow comes from decades of work started in the 1920s by Dr. William A. Albrecht at the University of Missouri. He actually started working there as a microbiologist and I believe he was initially studying inoculation of legumes with various Rhizobia bacteria. He came to the conclusion that the nutrients in the soil were having an impact on the quality and yield of the food crops, so he started researching the impact of nutrients and nutrient ratios on the crops.

He perfected the use of the base saturation test. A total base saturation of 75% means the CEC sites in our soil are occupied 75% by the bases and 25% by hydrogen. But more important to us are the specific numbers, and here's the magic formula. The ideal results are 60-75% calcium, 7-15% magnesium, 2-5% potassium, 0.5-3% sodium, and 10-15% hydrogen, and a few percentage points for all of the other micronutrient cations, such as iron and copper. We don't know precisely why nature has settled on these numbers. What we know is that often, the closer the soil gets to these numbers, the healthier the soil and plants become.

When I say we, I don't mean everyone. Some people disagree with this method, claiming there is not enough research proving its effectiveness. Their other main argument is that all soils are different and there is no one formula that fits them all. This is certainly true. We could use more research. What is also true is that this method has worked for thousands and thousands of people over at least the last 60 years.

It has worked for me, as well, because I've used a lab that is doing it right, using Albrecht's system or something similar. The soil labs mentioned previously are doing it right, as is Kinsey Agricultural Services. Neal Kinsey, co-author with Charles Walters of *Hands-On Agronomy*, has helped bring Albrecht's system to us. There are other labs doing a base saturation test without using Albrecht's system, and making fertilizer decisions based on those results may not be as effective. The only research I've seen that disproved the effectiveness of using the base saturation test for fertility management was poorly conducted, not even using Albrecht's system, among other issues. Albrecht's system does work in the hands of a good lab.

Back to the numbers. Again, these ideal percentages vary depending on who you ask and on testing procedures the lab is using. On sandy soil, calcium goes down closer to 60%, magnesium up to 10-20% and potassium potentially up to 6-8%. This is because the magnesium and potassium help the sandy soil to bind together. It may be that the numbers are different for some trees and ornamental plants, but I've never seen this data anywhere, so I've always applied them to all plants. They certainly work for various kinds of foods all over the world, from corn to bananas to other fruit trees to coffee.

It's very important to note that the amount of each nutrient in your soil is not as important as having the correct percentages. In fact, a lack of nutrients is not the problem in our soils. The nutrients are there. The problems are that they are out of balance and the soil food web is not healthy and diverse enough to extract what is there. If you were to take a soil sample from a healthy forest, a soil lab would probably tell you that soil was very low in nutrients. What the forest has is a highly functional soil food web to keep the nutrients recycling in the system. It certainly doesn't have anyone adding fertilizers.

Getting the soil food web working in our own soil is one of the most important goals on which we need to focus. And we don't need to add much in the way of fertilizers, but correcting the nutrient ratios is important to create an environment in which microbes and plants can flourish. We need to work on the biology and the nutrients at the same time. Here's a summary of the ideal soil nutrient percentages:

Ideal Soil Nutrients

60-75% calcium (60% for grasses and sandy soils)

7-15% magnesium (10-20% for grasses and sandy soils)

2-5% potassium

0.5-3% sodium

10-15% hydrogen

One reason you want to find a good lab and stick with it is because they will have their own precise set of ideal numbers based on the procedures they use. Neal Kinsey works with Albrecht's exact system, and he wants the numbers to be very close to 68% calcium and 12% magnesium. He says he won't give you recommendations based on another lab's test because he doesn't know the intricacies of their procedures. They may have found that 75% is the ideal calcium percentage based on their methods, and that's just fine. He finds if you get below 10% or above 12% magnesium on his test, you'll probably run into some issues.

It may seem somewhat arbitrary to focus on only these few nutrients. While it's true that there are many other nutrients needed mostly in smaller amounts, Albrecht arrived at the conclusion that these main ones are the most important to get right, especially in the beginning of a soil management program. Overall, Albrecht's work has been ignored by conventional agriculture, but championed by ecological farmers and gardeners. You won't learn about it in most gardening and farming courses, but buy some books from Acres U.S.A. or go to their annual conference and you will learn more about these topics.

One other criticism of this test is that in order to extract the minerals from the soil sample, labs use some fairly strong acids. They argue that these acids release nutrients that aren't really available to plants because they are so tightly held by the soil that plants can't extract them. This is partially true for many labs, but Albrecht didn't use the very strong acids that many labs use. They were certainly stronger than the acids used in the Reams test I'm going to show you next, but Albrecht was very concerned with finding the plant-available nutrients, too.

The analogy often given is that strong acids tell you what you have in your long-term soil savings account. Weaker acids tell you what's in your soil checking account, so which nutrients are more readily available to your plants. Using water instead of acids tells you what you have in your pocket, so which nutrients are available today, but not necessarily tomorrow. The strong acids pull too many nutrients and the water-soluble tests don't pull enough. The weak acids are the most useful, and while I agree this Albrecht test is not perfect, I've seen how it's useful to compare year after year results and look at the trends.

This test helps us determine what mineral fertilizers we will apply to build the base foundation of the soil in the long term. It's important to still look at what weeds you have growing to see if they are telling you what the soil test is telling you. You may have 75% calcium from your test, but your garden is full of grassy weeds that indicate a calcium deficiency. That's one reason why we do more than just the Albrecht test. The more sources of information we have, the better.

Soil Exchange Capacity

To determine a soil's productive potential, start by determining the total exchange capacity. That is the first thing we need to know. Then, after we know the capacity of the soil to hold plant nutrients, there is another portion of the test that goes hand-in-hand — the base saturation percent. The reason it comes second is because you can never establish the base saturations unless you know the exchange capacity. Base saturation teaches us that in each soil there is a specific percentage of nutrients that grows crops best, and that it is not the soil that receives the most pounds per acres that always delivers the best crop.

The longer a farmer works with this program, the more this will become plain. Anatomically, you use the pounds to get the percentages, and percentages tell how a soil is going to perform. Yield and quality are determined by the percentages, not the pounds. Thus our bottom line: base saturation percentage tells us what the soil is composed of in terms of cations — calcium, magnesium, potassium and sodium. It also tells us that the availability of these nutrients to plants generally increases with their percent saturation.

Magnesium and manganese are exceptions. A higher percent saturation of magnesium in a soil does not necessarily mean that this nutrient is more available. It is possible to get to the point where the percent of magnesium — as it goes up — actually makes less magnesium available

> to the plant. Here is the optimum percentage base saturation of cations
> generally for most soils. The cation calcium should be 60 to 70% of the
> saturation of the soil. In other words, 60% of the minerals attached to the
> colloids should be calcium. That is on a light, sandy soil. On a heavy clay
> soil, 70% would be optimum. The correct number for magnesium should
> be between 10 and 20%. On a heavy clay soil, it would be better at 10%.
> The ideal is for calcium and magnesium to total 80%. In high clay soil, 70
> + 10 = 80, and in a light sand, 60 + 20 = 80.
>
> — Neal Kinsey and Charles Walters in *Hands-On Agronomy*

Anions

Along with the base saturation test, you may have some anions
tested, such as phosphorus and the nitrate form of nitrogen. Organic
matter isn't generally tested for minerals on a soil test. The nitrogen
test, therefore, is not especially reliable because about 98% of soil nitrogen is tied up in the organic matter. There are other factors that make
it difficult to get an accurate result. Some labs ask you to bring in a
sample at just a couple of degrees above freezing to improve the results,
but it's just not feasible for most of us.

That being said, labs do give you a number for nitrogen. In theory,
nitrate nitrogen levels that are too high may contribute to increased blos-
som drop, decreased fruit set, and increased frost damage and winter
kill. If the cation form of nitrogen — ammonia nitrogen — is low, which
is very common, it indicates a lacking soil food web. That needs to be
addressed in order to bring the level of this form of nitrogen up, which
is necessary for optimal fruiting and flowering. More important to us is
how much organic matter we have in the soil and whether we have the
microbes to convert some of it into usable nitrogen.

Phosphorus is another tricky one. There are a few different tests

Soil Test Sample — Base Saturation Test

Nutrient	Actual
Phosphorus	
• Bray I Test	67
• Olsen Test	36.6
Potassium	111
Calcium	1182.12
Magnesium	176.99
Sodium	6
Organic Matter	2.92
pH	6.5

Nutrients	Units	Ideal	Actual
K	**%**	**2-5**	**2.2**
Ca	**%**	**60-70**	**36.6**
Mg	**%**	**10-20**	**11.6**
Na	**%**	**0.5-3**	**0.2**
CEC	**mEq/100g**		**7.7**

Note: The bold results show base saturations. This is the only part of this soil test result that I really think is important.

used to determine how much phosphorus is in the soil, but it's difficult to get an accurate picture. The interpretation of a phosphorus test is again very challenging because phosphorus uptake by plants is many times higher from organic matter than from mineral soil. There is a better nitrogen and phosphorus test coming up in the next section.

On the previous page is an example of a test with some cations, anions and — the only part I pay much attention to — the base saturations, in bold. Note that while it doesn't tell me the hydrogen base saturation number, I can deduce that it's most of the remaining 49.4% because I know this is a base saturation test. I know the numbers have to add up to 100% and hydrogen is most of the remainder.

If you look at the parts that aren't bold, you may notice some inconsistencies. The numbers for calcium, magnesium and potassium aren't in the same ratios as they are in the bold part. This may be because the units of measurement are different. I'm not sure. The easiest way to get around it is to not look at the parts that aren't bold. The bold part is what's important.

Looking at these results, we can see we have about a 3:1 calcium to magnesium ratio, not at all uncommon and as we will see, probably not good. This soil and the plants in it are going to have problems. Sodium is also low, as is the CEC. It's probably a fairly sandy soil with this low CEC. We'll look at the next test to confirm this and get more detail.

The Reams Test — My Favorite

This is the second test I do. The Albrecht test is good, but we don't want to stop there. Carey Reams was one of the most influential scientists for ecological agriculture, an outside-the-box thinker. He developed a testing system to give you an indication of what your plants might actually get from the soil, even more so than the Albrecht test. The Reams test lets you know more about which nutrients are biologically active in your soil.

To be clear, we've been looking at two different testing procedures — the test championed by William A. Albrecht uses stronger extractants to measure CEC, cations and anions, while the Reams test uses weaker extractants to measure nutrients. I ignore the anions such as nitrate and phosphate from the base saturation test, but rely on them more from the Reams test.

The Reams test uses the Morgan procedure and the relatively weak acids from the LaMotte testing kit. These acids are more like those produced by plant roots, therefore the test reveals more about what the plant can actually get from the soil, regardless of how much of each nutrient is in the soil. You could be sitting on a bed of limestone that might show up as having a lot of calcium in a base saturation soil test, but a Reams test may indicate it's not available to plants. Some labs use different testing solutions than the LaMotte kit, but as long as they are following guidelines similar to those of Reams, it works for me.

Incidentally, it won't say Reams test on the paper, but if you look for these numbers I have below all lumped together, you've found it. After many years of observation, analysis and the help of colleagues and students, Reams settled on the following as being the amounts to strive for in pounds per acre using his test.

Reams-Based Ideal Nutrient Levels in Soil

Calcium	2,000-6,000 lb./acre
Magnesium	14% of calcium
Phosphate	400 lb./acre
Potash	200 lb./acre
Sulfate	200 lb./acre
Nitrate nitrogen	40 lb./acre
Ammonium nitrogen	40 lb./acre
Sodium	20-70 ppm

Again, these numbers are for food, but I use them for all soils. There's no need to memorize them, as you have them right here. When you get a Reams soil test back from a lab, you can compare your results to these numbers, (and they probably have even done that for you). They may use slightly different numbers depending on their methods and on your plants. They also may give the numbers in ppm instead of pounds per acre, where 1 ppm equals 2 pounds per acre, so ideal phosphate would be listed as 200 instead of 400, for example. From there, the lab will tell you which fertilizers to add to the soil in what amounts. They may give it to you in tons per acre. One ton per acre equals about 45 pounds per thousand square feet.

With this test, you're aiming for a 10:1 calcium to magnesium ratio, or 7:1 for grasses/grains and for very sandy soil. The lower the ratio gets below 7:1, the more potential for compaction and drainage issues, as well as poor microbial life and unhealthy plants. If you see grass weeds such as crabgrass, it's probably because it's come along to help make calcium available.

You're aiming for a 2:1 phosphate to potash ratio, or 4:1 on sandy soils. If they give you the numbers as phosphorus and potassium instead of phosphate and potash, it's a 1:1 ratio you want, or 2:1 on sandy soils. The calcium to magnesium and phosphate to potash ratio are the most important to balance, so worry about them first. You're also aiming for a 1:1 potash to sulfate ratio. You may also get a few micronutrients tested. I don't worry about correcting them until I've corrected the main ratios, because I've found some of the micronutrients will fall in line when the main ratios are good.

A summary of the ideal ratios follows. Like the base saturation test, the specific amount of each nutrient in the soil is often not as important as their relationship to each other.

Ideal Nutrient Ratios

10:1 calcium to magnesium (7:1 for grasses and sandy soil)
2:1 phosphate to potash (4:1 for grasses and sandy soil)
1:1 potash to sulfate

Below is an excerpt from the same soil test sample given previously. Other than potassium, all of the major nutrients are low — nitrogen, phosphorus, calcium and magnesium. The ratios are also skewed. Based on the calcium to magnesium ratio, there may be compaction, grassy weeds, plant predators and unhealthy plants. The phosphate to potash ratio indicates the same problems, as well as potential broadleaf weeds. We'll look at how to fix this throughout the rest of the book.

Soil Test Sample — Reams Test

Nutrient	Desired Ratio	Desired Level	Lab Results	Notes
Humus		40	8	
Nitrates		40	15	
Ammonia		40	6	
Phosphorus	1:1 P:K*	200	61	1:4 P:K
Potassium		100	241	
Calcium	10:1 Ca:Mg	>2000	451	2:1 Ca:Mg
Magnesium	14% Ca	280	219	
Sodium		<70	6	Very Low
pH		6.5	6.5	
ORP		28	24	
ERGS		200	75	Very Low
Copper		0.8 - 2.5	3.5	Very High
Iron		10 - 25	175.3	Very High
Zinc		1 - 6	3.4	
Manganese		8 - 30	10.9	Medium

* Soil labs may say 1:1 phosphorus to potassium or 2:1 phosphate to potash, but they mean the same thing. Likewise the desired level may say 200 and 100, or 400 and 200.

Note: Sulfur/sulfate was not measured on this test.

Organic Matter, ORP, pH and ERGS

You'll probably get a number for organic matter on your soil test. The environmentally friendly way of determining this is to bake the soil and measure the weight loss, because the carbon burns off. Labs are moving to that over the old method, which used toxic chromium. Still, some labs measure humus, while some measure total carbon, and some labs just guess based on the color, so it's difficult to know what the number means. Mostly, I use this number to see the trend — whether or not it's going up with my management practices.

For most people, your soil organic matter will be low, perhaps even down in the 1-2% range. If you've been working on your soil for a while, it can be around 5% or even higher. I prefer just looking at my soil color, and looking and seeing how well it's aggregating and holding moisture and so on. It just takes a bit of experience looking at the soil to be able to judge the amount of organic matter present.

Oxidation reduction potential (ORP) is a number that has been traditionally used more for determining compost stability, but it's also being used for soil. It basically measures the state of soil oxidation. The ideal range is 25-30. Too low and the soil is lacking oxygen, it's anaerobic. Too high and the soil has so much oxygen that organic matter may be burning up too fast. Like pH, I don't use ORP for soil management decisions, but you may see it on a soil test.

While pH is important, we've already seen how knowing the number isn't particularly useful to us other than to monitor changes over time. ERGS, energy released per gram of soil, is another number often shown in tests that is covered later in the energy chapter.

Soil Contamination

Some soils, especially in urban environments, are contaminated with radionuclides, chlorinated solvents, petroleum hydrocarbons, PCBs, PAHs, and heavy metals such as lead, mercury, cadmium and chromium. Many of these come from human activities such as waste disposal, "inert" ingredients in chemical fertilizers, and industrial mining, agricultural and recreational pollution. To determine if your soil is contaminated, find a local lab that does this kind of testing.

If you have soil contamination, then comes the task of remediation. Many of the chemical and physical methods of reclaiming polluted soil require a lot of energy and often leave the soil lifeless and unproductive. Some methods go so far as to remove the soil and treat it as hazardous waste. Another approach is to work with nature by using microorganisms (bioremediation) and plants (phytoremediation) to help with the process. Though it takes longer, these actually improve the soil, while chemical and physical processes can be very destructive.

Fungi are especially adept at breaking down hydrocarbons such as those found in oil. Even the oyster mushrooms I've grown in my home are good at this. The book, *Mycelium Running* by Paul Stamets is an excellent introduction to using fungi in your garden and for soil remediation.

Certain plants can pick up nearly all of the heavy metals from a soil. Research, for example, suggests that *Brassica juncea* (Indian mustard), can take up lead, cadmium and nickel from the soil into its above ground parts. It can then be harvested and disposed of elsewhere. Other common plants such as corn, alfalfa and sunflower can be useful for this same purpose because of how fast they grow a lot of biomass. Admittedly, this process just moves the problem elsewhere, but that's the way it is with minerals. They can't be broken down like organic molecules. Some argue that lead cannot be effectively taken up by plants, but that fungi may be able to do a good job of removing it.

The specifics of remediation are beyond the scope of this book because I've never knowingly dealt with a contaminated soil, but I believe testing for and fixing contamination is very important.

Summary

- Most food growers should test soil once a year, but if you don't want to do that, just one time at the beginning is much better than not at all.
- Be sure to take a good, clean sample and send it to a good lab that is doing Reams-style testing and giving organic recommendations.
- While you may get numbers for pH, anions and organic matter, the most important numbers are the base saturation test and the Reams test.
- From the base saturation test, focus on the percentages of calcium, magnesium, potassium and sodium.
- From the Reams test, focus on the availability of nutrients, both cations and anions, as well as the ratios between them.

Six Steps to Creating Healthy Soil

In a well-balanced ecosystem, external inputs aren't necessary. Granted, even when our garden is healthy, we still may bring in some inputs in order to maximize health and yield, but nature does most of the work. Some people might argue it doesn't make sense that we should have to bring external inputs into a garden at all. After all, nature doesn't do this.

I agree that it's unfortunate to have to go to this extra work, but here's the thing. First of all, we're probably trying to grow things that wouldn't grow naturally. Second, our soil has been so abused in the past by deforestation, farming methods, tilling, chemical use and on and on to the point that we need to actively fix it, fast. We don't want to wait 10 or 100 years to be able to grow healthy food.

This is why we may concede, for example, to ship some lime halfway across the country to get more calcium into our soil. Being environmentally conscience, we don't want to ship this lime and we may not want this rock to be mined in the first place. This is a complex topic that merits debate, but I believe we need to do it. We need healthy plants and we need healthy food.

We've now looked at the basics of the soil food web. We've peeked into the lives of the different organisms that live there. We've seen why insects, diseases and weeds show up on the scene. We've looked at the fundamentals of soil, and how to learn about it through some simple at-home digging and testing through a lab.

Now it's time to see what to do about it. This section covers the six steps to creating healthy soil and abundance in your organic garden.

Chapter 6

Water

STEP 1

We can't look at soil management without also looking at water management. This chapter isn't a complete summary of strategies, but it does cover the most important points we need to know. While perhaps not as exciting as say, the latest fertilizer or microbial inoculant, water is more important. Proper water management comes before these other topics and is one of the most important things we do.

Water is essential to life. Not only do we drink it — we are made of it. Throughout the course of our life, our bodies contain between 50 and 80% water. We know our plants are made of water, too, and they need it for photosynthesis and cooling. What is often overlooked is that all living species in our garden need water. Sure, it's a great idea to provide a water source for birds and other animals, but I'm referring here to the soil life. Insects, earthworms and microbes all need water. It's vital for the health of the garden that they have enough water. Remember, they make good soil and feed and protect plants. And interestingly, a biologically active, nutritionally balanced garden will also attract more water in the form of dew.

Not enough water in the garden is devastating and very common. Too much water is also common; more specifically, frequent, shallow watering. Irrigating daily for 20 minutes often encourages roots to stay comfortably along the surface of the soil instead of searching further and deeper, which is important for a sustainable, healthy garden.

Water Contamination

If you irrigate with water that is cleaned by the city, it probably isn't overly high in any of the trace elements, nitrates, salts or microbes such as *E. coli*, so you shouldn't need to test for that. It doesn't mean that it's high quality water — in fact, most of it isn't. Chlorine, fluoride and other toxins are generally used to clean it up before it gets to you.

That's why capturing rainwater is so important. Ideally, we would capture all the rainwater that falls on our roof and run it through a pond or series of ponds that clean it up using specific aquatic plants and microbes.

Wells and open ponds should be tested. They are all contaminated with pesticides now to some extent, but some more than others. You can test for some things yourself with special test strips, such as nitrates and salinity, but I would just get a lab to do that along with all the other important things. International Ag Labs does this water testing as well as soil and plant tissue testing.

Our Water Supply

Aquifers around the world are drying up, including in the U.S. and Canada. The gigantic Ogallala aquifer in the Great Plains, which gives the U.S. about 30% of its irrigation water, is being used at many times the rate it's being recharged and may be dry in as little as 25 years.

Half of the wetlands around the world have been lost since 1990. At least a third of rivers and streams in the U.S. are so polluted that fish contain toxins and are inedible, and swimming isn't safe. Lakes are worse off. Farming accounts for about half of this pollution. The majority of wells have pesticides and even more of them have pharmaceuticals and other man-made toxins. Even in rural areas, many of our wells are contaminated with pesticides and excess nutrients.

In the city, substances like fluorine, chlorine and chloramines are put in our water in an attempt to clean and improve it. Some of it is necessary and definitely helps make our water safe to drink, but some of it is unnecessary and harmful to us. None of it focuses on the root cause of the problem, which is the absurd chemicals we shouldn't be producing and disposing of in the first place.

The implications for you and me are that we need to stop using toxins in all areas of our lives and start protecting our water supply, find ways to collect and recycle water, and then responsibly use municipal or well water to make up for what we can't collect. You might also consider doing something to clean your drinking and irrigation water, some combination of ozone, ultraviolet light, carbon filtration, reverse osmosis, hydrogen peroxide, ion exchange or distillation. I have a relatively inexpensive filter for my drinking water that takes out 99% of the chlorine, lead, pesticides, cysts and many other compounds.

To protect our water, we can start by not using pesticides, chemical fertilizers and genetically modified products. We can also establish a garden that is teeming with plant and microbial life in order to clean up toxins and pollutants. There are certain microbes that specialize in doing just that, such as the *Rhodopseudomonas palustris* found in many microorganism inoculants.

Collecting Rainwater

Before we look at irrigation, let's first look at how we can save water. The first method is rain harvesting. While a rainwater barrel is a good starting point for water conservation, I find it interesting to actually run the math and see how little water they hold. I wonder if they are taking the limelight away from more important methods.

Heide Hermary of Gaia College showed me this. If your roof is 1,000 square feet (93 square metres) and you get one inch of rain on a spring afternoon, you'll have 625 gallons of water coming off that roof. Where I live, one inch of rain is fairly common during a storm.

Let's say you're collecting that rain into only a 60 gallon rainwater barrel. It will get nice and full and you can use it to water your tomatoes another day, but 90% of that rainwater is going elsewhere, maybe into your city's storm drain system. Your barrel can only take ⅒ inch of rain from that 1,000 square foot roof, so while I like the 60 gallon rainwater barrel, I think there are better solutions, especially if you have long dry spells during the summer. A 600 gallon rainwater cistern could handle almost a full inch and a 1,500 gallon cistern could easily take two inches of rain. Think of it as a giant rainwater barrel. Ideally, almost every house would have one of these, the size dependent on the amount and seasonal patterns of rainfall in your area. If you don't like the sight of them, they can be cleverly hidden or even buried.

The thing is, they can also be expensive. A more attractive and potentially less expensive solution would be to build a small pond, bog or rain garden into which you can direct the roof water. A pond the size of a king-sized bed and four feet deep should hold an inch of rainwater off the roof. If constructed thoughtfully, it can also provide drinking water for insects and animals. Most gardens should have some open water for this purpose, with places for insects to stand while drinking so they don't drown. Mosquitoes aren't a problem if you keep the water moving and use larvae control methods.

Rain Harvesting Into the Soil

While cisterns and ponds are a better option than a rainwater barrel, we should mostly be focusing on the ultimate storage solution, the soil. The soil is the best way to hold onto water and makes rain harvesting using a rainwater barrel look like child's play.

A loamy sand without organic matter, which is 70-85% sand, and not very good at holding water, can hold at least two inches of water. Of course, just how much depends on how wet it is already, the health of the soil food web, compaction and so on. This loamy sand could potentially store that inch of rain, plus the extra inch from our roof, if we could somehow direct that inch evenly over 1,000 square feet, which we probably can't, and if the infiltration rate of the soil is high enough, which it may or may not be.

Soils higher in silt and clay can hold four to five inches of water, but infiltration rates on these soils are generally much lower than a downpour of one inch of rain per hour, so they may have enough to handle with the rain alone, unless it comes gradually over a few days. So what to do?

There's one thing we can put in and on our soil that will hold the extra water, and that is organic matter. Organic matter is a rain harvesting bonanza. Various research has tried to determine how much water organic matter can hold, often concluding it can hold tens or even hundreds of times more water and nutrients than the same amount of soil. Even if it holds only four times its weight in water, you can hold nearly an extra inch of water if you can increase the organic matter content of your soil by just 1.5%, and this is easily doable.

A study in the *Journal of Soil and Water Conservation* found that regardless of the type of soil, "as organic matter increased from 1-3%, the available water capacity approximately doubled." That means we can now be harvesting two or three inches of rain from the roof, 20-30 times more than a 60 gallon rainwater barrel can hold.

Organic matter can be brought in as compost and mulch. Even incorporating two inches of good compost into the top 12 inches of a new garden bed will often increase the organic matter content by 2-3%. It won't increase the stable humus that much, but I'm just talking about any organic matter here. Mulch goes on top of the soil, but it holds a lot of water, as well. Your soil should always be covered in mulch, and when possible, plants. This improves water infiltration and decreases evaporation. Now all that's left is to direct the runoff to your gardens with gutters, and perhaps slight grading of the ground, using techniques such as swales and berms.

Vegetation

Another of our goals is to keep continual plant cover in the garden. This vastly improves the ability of the soil to hold onto water. It slows down rainwater, giving the soil more time to absorb it. Plant root systems open up channels in the soil that allow water to infiltrate more easily and deeply. The plant canopy decreases evaporation.

Plants are often blamed for using too much water. Interestingly, in places where large amounts of forest are being cut down, the rivers are drying up and the precipitation in the region is often decreasing drastically. We actually need these plants and microorganisms all to be happy and healthy in order to have a healthy water supply. A multi-level planting made up of groundcovers, flowers, shrubs and trees may use more water, but it will also improve soil conditions so the soil can hold more water.

Drip Irrigation

Drip irrigation was developed to save water by dripping it directly to the roots of plants, rather than spraying the entire landscape. Note that I'm not talking about soaker hoses, or microsprays. Drip irrigation is where tubing brings water to tiny nozzles that drip water directly into pots or right onto the soil beside each plant in the garden. There are new systems that can distribute the water further, but the classical approach is delivery just to the plants.

Drip irrigation was designed for farming in very dry climates where water is scarce. If calibrated correctly and properly managed, it can work to save water in an agricultural monoculture situation. In fact, some people think it was one of the most important technological developments for agriculture. It's useful for the above purpose, but it has made its way into residential gardens where most of the time it's inappropriate because it waters a tiny area right around the plant, ignoring the rest of the soil. This is problematic for two reasons.

Roots look for moisture and stay away from areas that are dry. With the frequent, shallow watering of drip irrigation, the majority of the roots will tend to stay right by the plant instead of reaching further into the soil for water and nutrients. This means most plants will never reach a state of optimal health. Instead, there's a good chance they will be unstable and unhealthy, covered in insects and disease and on their way to an early death. Many times I have put a shovel into the soil 18 inches away from a drip emitter and found it to be totally dry.

The rest of the soil needs water just as much as the plant because the microorganisms, earthworms and insects need water, not only for their own health, but also in order to give the plants nutrients, water, a healthy organic soil environment, and protection from plant-feeding organisms. Remember, plants get all of these services from the organisms in the soil. Drip irrigation may save water in the garden, but at the expense of the plants we're trying to grow. Also once grown these plants would actually attract water into the landscape, sequester carbon, produce oxygen, feed bees, butterflies and other animals, and cool our houses and cities.

That being said, enough people are successfully using drip irrigation to grow food for me to mention that it's not only possible, but may become very important as our fresh water sources continue to dwindle. These folks should be commended for finding these kinds of solutions that may become necessary. One alternative method is to make the top three to six inches of soil dry and not use mulch, thereby decreasing evaporation from the soil surface and saving a lot of water. This method generally requires chemical salt fertilizer use, so as I see it, there's a good chance of producing food that is substantially less nutritious in the long run. My viewpoint is that if we're ultimately decreasing the organic content of the soil, killing the soil food web, and supplementing with imbalanced nutrition, our food will reflect this.

Providing the Right Amount of Water

Of course, we definitely want to save water. It's absurd how much water goes into our gardens — especially our lawns. That's why I think about collecting and storing rainwater before I think about irrigation. Most of us will need to irrigate, especially when we're establishing new gardens or growing food. We can use captured rainwater for a lot of this.

I recommend irrigating with anything that provides water to the entire landscape: by hand, with a sprinkler, microspray heads, or even soaker hoses if they overlap enough, although the latter really only have occasional usefulness. I wouldn't worry too much about evaporation with overhead watering, as research from the University of Nebraska shows this to be a less than 4% loss. Some gardeners don't like to apply water to the leaves because the conventional wisdom is that it promotes some disease. It does make sense to avoid watering at night for this reason, as night time conditions are better for many disease organisms, but we have also seen the true cause of disease is more a function of a lack of plant health.

I like to apply water from a sprinkler that gets the leaves wet because that's how it happens in nature when it rains. I do this in the morning. If I'm using chlorinated city water, however, I may apply it more to the soil to avoid killing microbes on the leaves. Of course, the microbes on the soil surface won't be too happy, but we work with what we have, right?

It's difficult to determine exactly how much water to apply. People have developed mathematical equations and charts and calculators to help with this, and while these tools are helpful, it's hard to find accurate parameters that you need to feed into these calculations. For example, how deep do your plant roots go? This is especially difficult to figure out when we're growing many different kinds of plants. How much water does your sprinkler apply per minute? What is the evapotranspiration of your area?

You can find these things out and it's important to do so in a landscape where you're designing an automated irrigation system that has to work without you being there, but for home and market gardeners who can pay more attention to our gardens, I prefer to go by feel. You want to water deeply to encourage the roots to go down, and then allow some time for the soil to partially dry out, but not entirely. It should be thoroughly wet after you water it, but not to the point of run off. Even though you should water more deeply and less often, your mulch layer should generally stay good and moist.

A slope may need to be watered in stages, such as 10 minutes on and 10 minutes off for an hour, in order to allow time for the water to infiltrate rather than run off. Sandy soils can't hold as much water, so they need to be watered more often throughout the week with less water. Silt and clay soils are watered less often with more water, although if they have low infiltration, they may need to be watered in stages like a sloped garden.

As your soil organic matter and biology improves, you will be able to water substantially less. In fact, you'll have to, or you may drown the life in the soil. The soil will hold water just so much better as it comes alive.

Summary

- All organisms in the garden need water, which is why drip irrigation is generally inappropriate for our purposes.
- Everyone should collect rainwater in cisterns and ponds. Best of all, though to soak up water is to have a soil with lots of organic matter and vegetation, including multi-level plantings where possible.
- Water with anything that deeply wets the entire soil, adjusting it based on the soil texture, infiltration rate and organic matter content, and keep that mulch layer moist.

Chapter 7

Organic Matter
STEP 2

Despite some claims, plants and microbes really do care about the source of their nutrients. They prefer and often do better with organic forms of the elements instead of synthetic chemical forms. They prefer compost to synthetic nitrogen. While I definitely recommend using products such as lime in certain circumstances, the thing most of us need to do before all of that is start a regimen of deliberately increasing the organic matter content of our soil. We can do this with leaves, compost and other organic materials, even cover crops. After we've removed the threats and determined how we'll supply water to the whole garden, we can start increasing the organic matter content of our soil.

In the last century, we've burned up more than 90% of the organic matter in many of our soils through tilling, applying chemicals, and clearing plant residue without allowing organic matter to decompose. Humus is our ultimate goal, but we also want a supply of fresh organic residue as food and shelter for microbes and animals. As this residue is broken down, carbon dioxide becomes available to plants. Conventional agriculture has largely ignored organic matter, and organic gardeners have relied on it perhaps too much at the expense of other management practices. Still, increasing organic matter and humus should be one of our most important goals.

Humus, made up of biologically active complex carbon chains, is critically important in the soil. While the term is often used interchangeably with organic matter, it's really organic matter that has been broken down by multiple organisms to the point where it won't get broken down much more. Humus holds nutrients in the soil, including the fertilizers we apply. According to some, it particularly holds calcium, which otherwise likes to sink down in the soil profile below most of the other minerals. It definitely holds water. Walk into your garden in the middle of a rainless summer night and your shoes may very well get soaking wet, if you have enough humus in your soil. It has many other important functions, such as tying up toxins, contributing to better soil structure, moderating soil temperatures and stimulating microbes.

When we build up our organic matter content in the soil with mulch and compost, it decreases the amount of fertilizers we need to apply because these organic matter sources are full of nutrients. Also, the more carbon you have in your soil, the less fertilizers you need to apply because the fertilizers will stay in the soil longer and will become chelated. Chelated means they are bound with organic compounds, and consequently are more available for microbes and plants. Let's look at our main sources of organic matter, mostly for mulching purposes. In the next chapters, we'll look specifically at composting and cover cropping to create humus.

Mulch

Thick, dense mulching in the garden with the right material provides a huge array of benefits. You can certainly say goodbye to most of your weeds when you apply a thick mulch. Not only does it smother them out both physically and sometimes biochemically by tying up nutrients on the soil surface, it makes the ones that do find their way through so much easier to pull, especially if you've been clever enough to hit the garden and the mulch with some water. Note that it may be necessary to kill some tap-rooted or perennial weeds before placing the mulch on top of them.

When we mulch, we create homes for insects and other animals and provide them (and microbes) with food. They take this food and turn it into available minerals and humus, incorporating it into the soil to create amazing soil structure. Then all of the other benefits of good organic matter begin to accrue — increased CEC, water-holding capacity and fertility, and decreased compaction.

The mulch itself serves to decrease the compaction caused by us walking on the soil and from heavy rains, and can help to prevent erosion. It moderates the soil temperature, benefiting everyone living there. Some studies have concluded that mulches and cover crops make soil cold in the winter and increase frost damage, but these studies are using dead soil, and this does not happen on real, organic soil that is actually kept warmer during the winter due to the insulating capacity of the mulch and the activity of microbes and animals.

So mulch actually improves the biodiversity of your entire soil ecosystem by giving all manner of critters a place to live, food to eat and water to drink.

Why not just use compost? A little bit of thought tells us why. It does a lot of things right, but fails to stop the weeds. The same goes for manure. Manure can be a very useful soil amendment, but it needs to be well composted and should really be mixed in a proper compost pile. On its own, it isn't a valuable, balanced nutrient source, since the animal kept most of the trace minerals for itself and gave up excess nitrogen and salts. Indeed, many studies have shown that soils continually amended with the same manure will eventually produce unhealthy plants. We can use compost and manure, but they don't make the best mulch. We'll look at them in the next chapter.

Mulch is often applied two to three inches thick, and should be kept away from tree trunks, which don't want to be covered in anything. If you want to promote fungi, such as in a perennial or shrub garden or around trees, put the mulch on the surface. If you want to promote bacteria, such as in an annual or vegetable garden, incorporate it lightly into the top few inches of soil to give the bacteria better access. For bacteria, also consider chopping or grinding up the mulch into smaller pieces, and make sure it's plenty wet, as bacteria need moisture more than fungi.

Let's start with mulches that satisfy very few of our healthy soil conditions and get rid of them right away.

Landscaping Fabric

Landscaping fabric is considered part of our mulch layer because it's often placed on the soil under various mulch types in order to help control weeds. The cheap stuff doesn't work very well, but thicker fabric can work for awhile before weeds start to find their way through the cracks or just start growing on top.

Unfortunately, that thick landscaping fabric can also stop water from getting down to the soil, especially on a slope where the water just slides down the fabric to the bottom of the hill. It doesn't take long for the landscape to show signs of suffering in this case. But the biggest problem with this fabric is that it doesn't allow organic matter to recycle into the soil. When you put landscaping fabric on your garden, it means your soil doesn't get to eat anymore. This is definitely not an appropriate mulch, except under pathways and patios.

As we've seen, soil needs to be consistently replenished with organic matter, so any of the mulch types we choose have to be composed of organic matter. Soil is replenished in nature and in our gardens when leaves fall to the ground. Since many of our gardens are low in organic matter anyway, it also happens when we intentionally bring in more leaves, straw, compost and other organic matter to improve the soil.

Putting landscaping fabric in the garden stops all of this and slowly kills the fertility and structure of the soil, and everything living in it. In fact, you should take it out if there's some in your garden. I've done that for many of my clients.

Stones

Stones and gravel provide some benefits in that they protect the soil from erosion and decrease evaporation, but they don't breakdown into humus and don't allow organic matter to get down to the soil, so they don't do much to improve soil health.

That being said, there is an aside here. If you have certain bigger plants that are special to you, like a new fruit tree for example, there is a technique called rock mulching that can improve the soil extremely quickly, resulting in amazing plant growth. Place a few inches of leaves around the root zone of the new tree, which might be a few feet in diameter. Cover those leaves with round stones or flagstones that are small enough so that you can handle them, but big enough to cover some of the leaves, i.e. not pebbles and not 50 pound boulders.

Doing this facilitates rapid breakdown of the leaves. They may take, for example, eight months to break down normally, but the rock might bring it down to two months or even less. Whether it is because of the pressure exerted on the leaves, or the prolonged moisture the stone cover provides, or the heat stored by the rocks during the day and radiated back to the soil overnight, or the explosion in the earthworm population under them that often happens, I don't know, but it works.

The key to success here is doing it a few times. Yes, you have to remove the rocks by hand every couple of months and apply more leaves and place the rocks back by hand. The first time, the leaves may disappear fairly quickly and that will be interesting enough on its own. But subsequent times, you'll start to notice a thick layer of worm castings where the leaves once were. This is a bit of work. Not much, but it might take 15 minutes to do a tree. It's not a practice most of us will wish to do long term, but we may want to do it for the first growing season to give the trees an incredible boost in organic matter.

Peat Moss and Coir

Peat is organic matter — plants, microbes and even insects and other animals — that has been broken down in wet, anaerobic conditions, generally in marshy areas. In fact, peat bogs can preserve animals extremely well, and were used for human sacrifices back in the Iron Age.

There are different kinds of peat moss. While it's often thought of as a sterile medium, this isn't always the case. Some peat is low in microbes and some of it is extremely high in microbes. Some of it is 90% organic matter and some closer to 30%. While some is high in minerals and some is low, all peat has a high CEC and water-holding capacity. Sphagnum peat is the most common variety. It's very acidic, low in nutrients, and high in oils that repel water. Though it holds a lot of water, once it dries out, it needs to be soaked to wet it again. It's not useful to us a mulch, nor as a soil amendment.

More importantly, peat bogs are unique, vitally important ecosystems for this planet. When they are harvested for their peat unsustainably or to create farmland, these ecosystems are gone, species go extinct, and a huge amount of greenhouse gases are emitted. The bogs are supposed to be restored after harvest, but many aren't, and some scientists propose that it's impossible to restore them properly. Shipping peat across the country or the planet isn't environmentally sustainable. One could argue the same thing for any fertilizer, but peat is very heavy for the surface area it covers, and for the lack of real benefits it provides.

Coir is ground coconut fibre husk, a by-product of the coconut industry. It doesn't have the high CEC of peat, but it also doesn't have the water and pH problems. There are sustainability issues with coir, too — do you have coconuts growing where you live? Is the coir coming from them? Most of the coir you see in your garden center is coming from far away. I see no need for shipping this stuff around the world when we have organic matter locally.

Bark Mulch, Wood Chips and Sawdust

Bark mulch and wood chips are some of the most commonly used mulching materials in the garden. They can be useful or harmful, depending on the source and the use. They can be found in bags or bulk bins at the garden center. They satisfy many of our mulching goals, but unfortunately, they have a couple of potential problems making them one of the mulch types I don't generally use.

Bark contains oils that repel water and wood chips can become hydrophobic, preventing water from getting through to the soil. Bark in particular is low in nutrients, so it doesn't improve soil fertility as much as other mulches. Conifer bark such as cedar and fir can be high in toxins, as conifers have evolved a strong arsenal of compounds that are their first line of defense against insects and diseases. These chemicals can also cause toxicity problems in the soil.

Wood, including both chips and sawdust, is very high in carbon and very low in nitrogen. This means microbes have to pull much of the available nitrogen from the surrounding area in order to break down the wood, which can end up causing a nitrogen deficiency in your plants. If you first include this wood as the carbon source in your compost pile, this situation can be avoided. Otherwise, you may need to bring in a source of nitrogen regularly.

However, if you have shrubs and trees that like a fungal environment, wood chips will promote that, especially if you don't overwater. Fungi still need water, but not as much as bacteria. If they are coarse wood chips and if you put on just a couple of inches and leave them on the surface without digging them in, the nitrogen shortage may not be a big problem.

Wood chips from the non-bark part of the tree and even sawdust can have some good nutrition in them, so they're a great addition to composts where they can be properly mixed with nitrogen materials. As long as they're from non-treated wood, they can even be used lightly in gardens, especially if mixed with leaves; but on their own, they have the same high carbon problem. Sawdust breaks down more quickly and can decrease the amount of air and water that enters the soil if you use too much as a mulch.

All of this being said, if you have access to a large amount of local bark mulch or wood chips at a good price (or free), and you have room to store them, feel free to take them and compost them or pile them and let them compost for a few years. They can become good organic matter. I often work with what I have and try to use local materials. Also, both bark mulch and wood chips can definitely be used in paths, where I am not trying to create a balanced soil environment. They can do a decent job of controlling weeds there if you apply a few inches and keep this mulch topped up.

Straw, Hay and Grass Clippings

Straw and hay aren't the most aesthetically pleasing, but they are fairly good mulch types if you can find a source. You may not want to use straw or hay from ryegrass as it has toxins in it, nor from grass that has been sprayed with pesticides, which is common in many countries. The difference between straw and hay is that straw is just stalks from harvested grain, while hay is finer and has seeds, so hay will often actually produce extra weeds. You can deal with this by composting it in a hot compost to kill the weed seeds, but make sure you get all the seeds into a hot enough part of the compost pile.

Grass clippings aren't the best mulch to use in the garden in abundance because they can get so tightly packed together that they inhibit air circulation. Besides, they're far too important for the soil below your grass plants than to remove them and bring them into the flower or vegetable garden as mulch. They don't cause thatch or any other lawn problems, but they provide many benefits so please let grass clippings lie in place.

If you have left a little bit too much time between cuts and you simply have too many clippings, add them to the compost pile. Just make sure they're thoroughly integrated into the pile, because if they are left in a big clump, they may promote anaerobic decomposition.

Leaves

Of all the mulch types, by far the best is leaves. They do absolutely everything right. That's why when designing gardens I want to make sure to use plants that make a lot of leaves — not just evergreens — and I want to design the beds to catch all of these leaves too.

Leaves that fall on the lawn and on non-garden surfaces can be raked into the gardens or mowed and left right on the lawn. If you don't have enough leaves, your neighbors will usually be happy to give you theirs. When I worked as an organic gardener on residential properties, I would go to the neighbors of my clients and ask for their leaves too. In many cities, you can rake your leaves to the curb and a big truck will come by to pick them up. But why would you want to give away the best garden mulch ingredient?

Ironically, some organic gardeners do get rid of their leaves and then pay a fortune to buy the leaves back as leaf mold in the spring. Leaf mold is just leaves that have been slightly decomposed. It's one of the best mulch types, too, but in most cases, the gardener would have done much better to save the money and keep the leaves in the garden over winter where they can have the benefit of protecting the soil.

If you have a layer of leaves in your garden that's thick enough, say two to four inches, many weeds will be smothered. You'll still get some weeds, but they'll be so easy to pull out that it won't matter. You can just drop them back on top of the leaves (if they don't have seeds) to become part of the mulch.

Some people think leaves are not one of the most attractive mulch types for the garden, but is a forest floor unattractive? Is the forest floor covered in two inches of bark? We've been conditioned to think that bark mulch or bare soil is the most aesthetically pleasing, but if you cover your garden in a rainbow of autumn leaves, I think you'll see it differently, especially now that you know all the benefits they provide. When we remove the leaves, we are breaking nature's cycle and creating more work for ourselves.

So leaves are the number one best mulch type, but there are exceptions. In some climates, a thick layer of leaves over the winter may promote such wet conditions that disease is actually increased. It's possible to have too many leaves if you have a lot of big trees or if your beds are already covered in groundcovers and you don't want to totally smother them. In that case, you may just have to compost them or give some away, to a friend or to the city, although I have mulched 12 inches of leaves into some lawns with great success.

Actually, when I was a kid, I recall my dad would pile a bunch of leaves in the back of the pickup truck, head down our rural street to where there were no houses, drop the tailgate, and hit the gas. It was so much fun watching the leaves get caught by the wind and cover the sky like a thousand red and yellow butterflies. In hindsight, I have no idea why we did this, but it was fun at the time. In fact, I suppose that's why we did it.

You can also rake some of them into their own pile and moisten them to make leaf mold. It can take a solid year to make a good leaf mold, but it is a beautiful mulch. It's made largely by facultative anaerobic microbes, similar to the ones in beer and wine, which is why it smells like yeast.

For most of us, too few leaves is the problem, and this is a design issue. If you find yourself short on leaves, get some plants that produce a lot of leaves. I'm talking about fast-growing annual or perennial plants that get big and provide a lot of leaves in the fall, such as cardoon, rhubarb and ferns.

Now a bit about about oak leaves. I've never had a problem because oak leaves don't break down quickly. I've always enjoyed that about them because it just means my mulch stays around longer. And, they don't acidify the soil to any notable degree, but again, if you have too many, don't force it. Walnut leaves, on the other hand, aren't the best mulch because juglone, a plant toxin, does show up in the leaves and can cause some issues.

Seaweed is another incredible mulch that we often think of as leaves, although it's not technically a plant. It's a great mulch for people living by the ocean. It often breaks down very quickly, giving you another excuse to visit the beach. There are two main problems I see with using seaweed. The first is that it may be important to leave most of it on the beach, because it may be food for many organisms. The second is that there is actually a worldwide shortage of kelp because it's been overharvested just like fish. It may be that the kelp in your area is abundant, but overall, we're running out. This information is new to me, but I'm starting to rethink my use of kelp.

Summary

- Increasing the organic matter and humus content of our soil is one of our most important goals.
- Landscaping fabric should only be used on paths, not gardens, and should actually be taken out of gardens if it's already there.
- Stones and rocks aren't a particularly helpful mulch because they do not improve the organic matter content of the soil, but they can be used short term on top of a layer of leaves around a tree or shrub to hasten decomposition.
- I don't tend to use bark mulch, wood chips or sawdust as mulch because they can cause more problems than benefits, but they can be composted or used as a light mulch in perennial gardens to encourage fungi.
- Straw makes a great mulch. Hay is better composted to get rid of weed seeds, and grass clippings are best left on the lawn.
- Leaves are the best mulch, supplying nutrients, organic matter, a balanced carbon to nitrogen ratio, weed control, a good water-holding capacity, decreased evaporation, homes for critters, and all of the things a good mulch should provide.

Chapter 8

Compost

Compost is our way of mimicking nature, yet speeding it up substantially. Whereas nature slowly decomposes animal manure, leaves and other organic matter all over the ground, we put a large amount of these things into a pile, in specific combinations and ratios, to make it happen quickly.

Compost is not natural. I love making and using compost, but we should remember that fact. Nature makes humus by covering the ground in plants that continually grow and die throughout the seasons and years. Masanobu Fukuoka points out in *The One-Straw Revolution* that we don't need to compost if we maintain plant cover and mulch. This is true. The reason we compost is just to speed things up a little bit, particularly when we're dealing with degraded soils. It works, but it doesn't mean we should forget about mulching and maintaining plant cover.

We add compost to our soil to quickly increase the number and diversity of microbes and small animals, organic matter content, and nutrients in our soil, all of which are often low because of past gardening or other land use practices. A lot of resources refer to the organic matter and nutrients, but fail to focus on the microbes. The way compost breaks down is through the action of microbes, earthworms and insects. Their numbers multiply many times in the pile, and to me, they are the number one reason to compost. For most of us, getting that biology back into the soil is more important than using fertilizers.

How much compost should you make? As much as you're willing to make. I've never heard a gardener complain of having too much compost. That being said, it's better to concentrate your efforts on one properly managed pile than many, poorly managed piles. As you'll see, you actually need very little compost to get big benefits. And you don't have to get too scientific about it, but you do need to do a few things right. Poorly made compost can be plant-toxic putrefying organic matter.

Materials

I'm not going to list all of the materials you can use in your compost. Obviously use good judgement, but pretty much anything that was once alive can go in there. The more variety in your raw materials, the more diverse the resulting compost. As you'll see, I don't use any genetically modified materials (GMOs), or a few others discussed in the upcoming chapter on supplementing nutrients.

The three most important ingredients in compost are plant parts such as leaves, weeds, grass clippings, and straw; manure; and food scraps. Useful supplementary materials include newspaper, cardboard, wood chips and sawdust. You can also throw in drier lint, tea bags, animal hair, vacuum cleaner dust and so on, but these will make up just a tiny portion of the pile.

There are dozens of materials out there. Some of them are available only in certain regions. Perhaps you have a beet processing plant or an apple cider producer near your house. These processes make wastes that can be composted, as does residue from cocoa beans, coffee, wineries and breweries. I taught a composting class for Gaia College where we used a nitrogen-rich material called okara, a soybean by-product from the manufacture of soymilk, tofu and tempeh.

You may not have enough stuff on your property to keep a good pile going. For this, get food scraps from your friends and neighbors and offer to take their leaves in the fall. Find a farm or orchard with some spoiled hay or fruit. While you're out there, find a source of animal manure from a farm or stable. This isn't absolutely necessary for the pile, but will definitely improve it. If you have many forests in your area, you'll probably find someone selling or giving away sawdust or wood chips. In the city, find breweries, canneries or other food processors.

In the long term, a good goal for achieving a more sustainable garden is to use at least 50% of your garden beds to grow this biomass. Some of it can be turned into the soil, and some of it can be composted. Grasses and legumes are the best for this, and we'll look at them in the cover crops chapter. To be as close to being sustainable as possible, we should really be composting our own human manure, too, and maybe even have some of our own animals that make manure for the garden.

Carbon and Nitrogen

We loosely categorize our materials as being carbon materials and nitrogen materials. Carbon materials tend to be yellow-brown and dry, so they're often referred to as "browns." They can have anywhere from a 30:1 carbon to nitrogen ratio to hundreds of times as much carbon as nitrogen. Nitrogen materials tend to be wet and often green, so they're often called "greens."

Despite the "greens" name, they still have more carbon than nitrogen, but the ratio is generally much lower — between 10:1 and 30:1. Just because something is actually brown in color doesn't mean it's necessarily a high-carbon material. Chicken manure, for example, is definitely a "green," though if it actually looks green you should check what you're feeding your chickens.

Carbon materials, roughly in order of increasing carbon content, include leaves, straw, hay, paper/cardboard, and wood/sawdust. Nitrogen materials, roughly in order of increasing nitrogen content, include manure, seaweed, grass clippings, alfalfa hay and food scraps, although manure varies depending on the animal and the freshness. In reality, all of these materials vary based on different factors. Kitchen scraps, for example, can range from being high in nitrogen to a moderate 25:1 carbon to nitrogen ratio. You can find many reference charts online with carbon to nitrogen ratios for common materials. It's worth checking more than one, since they don't always agree with each other's estimates.

Other Materials

Most experts tell you not to compost cat and dog manure because they contain pathogens. I think we just need to know how to make a good pile that will kill most of the pathogens. Obviously we don't want our pile to be 50% dog manure. It will more likely be 2% dog manure, and that's just fine. It's true that these manures contain pathogens. Cat manure contains a microbe that is hazardous to children and fetuses in the womb. It's just as hazardous in the litter box and out on the lawn, so my opinion is that composting it is fine, as long as you're building a proper compost.

Experts also say not to compost diseased plants, but I disagree. First of all, most pathogens will be killed in a well-made pile, and perhaps more importantly, their predators will be given a reason to flourish if their food source is around. We need some disease around in order to keep the predators that eat that disease around, so I put all diseased plants right into the pile.

About the only things I don't compost are toxic materials such as colored paper and carpet, and noxious weeds such as quack grass and bindweed that may survive the composting process and be subsequently spread throughout the garden. But yes, I use oak leaves, pine needles, cooking oil, ashes, and even a small amount of meat in the middle of the pile.

If all of this sounds like a bit of work, it is. If you have more money than time, you can pay someone else to do it for you or buy compost, as long as it gets done. Using compost may be one of the most important things you can do for your garden.

Activators

Activators are extra substances that stimulate the composting process. They can be synthetic substances, which I don't recommend using, or they can be natural such as blood meal or bone meal. I don't use these either because of mad cow disease concerns, but I do use a few things.

Activators aren't crucial, so if you want to keep the external inputs to a minimum, you don't need them. People who are really into making the best compost may enjoy using some of them, but there is something to be said for keeping compost simple and using materials from your site as much as possible. Some of the potential benefits of using activators are a faster time for the pile to finish, a better finished product and less odor. Some activators such as clay, humates, calcitic lime and gypsum also decrease nutrient loss from the pile, especially nitrogen, which is a big deal.

When I'm building a new pile, I inoculate it with finished compost, generally as much as 10% of the pile or even just a few shovels if that's all I have. I'll also add as much as five pounds of humates per yard of raw materials, although that can get expensive. You'll read more about humates in the biostimulants chapter. It seems counterintuitive to add them when the ultimate goal of compost is moving it towards becoming humus, but adding humates can drastically improve the composting process.

I use as much as 10% clay in the pile. You don't want to add clay directly to sandy soil, but composting it gives it a chance to form a clay-humus complex. Even if I have clay soil, I'll add some to the pile to get this complex happening, because it helps the organic matter stay in the soil. Bags of bentonite clay are great, or even just a clay loam soil works well. This can get expensive, too, but even a small amount of clay is very useful.

I'll cover Effective Microorganisms (EM) and biostimulants later in the book, but I will mention here that inoculating the compost with

EM will speed up the process and may contribute to a decomposition that is more controlled and less oxidative so that nutrients are better retained. Odors are also greatly reduced. EM can be mixed with an equal amount of molasses and 100 parts water and sprayed onto compost until the desired moisture is obtained. That's 2 teaspoons each of EM and molasses per quart of water. I do this whenever I'm spraying the rest of my garden, which might be monthly.

Rock dust, covered in detail in the chapter on supplementing nutrients, is an incredible addition to the compost. Just sprinkle it in as you build the compost or work it in from the top. The nutrients have an opportunity to bind with the organic matter and are thus more effective when they're eventually incorporated into the soil. The dust will also improve the composting process. Different experts say to apply anywhere from 2 to 50 pounds of dust per cubic yard of compost. I use 20 pounds and I use a non-quartz dust such as basalt rather than something like granite. Quartz contributes less value to the pile and can inhibit proper humus formation.

If you've determined from a soil test that you need certain nutrients in your soil, it's great if you can first add them to your compost. Products such as calcitic lime and soft rock phosphate will bind with the organic matter, just like the rock dust. In fact, even without a soil test, it would be entirely appropriate to add five pounds of calcitic lime per yard of raw materials when building the compost, as it is so crucial to the microbes in the pile. Alternatively, five pounds of gypsum works well to get things moving, perhaps because of the sulfur. Otherwise, don't indiscriminately add mineral fertilizers because we may not want the nutrients contained therein. Urine, on the other hand, is exceptionally good for the compost, admittedly a bit easier for guys.

Penergetic is a homeopathic product that helps stabilize the composting process and bind nutrients. It's easiest to mix it in water and apply it that way. It can be mixed with the EM previously mentioned, but doesn't always go through a sprayer all that well. Along the same lines, I have used a series of preparations from the biodynamic world. More on these soon, too.

Manure

It's a bit of work for city folks to find manure, but it does play an important role in the compost pile for its nitrogen content and microbe population. A pile can be made without manure, but it can be difficult to find enough food scraps and fresh plant matter to supply adequate nitrogen. That being said, I've spent the last few years as a vegetarian and a vegan, and certainly support using compost that doesn't contain manure if you prefer. In fact, some research has shown that mad cow disease can be transferred from manure to mice. Consequently, I have used horse manure instead of cow manure, but I can't find any information showing which animal manures are safe from this point of view.

Fresh manure should not be applied directly to the soil for several reasons. The high nitrogen content can burn plants, and nitrogen can leach into the water table and volatize into the air. The high salt content can also cause problems. Other excess nutrients such as potassium can imbalance the soil. Weed seeds that weren't broken down by the animals' digestive processes can be spread throughout your garden too. Composting the manure in a well-made compost pile helps with many of these problems. Some nitrogen is still leached and volatized, but much of it ends up in the bodies of microbes. Composting manure first means salt and excess nutrients are buffered and weed seeds are killed.

Different manures have different characteristics. A mixture of manures is ideal, but just go with whatever kind you can get your hands on, keeping in mind the health of the source animals. Non-organic farm animals receive antibiotics, hormones and dewormers, some of which can survive the composting process. They certainly decrease the amount of beneficial microbes that end up in the manure. Chickens may be fed arsenic and their manure may have been treated with alum, which ties up the phosphorus, rendering it unavailable to plants. Mushroom manure is horse manure that has been used to grow mushrooms. It may contain huge amounts of pesticides and excess calcium, which is added to grow the mushrooms. Basically, we want organic manure.

Chicken, sheep and rabbit manure are generally considered the highest in nitrogen, and horse can be good, too. Pig and cattle manure are lower in nitrogen, but cattle manure is said to be rich in microbes. Even your own manure can be used if you're not taking pharmaceuticals. The best places to go are where there will be manure that isn't going to be used. Horse stables are a good bet and the manure is already mixed with straw, so it's very easy to handle. Poultry and dairy farms are okay, too. Small hobby farms aren't as good because they probably use all of their manure on site. You can even go ahead and buy a few bags of manure at your garden center, but it's already been composted and it may have nasty substances added. Check the label.

Buying Compost

Many gardeners will prefer buying compost from a garden center or the municipality. I have never lived in a city where I found great compost, but there is usually something acceptable. I lived in one city where gardeners flocked to pay $75 per yard for a compost made with fish waste and coniferous bark, complete with coniferous toxins. I didn't like the stuff much and gardening friends determined it had a calcium deficiency, but other people loved it and used it successfully.

When buying compost, it should smell good, not like garbage. I shouldn't have to say it, but it should not *contain* garbage. I once received a load of 15 yards of compost that was full of pieces of plastic, produced by a recycling company. I got my money back. Most purchased compost will not have been properly cured, so although I know it's not often feasible, if you have a month or two to let it continue composting on your property, that would be good.

Ask about the raw materials. Is there toxic paper mill waste or household waste, or pesticide-laden grass clippings in it? Don't use compost that has been made with sewage sludge. Yes, an argument can definitely be made that we should be composting this stuff rather than sending it raw to the landfill or our waterways, but we shouldn't be putting it in our gardens. Most of the pathogens can be destroyed, but a smorgasbord of heavy metals, pesticides and other chemicals survive the process and end up increasing in concentration. The sewage sludge industry may try to tell you differently, but there is plenty of research available on this.

Using Compost

The best time to apply compost is in the spring and fall when the conditions are best for the microbes, although if you're doing intensive composting throughout the year, you may apply it every month. In the spring, I apply it at least two weeks before planting to give some time for it to get acquainted with the soil. You can apply compost in the fall, but if you live in an area of high rainfall, you may want to cover your compost pile for the winter and wait until the spring to apply it, in order to avoid leaching some of the valuable nutrients from it.

If I'm using compost to make a new garden bed or install a new lawn in a soil without much organic matter, I'll often till two to three inches of compost into the top 8-10 inches of soil. That's generally too much compost to use more than once in the same garden, but for a soil that is low in organic matter, it's useful to get that in there in the beginning. For maintenance on existing beds, I'll apply between ⅛ inch and ¼ inch to the surface. I may lightly incorporate it, but I don't do much tilling for maintenance. For an existing lawn, you can screen out sticks and big clumps and apply it at ¼ inch thick. If possible, do this as often as in the spring and fall each year.

As I said, for maintaining nutrients and microbes, two to three inches is much more than needed. The Luebke's, who developed Controlled Microbial Compost on their organic farm in Austria recommend 10-12 tons per acre to start and then down to 3-8 tons for maintenance. Elaine Ingham recommends a maximum of 10 tons per acre and more like 1-5 tons per acre for maintenance. By my math, 12 tons per acre is only about ⅔ yard of compost (⅛ inch thick) per 1,000 square feet and 1 ton per acre is only about seven gallons of compost (¹⁄₉₀ inch thick) per 1,000 square feet.

You can see that even a tiny amount of compost is beneficial, so you don't need to worry about making or purchasing tons and tons. Instead, most home gardeners need only make or buy 1 yard of high quality compost each year. While the organic matter is important to get in there in the beginning, the nutrients and microbes may be the most important part and even seven gallons of good compost can supply plenty of them. Many gardeners and farmers apply too much compost, which results in nutrient imbalances, nutrient leaching and subsequent pollution of our waterways, and volatization into the atmosphere as greenhouse gases.

When planting trees and shrubs, rather than backfilling the hole with compost, amend the entire planting area at least twice as wide as the planting hole by incorporating compost into the soil. We want to enrich the soil, but we don't want to make the planting hole so rich that the roots don't leave it. Finished compost can be used as part of a potting mixture and for seed starting at about ⅓ compost, ⅓ sand and ⅓ soil. If possible, let this mixture age for a month or two before planting into it.

Summary

- Leaves, weeds, grass clippings, straw, manure and food scraps are the main compost ingredients, along with supplementary materials such as newspaper, cardboard, wood chips and sawdust.
- Compost, urine, humates, clay, EM, biostimulants, rock dust, mineral fertilizers, Penergetic and biodynamic preparations are activators that can improve the composting process.
- Manure is one of the most important ingredients for its nitrogen content and microbe population, as long as it is from animals that are healthy, happy and drug-free.
- I often use two to three inches of compost in a new bed, but as little as $\frac{1}{90}^{th}$ of an inch can be extremely beneficial.

Chapter 9

Making Compost

There are many composting methods, but the most common is probably the outdoor, above-ground compost pile. It's a good method. The size of the pile is important. Too small and it won't heat up properly, but too big and it won't get enough air. The best dimensions are three to five feet long, wide and high.

Although it isn't always necessary, an enclosure can keep out critters, prevent the pile drying from wind and look a little more tidy. It can be made of used wood pallets or fresh wood, concrete blocks or anything else that holds the compost in place. Some gardeners have two or three such enclosures for different stages of the pile, such as raw materials, in-process compost, and finished compost.

Compost is easy because microbes do the work. All we need to do is construct the pile to have the correct air, moisture, temperature and carbon to nitrogen ratio.

Air

Oxygen is important because we're making aerobic compost. We want to select for aerobic microbes because they're the most beneficial. It's not that anaerobic microbes are inherently bad, it's just that the way their metabolism works, they often give off gases that are toxic to plants. So the oxygen content should be at least 5% and preferably above 10%, although I don't actually keep track of it that scientifically.

Interestingly, the original Indore method perfected by Sir Albert Howard in India in the beginning of the 20th century, the foundation for how we compost today, was largely anaerobic because the pile was not turned very often. Most compost piles spend some of their time anaerobic. In fact, properly made anaerobic compost has some advantages, such as less nutrient loss, and therefore has some strong proponents. Still, most composters are going to try to promote aerobic conditions some of the time.

There are two basic methods to ensure there's enough air, and you can use either or both. The first is to put a layer of brush, branches and sticks on the ground under the pile that is at least a few inches high. Along with this, if I'm not looking for a finely screened compost, I'll include up to 10% twigs in the pile. They won't break down, but they will help with aeration. Depending on the end use, I may screen those out afterwords, or not.

The second method is to turn the pile over once in a while. You can turn it into a second bin or bring it out of the bin and back in again. For the fastest decomposition, this is done whenever the pile starts to cool down from it's hot phase, usually every three to seven days. Even turning a pile once each season is helpful. In fact, when I'm not in a hurry, this is what I do because while an unturned or little-turned compost pile takes longer to finish, it retains more nutrients. If you don't want to go through the trouble of turning the pile, using a pitchfork or other tool to introduce some air can help.

If you don't want to turn, but need your compost to be done more quickly, you can put perforated pipe into the pile both horizontally and vertically, or even just put some poles vertically into the pile that you can pull out after the pile is made. You can use ABS pipe if you're concerned about toxic PVC. The fastest way to get it done, however, is to turn it regularly. A "hot" compost pile can be largely done in four weeks. Most weed seeds and pathogens can be killed in this time. Many nutrients may be lost, but if you have enough materials, you can make a huge amount of compost in a year using this method. Of course, it's a lot of work turning the pile and it does contribute many more greenhouse gas emissions.

Some gardeners want fast compost, but don't want to turn the pile often. I don't blame them. In this case, you can spend more time ensuring aeration right from the beginning, using the method above and even building the pile one foot off the ground with a sturdy floor of wood and mesh.

If you don't need as much compost or if you don't want to do all of this turning, a slow compost pile has big advantages. Not only does it retain many more nutrients, but research shows it's more able to suppress disease, probably because more beneficial microbes survive the composting process, especially the fungi ones.

We can also allow the pile to go through a maturation phase, where it's already looking like finished compost, but sits for another perhaps six weeks at a cooler temperature allowing many microbes to multiply. This curing time is vital to make the best compost. Many adherents and some research projects have concluded that the extra work involved in the very intensive management, such as turning several times a week, is not worth the effort. There are strong opinions on both sides.

Moisture

A compost pile should be moist like a wrung-out sponge. This means when you take a fist full and squeeze it, it should feel wet but not drip water. This is somewhere between 30% and 70% moisture, with 50-60% generally considered ideal. If it's too moist, it can turn anaerobic and promote the wrong microbes, as well as leach a lot of nutrients. If it's not moist enough, decomposition will be very slow, but this is a better problem than too much moisture, which takes more effort to fix.

You'll probably need to have a hose handy while you build the pile so you can occasionally spray it with some water as you build it. I generally like to cover my pile when it's done being put together. In a dry climate, it helps decrease evaporation and in a wet climate, it protects the pile from too much moisture.

If the pile gets too moist or if it starts to smell bad, you can take it apart, air it out, and then add more carbon materials when you put it back together. If it gets too dry, water it and perhaps apply more nitrogen materials. You may need to take it apart here, too, in order to get it sufficiently wet. Hay and straw, for example, can keep water out of the pile. Actually, this can be used to your advantage in a wet climate because straw can act as a natural tarp if you put a layer on top.

Temperature

Compost goes through three stages of temperature that coincide with different microbes. The easiest way to kill weed seeds and pathogens is to ensure the pile gets up to a certain temperature for a certain amount of time. If you want to get technical, you can buy a compost thermometer and measure the temperature to make sure you're okay, or you can learn by experience.

Different studies have come up with different ideal temperatures, but it's generally agreed that 130-150F (55-65C) for several days is adequate. If you're judging with your hand, it should be too hot in the pile to keep your hand there for long. We don't want it to go above 150F because that degrades humus and humic acid complexes, as well as scaring off a lot of microbes. Ideally, it would be allowed to finish for six weeks at cooler temperatures. Still, significant reductions in pathogens have happened when the compost pile never went above 104F (40C). Even a cool compost, if well-made and left to mature, can control pathogens to safe levels.

To get the higher temperature, the pile should be at least 3 by 3 by 3 feet as a bare minimum, and as much as 5 by 5 by 5 feet, although some people even build 10 feet wide. If you're making a lot more compost, therefore, you can make a row that is 5 feet high by 10 feet wide by whatever length you have room for. At my parents' tree farm, we have a compost "windrow" that is probably 50 feet long.

The thermometer can also be used to tell you when to turn the compost, if you're looking for fast decomposition. Turn it whenever it goes below 104F (40C) or if it gets too hot at 150F (65C).

Compost that gets too hot will lose even more carbon as carbon dioxide than usual, or as methane if the pile is anaerobic. Nitrogen is lost as ammonia and other compounds, and sulfur as hydrogen sulfide — one of the highly toxic "sewer gases" that makes a poorly built compost smell bad. For the most part, the more frequently a pile is turned, the hotter it tends to get and the hotter it stays, although the most important part of reaching high temperatures is the right amount of moisture, proper pile size, and balanced carbon to nitrogen ratio. That being said, if the pile stays hot for months and is rather wet, that probably means it's anaerobic.

Carbon to Nitrogen (C:N) Ratio

Microbes need nitrogen for growth, and carbon for energy. If a pile has too much nitrogen, it may turn anaerobic, create bad compost and smell awful. Some people still feel that too much nitrogen is better than too much carbon as long as it doesn't smell. Some people feel that too much carbon is better because it will still compost, albeit very slowly over several years, but at least it shouldn't go anaerobic. If the pile doesn't heat up, you may need to add more nitrogen materials.

The ideal carbon to nitrogen ratio of a new pile is somewhere between 25:1 and 30:1, by weight, not volume. We don't have to get it exactly right, but that's what we're going for. The way to get this ratio is to use between two and four times as much carbon materials as nitrogen materials. If you're using very high-carbon materials like sawdust and wood chips, you may even end up using an equal volume of nitrogen and carbon materials.

If you have a lot of chicken manure and food scraps with their very low carbon to nitrogen ratio, and aren't using too many very high carbon materials like sawdust, you may use four times as many carbon materials as nitrogen materials. By the end of the composting process, the ratio in the pile goes down to somewhere around 10:1, because carbon is released as carbon dioxide.

Incidentally, this end ratio is approximately what the soil needs, too. If we pile on too much carbonaceous mulch, the microbes may steal most of the nitrogen from the surrounding soil in order to break that carbon down, resulting in deficiencies in plants. Conversely, if we add too much nitrogen, the microbes may burn up soil carbon faster than we want.

Building the Pile

There are many variations on how to build a compost pile. Here is how I do it, step-by-step. This is for a 3 by 3 by 3 foot pile that makes a 1 square yard or 27 square feet pile of organic matter, but if your pile will be going through a cold winter and you can get enough materials, you might go for a 5 by 5 by 5 foot pile. Build it in an area with lots of room so you can get in and out of the bin and turn the pile, and make sure your hose can reach it. If your city uses a lot of chlorine in the water, it may be better to use rainwater to moisten the pile.

I build my pile all at once in order to create the best possible pile. It doesn't work as well to just throw scraps in as they come because it's more difficult to get the mass required and the correct C:N ratio, so I make sure I have all of my materials ready at the start. If you're generating compostable materials like garden waste and food scraps high in nitrogen on a more continuous basis, they can be occasionally put in the pile without changing the C:N ratio too much, although it's nice to have a carbon material to add at the same time, such as straw.

I tend to use manure, kitchen scraps, leaves and straw as my basic materials, along with whatever other organics I can get, such as waste from a brewery, orchard or winery. The composting process will be much faster if big materials are shredded or chopped, but if chopped too fine, the pile will go anaerobic.

I tend to place my pile in the sun, although this isn't crucial. If I lived in a hotter climate, I would probably place it in the shade. I build my pile right on the ground to invite earthworms and other soil insects up into it. I water the ground first and put a base layer of branches and brush three feet wide and long.

Some people like to build in layers. I just take turns putting carbon- and nitrogen-rich materials into the pile. I usually put two or three shovels of carbon material for every shovel of nitrogen material. If you have neighbors who are intolerant of any odor, you can use four shovels of carbon material to be safe. I may also try to have a carbon layer on all sides of the pile to control odor and discourage animals and flies from hanging out around the compost.

I occasionally sprinkle in my activators throughout this process, and hit the pile with some water every once in awhile. These activators may include any of the following: compost, humates, clay, EM, sea minerals, liquid kelp, rock dust, calcitic lime, gypsum, other mineral fertilizers, urine, and biodynamic preps and other energizers. If I have any metal poles or long, broken shovel handles around, I stick them vertically into the pile and pull them out after the pile is made.

I top it off with a layer of leaves or straw and tarp it during the rainy season or the sunny, hot season to decrease evaporation. I also like to make the compost pile a centerpiece in my garden and in that case, I don't like having an ugly blue plastic tarp on top. The straw will keep moisture and wind out.

If I'm in a hurry, I turn this pile every three to seven days. Otherwise, I turn it every three months or so, except winter. I may put food scraps into the inside of the pile once a week, adding some carbon material at the same time. If the compost isn't working or smells bad, it could be the wrong moisture balance, not enough air, too small size, or an improper carbon to nitrogen ratio. The pile will shrink by as much as 75% by the time it's done.

Sheet Mulching

Sheet mulching is kind of like composting right in the garden, mostly to create new garden beds and in existing vegetable beds during the fallow season. The ingredients are the same, with the addition of a weed barrier layer made of some kind of easily available natural material — cardboard and newspaper are most commonly used. Some people are concerned about the glues in cardboard and inks in newspaper, but they're mostly fairly benign and should be broken down by microbes. I wouldn't use glossy or colored paper.

Sheet mulching is an amazing way to smother weeds and build fertility and structure at the same time by layering various materials as high as 18 inches. It has a few advantages over composting, perhaps the biggest being that it's less work. Once you put the materials down, that's where they stay, whereas with composting you generally turn it a few times and then have to move it into the garden. It takes longer to break down than compost, but that also means it lasts longer as a mulch.

At the same time, it generally doesn't get hot enough to kill weed seeds and pathogens. If you keep a continuous mulch, most of the weeds will be taken care of anyway. If you're using a diversity of materials from good sources, the few pathogens you'll be introducing will be taken care of, too. Unfortunately, some tenacious weeds can be introduced with sheet mulch, giving you months and years of work to get them out, so for some people, a proper compost pile can be less work in the long run.

If you already have slugs, you'll probably have more when you build a sheet mulch. They love the stuff. That's one reason why I put my garden in a sunny, hot spot and don't over water, but a few seem to show up anyway. There are plenty of ways to take care of them organically.

There are many methods of making a sheet mulch. I start with a ½ inch layer of newspaper or cardboard on the ground to suppress weeds, and then water the heck out of it. There's no need to pull the weeds first. Even if you do this on a lawn, you don't have to till up the lawn first — just mow it short and leave the clippings there. In fact, a sheet mulch can be a handy way to deal with weeds you don't want to put in your compost or with turf you've removed from somewhere else in the garden — just throw them under the weed barrier layer.

Then use all the same ingredients you would in a compost pile. Many people like to build it in layers, which is why it's sometimes called a "lasagna" bed. From the bottom up, it might look something like this: fertilizers such as calcitic lime, cardboard, one inch depth of manure or other nitrogen materials, eight inches hay or straw, one to two inches compost, and two inches straw or leaves to top it off. I prefer to mix the manure/nitrogen materials and hay/straw together using two to three shovels of carbon material for every shovel of nitrogen material, but the bottom and top of the pile look about the same. I also use all of my other activators during the process and some water. It's much the same as building a compost pile.

If you're feeling impatient and want to plant some vegetables into it right away, dig your planting holes in the sheet mulch and put compost in them. Some plants will like this better than others — squash does great in a new sheet mulch. The plants will be growing in the mulch, not down in the ground. One exception to this is potatoes, which can be planted directly into the soil beneath the sheet mulch, if you cut holes into the cardboard for the shoots to come through. This works because seed potatoes are big compared to other seeds, so they have enough energy to make it up to the light through all that mulch, and can grow many tubers in the extra deep organic soil, without needing to mound up the soil around them like people often do.

It can be difficult to get enough materials to sheet mulch a big area, so it's often best done for a kitchen garden right near the house, which will end up covered in my most important foods for daily picking, such as herbs and greens. I may even do this inside a raised garden bed.

Personally, I use sheet mulching and always have a compost pile going, too. They're both just too useful to choose one over the other.

Summary

- Ensure sufficient air by putting sticks and brush on the bottom of and even throughout the pile, turning the pile, and generally keeping it a maximum of five feet wide and high.
- A pile should be kept at 50-60% moisture, like a wrung-out sponge. Control the amount of water that gets in with a cover on the top and have a hose nearby to add more as needed.
- Proper temperature is achieved by making the pile big enough, using a good ratio of carbon to nitrogen, and turning the pile when it gets too hot or cold.
- A starting carbon to nitrogen ratio of between 25:1 and 30:1 is usually achieved by using between two and four times as much carbon materials as nitrogen materials by volume.
- Sheet mulching is like composting right in the garden to save time and effort and builds up the soil and mulch without tilling.

Chapter 10

Indoor Composting

Perhaps you don't have the room or inclination to make a full-sized outdoor compost pile. As we've seen, even a small amount of compost can be highly beneficial. This chapter outlines two methods of composting your food scraps that can be done right in your house.

Bokashi

Bokashi is a fermented substrate such as rice bran or wheat bran, but it can be made with many other kinds of waste materials such as sawdust, grain mash from breweries, and other grain scraps. I've made a lot of bokashi with sawdust, just because that's what I had available. It's fermented by mixing it with the liquid microbial inoculant called Effective Microorganisms (EM). It's done today because it makes some of the most incredibly beneficial organic matter possible for the garden, but traditionally, it was also a method of making use of waste products.

It has many of the same benefits as compost, but the process is a fermentation, without air, like making wine or pickles. It's actually better for the environment than composting because no carbon dioxide, methane, nitrogen compounds or water vapor are volatized into the air during the process, and some people argue that the finished product is consequently more nutritious. The small bucket that I use to make it isn't going to make a big difference for the environment, but it can be done on a larger scale if you prefer.

Bokashi is made by filling a container such as a five-gallon pail approximately two-thirds full with the substrate in order to leave room for stirring. You can optionally add in some rock dust. Then you make a mixture of EM, molasses and water, generally at a ratio of 1:1:100, which is 2 teaspoons each of EM and molasses per quart of water. In this liquid, you can optionally mix liquid kelp, fish, and/or sea minerals. This liquid is thoroughly mixed in with the substrate in the pail until it is moist like a wrung-out sponge all the way through, just like your compost pile.

Then press the mixture firmly and cover it with a plastic bag and then a plate, and even a weight (if you have it) to keep the air out. I do the same thing when I make sauerkraut, another ferment product. The bokashi will now only take up perhaps ½ of the pail. We want this to ferment without air for one or two weeks, therefore no more stirring is done from now on. Some people let it go for months. It's better if you can keep it warm somehow, around 100F. Otherwise, it may take a few weeks, which is fine.

When it's done, it should have a pleasant sweet and sour smell, kind of like pickles. If it smells really bad, something went wrong. Perhaps the moisture level was too high and acid was developed. In this case, throw it on top of the compost pile, clean the bucket, and start again. Likewise, any smelly molds indicate something went wrong. It's alright to have some white fungi, but you should not see fuzzy green or gray molds.

Once your bokashi is finished, you can put it in the garden or store it in a cool, dark place. If stored anaerobically under the same conditions as it was made, it will keep many months, and can actually improve with time. When stored moist and not anaerobically, it seems to keep for about two to three weeks, and longer at cooler temperatures. If dried and then stored, it will keep for at least two months.

The bokashi can then be used as an incredible way to inoculate your soil with these beneficial microbes. The 2.5 gallons of final product left in that pail will inoculate 500 square feet of garden. It can be put on top of the soil or dug in. It can also be dried to increase storage time by spreading it out on a tarp in the sun for a few hours.

While bokashi is traditionally a good way to make use of waste materials, it is now often dried and used in the kitchen to help pickle fruit and vegetable waste. Every time you put the waste into a waste bucket, a small handful of dried bokashi is sprinkled on top. Odors are controlled extremely well. You can buy buckets that allow you to drain the excess water from the waste bucket, but they're rather pricey, so some people may want to just drill a couple of holes in the bottom of the bucket and let it drain into another container.

When the waste bucket is full, you can bury the waste in the garden or compost. Because it's infused with these microbes, it will break down extremely fast. You can even put meat and dairy in the bucket, which some people don't like to put in their compost. If made with bran, bokashi can also be fed to livestock at a rate of 3-5% of their food.

Worm Composting

Compost made by worms is called vermicompost. The finished product consists of their manure (castings) and some decayed organic matter. I've been making it for a few years, or I should say the red wiggler worms in my bin have been making it — I've just supplied some food, water and bedding. Of course, billions of microbes and hundreds of other small insects help them out. Vermicompost is a nice way to recycle your food scraps into beautiful compost. The worms dine on the food scraps largely to get the microbes covering the surface.

Unlike outdoor composting, this method definitely needs a bin to house the worms. I use a plastic storage container that's approximately 18 inches wide, 24 inches long, and 12 inches high, with a lid. This size easily allows for the four to five pounds of food scraps I need composted each week, perfect for two people. A wood box would be nice, too. To make your bin, drill 12 holes approximately 1/2 inch in diameter in the bottom and at least as many holes towards the top of the sides. Some people also like to drill holes in the lid. The holes allow for air and water vapor exchange, with the bottom holes also facilitating drainage. You'll need something underneath the bin to catch the water that drains out. Another upside-down lid is often the perfect size for this.

I don't need to go into much detail here on the materials, because they're basically the same as a regular compost pile. I don't use meat, dairy or oil, and the worms also don't like too much citrus or salty food. Since your food scraps are your nitrogen materials, you'll need to supply some other forms of carbon materials as bedding. I use a mixture of shredded newspaper, leaves and straw. A handful of sand (or soil containing sand) is also needed for the worms to be able to digest food properly. Most resources recommend adding lime to increase the pH. We've learned how that is incorrect reasoning, but I do believe 1/3 cup of calcitic lime per cubic foot of compost will probably be helpful for the calcium, just as it is in an outdoor compost pile. You can also add any of the activators outlined in the other composting chapters.

Just like a compost pile, your bin needs to have proper air, moisture, temperature and carbon to nitrogen ratio. The holes bring in air. You may want to raise the bin slightly off the ground to increase air flow through those bottom holes. While shredding the bedding materials is nice for the worms, leaving some of them more coarse will help avoid compressed, anaerobic conditions. The bedding should be wetter than a compost pile — at about 70-90% moisture. Basically, you want it very moist, but not waterlogged because the worms still need oxygen. It takes about three times as much water as bedding to get it moist enough. The temperature should be between 60F and 80F, out of direct sunlight. Just like an outdoor compost, if the bin is smelly or attracting fruit flies, it's time to add some carbon and perhaps stop adding food scraps for awhile.

When the bedding mixture is thoroughly moistened, you can add your red wiggler worms, *Eisenia fetida*. These are small worms that excel at living in this kind of environment. The red earthworm, *Lum-*

bricus rubellus will also work, but they're not ideal and are now causing problems in North American forests. Other earthworms won't work. I start with the most common recommendation of one cubic foot of bedding and one pound of worms. I have even used half a pound when worms were expensive.

After the worms have settled in for a couple of days, you can begin to add food scraps. Do this once or twice a week, burying them in a different spot in the bedding each time. I gave them 1.5 pounds of food scraps per week at the beginning. When the worm and microbe populations have multiplied, I give them four to five pounds per week. I like to work my way across the bedding every couple of weeks burying the food, and then when I start back at the beginning, the original food scraps are mostly decayed. Every month or so, I'll add more bedding to get some more carbon back in there.

After three to six months, you'll want to stop adding food scraps for a couple of weeks to let the worms really break down what's already there. Then, to use the finished compost, you need to separate it from the worms. There are several methods of harvesting the worms, two of which I've used. The first is to move everything into one half of the bin and start new bedding and food scraps in the other half of the bin. After two to four weeks, most of the worms will have migrated to the new side of the bin to get at the new food. You can then harvest the finished compost from the other half and use it in houseplants and the garden the same as you would use other compost.

The second method of harvesting is to empty the entire contents of the bin onto a tarp or garbage bag under a bright light. Worms don't like light, so they'll try to stay buried at the bottom of the pile. You can separate the compost into several small piles and harvest most of it from the top of these piles, occasionally waiting a few minutes while the worms delve deeper into the pile. In the end you'll be left with mostly just the worms, which you can return to new bedding in the bin. Make sure to do this quickly because they'll die if left in the light for long. Wear moist gloves because the oils on your hands can hurt them. Their eggs will be killed in this process.

Once in awhile, a worm will exit the bin. You don't have to worry about it setting up residence in your home, because it will generally die from dehydration and exposure to light right beside the bin. If many worms are exiting the bin, something is wrong. It may be too moist or not moist enough, or there may not be enough air. It may be that the compost is done. The worm castings are slightly toxic to them, so they don't want to stay around long when the food has run out and it's mostly just castings left. In rare cases, you may find the worms aren't eating the food or are rolling up together in a ball. It usually comes back to a problem with the oxygen, moisture, temperature, or carbon to nitrogen ratio.

Feel free to experiment with bokashi or worm composting, or both. I do both because I enjoy the process and know the resulting composts will be very different in terms of their microbial makeup, but I would say bokashi is easier to start with.

Summary

- Bokashi and worm composting are methods that can be used indoors to make a small batch of quality compost for use in the garden.
- Bokashi is EM-infused organic matter that is applied to the soil or mixed with food scraps to help break them down and control odors.
- A vermicompost bin is used to break down food scraps and bedding into a very nice finished compost.

Chapter 11

Cover Crops

Cover crops are traditionally thought of as plants used when the garden or field is empty, such as over winter and sometimes over summer, but I'd like to broaden this definition to also include plants used during the growing season, inter-planted with food crops or even in ornamental beds where they're sometimes called groundcovers or living mulch. They're also referred to as green manures, generally when they're going to be incorporated into the soil after a certain period of growth.

A good goal is to make sure your soil is always covered with plants, and cover crops help achieve this goal. Some soil experts consider this more important than composting. It's certainly more natural, and more feasible in large gardens and on farms where it's difficult to make enough compost to cover everything, let alone distribute it.

The main reasons home gardeners use cover crops are to improve soil fertility, increase organic matter and control weeds and plant predators. There are also many other uses, such as to prevent erosion, send roots deep to break up compaction, conserve moisture and increase water infiltration, attract insects and other animals, and even provide food for humans and animals. Let's look at the three main reasons.

Cover crops improve soil fertility in a couple of ways. The main benefit most people think of is the increase in nitrogen we can get from planting legumes, such as clover. Many leguminous plants and a few others form symbiotic relationships with nitrogen-fixing bacteria such as Rhizobia and Bradyrhizobium. The plant provides the bacteria with a home on its roots, as well as food. The bacteria give some nitrogen to the plant in return. Some of that nitrogen ends up in the soil when the plant is alive, and more when it eventually decays. I've read that 22 lbs. of fixed nitrogen is as good as applying 220 lbs. of ammonium sulfate or 1,100 lbs. of sulfate of ammonia because the fixed nitrogen is efficiently used as it's produced, whereas most of the chemical ammonia that is applied is leached and volatized.

Fertility is also improved by many cover crop plants that send deep roots into the soil and harvest minerals that aren't reached by other plants. Even if they don't send deep roots, just being there is hugely beneficial because many of the nutrients would otherwise leach. Cover crops can stop a lot of this leaching both by taking up some of the nutrients themselves and by taking up a lot of the water that would otherwise be heading back to the water table, bringing nutrients with it.

Nitrate nitrogen is a prime example of a leachable nutrient because it's water soluble, so it doesn't stay around for long in the soil when there's a lot of water moving through. While legumes fix the nitrogen, grasses and brassicas are much better than legumes at stopping it from leaching. Many other nutrients such as calcium and potassium can also leach without plants and organic matter to hang on to them.

The next big benefit is organic matter. Any plant will increase the organic matter content of the soil simply by the dropping of leaves (including evergreens) and the constant growth and death of roots, but cover crops are often turned into the soil to give a huge influx of biomass to it. Less talked about, but potentially more important, plants send a huge amount of carbon — as well as protein, amino acids and thousands of other substances — into the soil as exudates. Grasses are especially adept at quickly getting big and building soil. For example, cereal rye adds large amounts of organic matter, sorghum-sudangrass sends deep roots to break up compaction, and annual ryegrass is great for stabilizing and drying out wet soil.

Along with the addition of plant biomass is the increase, or at least maintenance, of microbial biomass. Without plants, many microbes will go to sleep, but if we keep plant cover on the soil they'll keep working, even through winter, albeit more slowly. This is especially important for mycorrhizal fungi, who need a host to stay active.

And then there is weed and pest control. Plants accomplish weed control by several mechanisms — competing for water and nutrients, shading out the soil, crowding out the soil below ground with their roots, and sending out chemicals to inhibit other plants from growing. Cereal rye is an overwintering crop that controls weeds both physically and chemically by producing compounds that are toxic to many other plants. Sorghum-sudangrass does the same in the summer. The chemicals can inhibit germination of your vegetable seeds — a process called allelopathy — so be sure to wait two to three weeks after incorporating the cover crop before seeding.

Plant predator control is achieved mainly by the cover crops inviting and hosting a diversity of microorganisms, nematodes and insects that keep the system more in balance, as well as producing their own antibacterial compounds. Some people worry about the cover crop crowding out their other plants. It's possible, but I like to have them touching so the beneficials climbing on the cover crop will move over to my other plants, too.

It's also true that cover crops can attract some predators. For example, cereal rye, orchardgrass and crimson clover may attract armyworms. This is one of the reasons I like to plant a combination of two or three cover crops, to create more diversity, decreasing the chance of one insect causing problems.

Some cover crop benefits, such as organic matter or fertility improvement, are only substantially noticeable after a couple of years of cover cropping, while others such as weed control and insect attraction are noticeable right away. I have my dad cover cropping his entire tree nursery with a mixture of grasses and legumes. It's work to keep it mowed, but it's slowly increasing organic matter, improving soil structure and fertility, controlling erosion and attracting insects and other small animals.

Cover crop selection is an involved decision for farmers and gardeners, who have to decide which of the above benefits are most important and select appropriate crops based on that, as well as choosing crops that are going to work in their climate conditions. We gardeners can spend a lot of time making this decision, but for most of us, I believe it's more important to just get something in the ground that will satisfy the main goals of increasing organic matter and soil fertility. We can also enjoy the by-products of this choice, including some weed control, and we can always experiment with some different crops to see what we like best.

That being said, I have a few tips to help the decision. While all cover crops have some ability to increase soil fertility and organic matter content, and to control weeds and plant predators, certain plants excel at certain tasks.

Legumes

Although there are several non-legume nitrogen-fixing plants, often working in partnership with a group of bacteria called Actinomycetes, most of our nitrogen-fixers are from the legume family, working with Rhizobium bacteria. It's usually a good idea to use a legume as a cover crop, such as vetch or clover. This is especially important when you're going to be planting crops that are considered to have a high demand for nitrogen, such as corn or other grasses, but almost all vegetable crops benefit from a legume. In fact, it's a great idea to grow one interspersed among your beds.

The root hairs of a legume search the soil for the right species of Rhizobium bacteria with which to partner. Certain strains of Rhizobia provide optimum nitrogen production for each legume. If the plant roots don't find their ideal match, they will work with the other strains, but they won't be able to produce as much nitrogen. The root encircles the bacteria colony and creates a nodule as big as a kernel of corn where the bacteria live. The bacteria make an enzyme that converts gaseous nitrogen to ammonia and the plant uses that ammonia to build amino acids. In return, the plant gives carbohydrates and other organic substances to the bacteria.

When the plant goes to seed, the nodules are discarded and the bacteria remain viable in the soil for three to five years waiting for the next legume to come along. Unfortunately, the bacteria may not be numerous enough to provide optimum nitrogen fixation when that next legume is planted. Since we don't know if we have the right bacteria in our soil and whether or not they are numerous enough, it's a very good idea to add them in with the seed or buy seed that has already been inoculated.

Each legume needs a different inoculant. Ideally, the garden center will have the right one or a mixture. If the folks in the garden center don't seem to know what you need, you may have to order it online. The two main forms of inocula are solid and liquid, with solid being the most common. Either of them can be mixed with the seed before you plant or applied in the furrow directly with the seeds.

Even though they're planted earlier than grasses in the fall in order to get them established before winter, legumes don't do much until spring, when they put on their growth and fix most of their nitrogen. Most of the nitrogen fixed by a legume isn't released to other plants until the legume decomposes. Even then, if the legume is allowed to produce seeds, much of the nitrogen will end up in the seed. This is great if you want the plant to reseed on its own, or if you want to leave it as a groundcover such as in an orchard, but it's not great if you want that nitrogen to be available to other plants.

What we often do, therefore, is cut the crop down right in the early- to mid-stages of blooming in the spring before we seed or transplant our vegetables. If you want to save seeds, you can keep just a few plants for this purpose, and cut the rest down. If you have bare soil during the summer, legumes work great to fill that in, too.

Legumes also contribute to an increase in organic matter and weed control, although not as much as grasses. Also, since they break down much faster than grasses when you knock them down, due to their relatively higher nitrogen content, they don't provide a long-lasting mulch. The positive side of that is that they do release their nutrients more quickly to plants than grasses.

If you're planning a lawn area and are a patient person, you might plant a legume cover crop such as clover or trefoil for a year before installing the lawn, for all of the above benefits. It's no fun trying to maintain a lawn that was planted in poor soil. You can seed right into that clover and watch each year as the grass slowly outcompetes the legume — provided your soil is healthy.

Grasses

Non-legumes used for cover cropping are often grasses. They're used when your main goals are creating a lot of organic matter, controlling weeds, and taking up nutrients — especially nitrogen — from the soil so that they don't leach. If you have a bed that was mostly planted with legumes such as peas and beans during the growing season, or even better, if you have a soil test showing a lot of nitrogen in the soil after harvest, it will probably be more beneficial to plant a grass cover crop. This grass will do a better job than a legume of keeping a lot of that nitrogen rather than allowing it to leach, and also acts as an excellent weed control and huge organic matter builder.

While legumes do help build humus, grasses and other grains really excel at this job. It's partly because they grow fast and get big, but also because they're composed of more cellulose and lignin, materials that contribute to humus. In contrast, an annual clover will break down more readily and become a much better short-term source of nitrogen and other nutrients for crops.

Grasses have a higher carbon to nitrogen ratio than legumes, so they break down more slowly, acting as a longer-term mulch, but this also means the microbes may need to steal nitrogen from the soil in order to break them down. The implication of that is you don't want to use too much grass in a garden that is nitrogen-deprived, or at least you want to turn it in earlier in spring, because the carbon content increases as the plant grows. The longer breakdown period of grasses also means the nutrients will not be as immediately available to the next crop.

Winter annual grasses are seeded in late summer or autumn. They grow before winter, go dormant during winter, and grow again in the spring before we usually cut them down. Summer annual grasses are occasionally grown during the summer if you've harvested everything out of a garden bed and aren't going to plant it again until fall.

Companion Plants and Polycultures

Ecological landscape designers often look to the native plant communities in their region to see which plants grow together naturally, in order to help determine suitable plant combinations for their designs. This is a form of companion planting, but plants need not have evolved together in order to benefit each other.

Companion planting in a vegetable garden involves pairing plants that may come from different regions, but nonetheless work well together. Examples are green beans and strawberries, carrots and tomatoes, and lettuce and spinach. Sometimes the plants simply work well together because they take up different areas above or below the soil. Sometimes one plant deters a predator of the other plant. Often, the benefits realized are not nearly as grand as some gardening books indicate, but usually, no harm is done.

A polyculture goes a step further. It involves planting many plants together to take advantage of various niches in the garden, much the way nature fosters this diversity. Some will grow tall and provide shade, while others hug the ground. Some are ready for harvest early, while others take longer, even within the same food group, such as lettuces or tomatoes. Some attract beneficial insects, while others repel plant predators. Some provide nitrogen for the soil, while others happily gobble it up.

Permaculture has embraced the polyculture philosophy by using multi-level plantings to take advantage of all the various opportunities in the garden. Another concept is the guild, where a central plant such as a fruit tree is surrounded by a group of plants that benefit the tree. For more information on permaculture and polycultures, a great place to start is *Gaia's Garden: A Guide To Home-Scale Permaculture* by Toby Hemenway.

I just wanted to point out here that plants provide fertility for each other. While legumes and grasses are the most common cover crops, especially over winter, ornamental and food gardens should be interplanted with plants that provide more benefits than just being beautiful. Examples of beneficial plants to use are yarrow, fennel, lemon balm and clover, and there are hundreds of others in books such as *Gaia's Garden* listed above.

Mixtures

Let's get back to legumes and grasses as off-season cover crops. Rather than choosing one, I almost always mix grasses and legumes in order to get the benefits of both. By planting them together and occasionally going as far as to plant several cultivars or varieties of each, there is a much greater chance that at least one or two of them will do well in your soil and climate conditions. For example, if you have a soil with a lot of excess nitrogen, your legume might not grow as much but your grass might be very happy, whereas a soil that is low in nitrogen may favor the legume. It's more complicated than that, but the idea is that one of them will be happier in your soil conditions.

If it's a wet season, even within one species, some cultivars will do much better than others. Same for dry, cold, windy weather, etc. Different plants also have different growth habits, so a mixture can better cover the soil, make full use of different levels of sunlight and even grow off each other. Vetch will climb up a tall grass for support to reach sunlight, which is one reason that it's often planted together with rye.

There are dozens of cover crops, each with their own strengths and weaknesses and some more appropriate for certain regions, but there are a few that are used nearly universally and I recommend you start with them, or find out what works in your area. Once you have success with the basics, you can try others. You can even experiment with cover-cropping year round, in between your rows. This is being done very successfully in many warm-climate countries where leaving fields fallow in only cover crops isn't economically feasible, because the opportunity cost of not growing cash crops is too great.

Gardeners and farmers use all kind of plants as cover crops: dandelion, fava beans, fennel/dill, yarrow, and even parsley, but let's start with the following: hairy vetch, clover, cereal rye and annual ryegrass.

Hairy Vetch (Legume)

Hairy vetch (*Vicia villosa*) is the king of nitrogen production and that alone makes it worthwhile. It doesn't grow much in the fall, but is a good survivor through winter (hardiness zones 4 and up). Come spring, hairy vetch can get big, contributing lots of organic matter and smothering weeds. It doesn't need particularly fertile soil and tolerates many soil conditions. A friend of mine has it growing on a steep slope as part of a mixture to help stabilize the soil.

Vetch does need moisture to get going, but after that it can handle drought. With sufficient moisture, it can be used in much of North America, but isn't used much in the Great Plains, Southwest and Northwest. Even in the Southeast, clover is better. While it can definitely survive the winter, planting it with a grass will greatly improve its chances.

After you cut it down, you can seed vegetables right into it, although if you've let it grow for quite awhile in the spring, you might take some excess to the compost pile. Woollypod vetch (*Vicia villosa* ssp. *dasycarpa*) might be more appropriate in areas with little rain or irrigation. It's used extensively in California, and up the West Coast.

Clovers (Legume)

Clovers don't generally produce as much nitrogen as vetch, but they've been used for hundreds of years, so they must do something right. Bees sure like many varieties. Here are just a couple of the most universal species. Your garden center should carry what's right for your area. Towards the end of the summer, you can try seeding clover or another nitrogen-fixer into a bed before you harvest most of your vegetables.

Red clover (*Trifolium pratense*) is used mostly in the eastern half of North America as a dependable winter annual, biennial or short-lived perennial (zone 4 and up) that creates a modest amount of nitrogen. It's not the fastest or biggest grower, but it's one of the best when it comes to handling a wide range or soil and climate types.

White clover (*Trifolium repens*) is raised as a perennial to hardiness zone 4, although it's used as a winter annual down south where drought and disease weaken it. It's the typical living mulch, used year round in orchards and even vegetable gardens. If it were up to me, it would be used more in ornamental gardens instead of plants like ivy. It stays fairly low at 6-12 inches, tolerates shade, cutting/mowing and foot traffic.

Yellow sweetclover (*Melilotus officinalis*) and white sweetclover (*M. albus*) can grow in most of North America. It's not a huge nitrogen producer when used as a winter annual, because it's mostly a biennial, doing much of its nitrogen production in year two. It can, however, live on infertile soil and survive drought and winter, although it's not a big fan of really wet soils. It has a taproot to break up compaction, and creates a lot of biomass with its abundant growth.

Rye (Grass)

Cereal rye (*Secale cereale*) is my favorite grass for cover cropping. It's an annual that grows well pretty much anywhere in North America other than the very Southwest. It can handle infertile soil and can be planted fairly late in the fall and still do well. It prefers lighter soils, but grows in clay, and can tolerate both dry and very wet soils.

Rye is the absolute best when it comes to retaining soil nitrogen, makes a huge amount of organic matter, and is great at controlling weeds. It also controls predators and attracts beneficials. It grows big and can get a high carbon to nitrogen ratio that can tie up carbon in the spring, so I combine it with a legume. I often use hairy vetch, which the rye protects over winter, at a 1:1 rye to vetch ratio by weight. You can also use it with clover at the same ratio.

An alternative for farmers and gardeners to deal with the carbon is to cut down the rye early in the spring, but in areas with high rainfall, your soil may get too wet after that and you may lose a lot of nitrogen. Keeping the rye growing longer would suck up the spring rains. A much better option for home and market gardeners who get a lot of spring rain would be to cut it down much later and just remove some of the clippings for our compost bins. Then we get the benefits of the grass staying in the soil longer — less nitrogen loss and drier soil — and we get to use all of that biomass.

Seed rye in late summer to autumn in hardiness zones 3-7 or even as late as mid-winter in zones 8 and up. The seed prefers to get down into the soil one to two inches so some light cultivation will be beneficial, but broadcasting on top of the soil is possible. While it depends greatly on your region and goals, a good time for most of us to cut it in the spring is when it's 12-18 inches tall, before setting seed. Wait three to four weeks to seed vegetables and at least a week before planting transplants.

Annual Ryegrass (Grass)

Annual ryegrass (*Lolium multiflorum*) is not the same as cereal rye, but it's another great crop to use for soil building, erosion prevention and weed control, across most of North America, other than the

Southwest, Northwest and Great Plains. It's inexpensive and fast to establish, although it may not make it through the winter in the north. Even there, if established early enough in the fall, it will produce some good biomass before winter and act as a great nurse crop to clover that you can plant at the same time at a 1:1 ratio by weight. A nurse plant is a plant that offers protection or assistance to another plant. Annual ryegrass can also be used over the summer.

Ryegrass likes fertile soil, so I wouldn't use it if you're just starting on poor subsoil. It also needs a lot of moisture, and generally shouldn't be left to grow between rows during the growing season unless you have plenty of water and fertility. In zone 5 and cooler, seed at least six weeks before the first hard frost to ensure the grass gets established.

The annual ryegrass is often half the price of the perennial rye and much easier to cut down in the spring with a hoe. Be sure to do that before it goes to seed or it can become weedy. I always chop it down before it gets eight inches tall. If you have a perennial garden, you might rather have a low-growing perennial such as white clover that will be there every year to protect and enrich the soil, and that won't get so big as to need much maintenance.

How to Seed and Care for Cover Crops

Cover crops are just plants. They're cared for much the same as other plants. If you're using them in a vegetable garden in the fall, they should be seeded right after your main harvest time or even a week or two before your harvest. Of course, many of us grow a mixture of vegetables that we continuously harvest, and in that case we just plant the cover crop towards the end of the season. I like to plant fall cover crops a couple of months before frost to get them firmly established.

If possible, it's best to get seeds into the soil. Small-seed legumes go about ¼ inch deep while larger seed legumes and small grains are planted 1 to 1½ inches deep. While generally not as successful, you can broadcast the seed for small-seed legumes on the soil at a higher rate and you should get germination if you keep the soil moist for the next week.

You'll probably be cutting down your cover crop before you seed or transplant. Farmers mostly do this with herbicides, but you can just use a hoe or various other tools. It's not a bad idea to leave some of the plants alive to produce seed, attract insects, and for many other benefits, but most of it will be cut down. It's generally a good idea to wait two to three weeks before you seed and one week before you transplant, to reduce allelopathy and potential predators and allow some nitrogen release from the plants. That being said, some cultures have kept soils going for thousands of years by skipping this downtime. If you use fish emulsion, you can spray that on the cover crop when you turn it in order to hasten decomposition.

We'll look more at tilling in a later chapter, but I'll mention here that you can lightly incorporate your cover crops into the top few inches of soil a couple of weeks before you plant. I believe in disturbing the soil as little as possible through no-till or low-till practices, but it's a good idea to lightly work a green manure into the top layer of soil to speed up the decomposition and decrease the amount of nitrogen lost to the air. Residue from a grass/legume mix will have a higher carbon to nitrogen than the legume alone, slowing the release of nitrogen so it's not as vulnerable to loss.

Summary

- Cover crops improve soil fertility, increase organic matter, control weeds and pests, prevent erosion, send deep roots to break up compaction, conserve moisture and increase water infiltration, attract insects and other animals, and even provide food for humans and animals.
- They can be used seasonally or on an ongoing basis through companion planting and polycultures.

- Legumes such as vetch and clover attract beneficial insects and partner with bacteria to convert gaseous nitrogen into a form plants can use, some of which makes its way into the soil when the crop is turned in.
- Grasses such as cereal rye and annual ryegrass retain nitrogen and other nutrients in the soil, soak up excess water, control weeds and can create a huge amount of organic matter to enrich the soil.
- A mixture of a legume and a grass contributes the benefits of each and is best seeded a couple of months before frost, incorporating into the top of the soil two to three weeks before seeding in the spring.

Chapter 12

Microbial Inoculants
STEP 3

Do you have too much compost? I know I don't. It's always in short supply. Most of us don't have too much organic matter in our soil either. In fact, most of us don't have nearly enough.

The same goes for microbes. We generally need more of them. It may be because we don't have enough organic matter for them to eat, we have big monocultures in our landscape, we've used pesticides or chemical fertilizers, we've used drip irrigation or otherwise withheld water from the landscape, we've been tilling our soil, or even because of the generally toxic environment we live in with pollution, antibiotics and other pharmaceuticals around. Most soils are lacking a healthy soil food web and we need to get the microbes back in there. Of course, we need to address these other issues at the same time too.

Remember, microbes make our soil healthy, feed and protect our plants, and clean our water. They even help to control weeds, insects and diseases just by improving the health of the soil. They're vital to the success of our garden, and we can bring them in through composting, but it takes time. Fortunately, there are some quick ways to inoculate our gardens with microbes. An additional benefit of using these methods over compost is that we can apply some of them not only to soil, but directly onto the leaves. Although it doesn't hurt to do this a few times a year, just doing it the first few times is the most important.

We've already seen how inoculants are important to use with your legumes, and when most people talk about inoculants, that's generally what they're talking about. There are new ones being developed all the time, but there are three I use regularly. Two of them — compost tea and Effective Microorganisms (EM) — deserve their own chapters, which follow. The third, mycorrhizal fungi, is below.

The reason I use these inoculants is that they're tried and true, and I believe them to be the most important. Many of the newer products are blends of just Bacillus species, which are beneficial, but in my opinion, are not even close to being as good as a mixture like EM. That being said, I'm sure there are some out there that are beneficial.

When to Use Microbial Inoculants

All of these inoculants are best used during the growing season, especially during certain times of year — planting, high-stress situations, disease-prone times and spring and fall when microbes can most happily flourish. It's best to apply them in the morning or evening when there is a lower solar index or on a cloudy day, but this isn't essential. It's also ideal to apply them right after rain or irrigation and after mowing the lawn.

If possible, compost tea and EM are preferably applied in relatively frequent, smaller doses, such as on a monthly basis, and weekly during stressful periods such as during disease season on grapes. If applied through an irrigation system, EM is often used daily, but if applying it manually, such as through a backpack sprayer or hose-end sprayer, it's often done monthly. For large areas, it may be done only two to three times per year.

If using spraying equipment, you'll want to filter the compost tea and EM to get out any rock dust and other solids that are used during the brewing process. With EM, if the product container has been sitting for awhile, the solids should have sunk to the bottom, so filtration may not be necessary until you get down to the bottom.

I always like to apply microbial inoculants along with other biostimulants such as sea minerals, kelp, fish, humic acids, and molasses, or even multiple inoculants at the same time.

Indigenous Microorganisms

Before we get to purchased products, I should note that we can get some local microbes for our garden. If you have a forest nearby, taking a few handfuls of soil and putting it into your compost pile or even into the garden will bring in some different microbes. A meadow or aquatic system will have yet other microbes. We don't want to be taking wheelbarrows full of soil out of these ecosystems, but a small amount won't hurt. This is a simple, effective way of increasing microbial diversity.

Even more fun, we can culture our own microorganisms. There are many methods, one of which is to gather Lactobacillus bacteria, which are especially beneficial microbes. Personally, I have mostly just done this for fun because they also come in EM, which I believe is much more useful. Still, culturing Lactobacillus is a fun experiment and is useful for people who can't or don't want to bring in many external inputs.

I discovered how to do this from reading a transcript of a talk given by Gil A. Carandang of Herbana Farms in the Philippines. The way to do it is with some rice and milk. Rinse a small amount of rice and pour that rinse water into a container, leaving the container 50-75% empty and putting on a loose lid so that air can still get in. The rice can be used elsewhere, but is not needed anymore for this process. Keep the container at room temperature out of the sun for seven days. Once you see a thin film on the surface, strain the liquid into a bigger container and add ten times as much milk. In another week or so you may have some solids floating on top that can go into the soil or compost, and a clear, yellow fluid underneath that contains the bacteria.

Separate this fluid into another container and add an equal amount of molasses to keep the bacteria well fed. Store it in the fridge until you're ready to use it. Mix it with 20 parts non-chlorinated water and spray it on plants, soil and compost. You'll learn how to dechlorinate water in the next chapter.

Mycorrhizal Fungi

Over 95% of plant species form symbiotic relationships with mycorrhizal fungi. The fungi provide nutrients and water to their host plants in exchange for carbohydrates and other goodies. In fact, plants will trade as much as 80% of their carbohydrates with these fungi and other microbes. Mycorrhizal fungi greatly improve soil characteristics, and are among the most important microbes that form relationships with plants.

This is another of those microbes that should be in our soil, but often isn't anymore. In soil that has been tilled, compacted, water logged, treated with chemicals, or left without plant cover, mycorrhizal fungi may be seriously lacking. They aren't present in imported topsoil or potting soil mixtures either, and don't multiply in compost. In any of these scenarios, microbes need to be added back to the soil, especially when planting or seeding, as they're essential for optimum plant health.

We can inoculate our plants with mycorrhizal fungi by taking just a small bucket of soil from a healthy environment that contains the right fungi, or by buying a product from a garden center or online. While the first method sounds like more fun to me, I've always gravitated to the second because I know what I'm getting.

There are two main categories of mycorrhizal fungi. Over 90% of plants form relationships with endomycorrhizal fungi, also called arbuscular mycorrhizal (AM) fungi. You need them for most of your vegetables, grasses and many ornamentals. About 5% of plants, including many conifers and some deciduous trees, form relationships with ectomycorrhizal fungi. When you're planting a mix of plants, you can often buy a mixture of endo/ecto fungi and just use that for everything.

There are some plants that generally do not form relationships with mycorrhizal fungi. The most important for vegetable gardeners is the

Brassicaceae family: broccoli, Brussels sprouts, cabbage, cauliflower, collards, kale, mustard and rutabaga; and members of the Amaranthaceae family: beets, swiss chard, lambsquarters, quinoa, spinach, purslane and amaranth. The Ericaceae family: rhododendrons, blueberries and cranberries forms relationships with a different kind of mycorrhizal fungi that can be difficult to find for purchase, but it is out there.

The best time to apply mycorrhizal fungi is at the nursery during the plant production stage, but since your plants probably didn't have that done, the next best time is at planting/seeding/sodding. This will allow you to establish contact between the fungi and plant roots, which is important because that's where the relationship occurs. There's no benefit to foliar feeding with mycorrhizal fungi, as they need to touch the roots. We can, however, mix them with biostimulants before application. This inoculant shouldn't need to be applied more than once, unless other factors are harming them.

Rub the fungi directly on the root ball if possible, or sprinkle in the planting hole. For seed, mix it dry with the seed before spreading. For sod, get a powder form of the fungi, mix with water, and spray it on the soil right before you lay the sod, or even better, spray right on the bottom of the sod rolls. You could spray it on afterwards as well and water it down to the root zone.

While not as good, the other choice is to apply the product to existing landscapes. The powder form is best for mixing with water to get the spores to infiltrate into the soil. For turf, it's better to do this right after aerating so more of the spores get down to the roots. Otherwise, it can be watered in, but will not be as effective on heavy clay or very compacted soils.

Other Inoculants

There are hundreds of new microbial inoculants coming onto the market. Some of the important microbes are in EM, but a few others are showing promise. I haven't seen any research that would lead me to believe they are better than EM, but they can provide many benefits and they're making their way into similar inoculants, such as the ones I like from Tainio Technology and Technique.

Azotobacter and Azospirillum are soil-dwelling, aerobic and facultative anaerobic microbes, some of which can fix nitrogen on their own, without needing a legume host. Perhaps more important than the nitrogen, they also manufacture B vitamins, hormones and many useful bioactive substances that both protect and feed plant roots.

Trichoderma is another kind of fungi that is receiving a lot of attention. They aren't mycorrhizal, but they colonize plant roots, improve plant growth and are especially noted for controlling nearly all types of soil diseases. They're present in all healthy soils and are often the most prevalent fungi. They can be purchased as an inoculant, as well.

Summary

- We generally need to increase the often lacking diversity and number of microbes in our soil food web because of low organic matter, insufficient water, pesticides and chemical fertilizers, tilling, pollution and other toxins, while also fixing these problems.
- Most inoculants are applied weekly, monthly or seasonally, especially during planting, high-stress situations and disease-prone times of the year.
- You can increase the diversity of your compost pile by adding handfuls of soil from other ecosystems.
- You can culture your own Lactobacillus bacteria and experiment with spraying them on plant leaves.
- Mycorrhizal fungi are among the most important microbes for plants, and an inoculant should be applied during planting when it's possible to get the spores on the roots.

Chapter 13
Compost Tea

There's a lot of excitement right now about the benefits of compost tea, and nearly as much confusion about what it is. The benefits are all the same as those things microbes do in the garden that were listed in the soil food web chapter, with insect and disease control and plant health being the main reasons people use it. The confusion happens because of the name. Gardeners have been making a form of compost tea for centuries by putting a small amount of compost in a pail of water, sometimes inside a burlap sack, stirring it once in a while for a few days, and then applying that water to the soil.

To me, that sounds like tea because it's a lot like making a cup of tea — put the tea bag in the cup, add water, stir and drink. That's tea. Nowadays, this method might be called non-aerated compost tea, or simply the bucket method, which is also confusing because we use a bucket for the new method, too. This older method can extract some nutrients and aerobic microbes from the compost if it remains aerobic, but the microbes generally won't be very active and won't stick to the leaf surfaces when applied.

Even worse, some funky teas can result from the old method that may harm plants. You can add foods to the tea to wake up the microbes, but in doing this then they use up more oxygen and the tea can quickly go anaerobic. Immature compost may also make an anaerobic tea. Anaerobic tea may have its special uses, but it will be mainly composed of anaerobic bacteria and yeasts, not particularly diverse, and lacking aerobic microbes like fungi, protists, and many bacteria. We want aerobic tea to restore more of the beneficial microbes.

So non-aerated compost tea can be helpful or harmful, and it's generally not optimal. There's also traditional manure tea, which isn't aerated. The potential to extract harmful microbes that exist in animal manure is greater, along with antibiotics, hormones and other things we feed animals that aren't organically raised. Then there's compost leachate, which is basically just the water that comes out of a compost pile that is too wet. Some people call that compost tea, but it's very often an anaerobic, potentially toxic stew.

There's a newer game in town that involves bubbling air through the water with some kind of air pump and adding specific foods to feed and multiply the microbes, and that is now called compost tea. It's more accurately called aerated compost tea or even actively aerated compost tea, but it's mostly just shortened to compost tea. I understand the confusion, but in this book, we're looking at this new version of compost tea.

What's so great about it? The new system can extract and multiply an astonishing number and diversity of beneficial, active, aerobic microbes. We mostly want the aerobes (aerobic organisms), because they're generally the beneficial ones. Really good compost tea can contain as many as 100 trillion bacteria per 0.03 oz. (1 ml).

One of the reasons we do this is to inoculate our soil with microbes when we don't have enough good compost available. The other main benefit is that we can actually inoculate the leaves of our plants, something we can't do with compost. With more experience, we can also get fancy and brew specific teas for specific circumstances. We may brew a tea to combat powdery mildew on grapes, or a tea to alter the microbial population in a soil in order to allow us to establish an orchard.

There has been some good research on compost tea over the past 10-15 years, mostly on a larger scale. Vineyards have achieved good control of mildews and even been able to harvest their grapes *several weeks* early, giving them a head start on wine making. Food growers have controlled diseases and documented many other benefits for plant health. Golf courses and parks have reduced pesticide, chemical fertilizer, and water use, substantially lowering costs while creating healthier turf. When I started using it in my gardening business in 2006, I didn't personally know any other gardeners or landscapers using it. It's catching on now, but there are still very few professionals taking advantage of these great benefits of compost tea.

Even Harvard University is using compost tea. They did a one acre test of mostly turf in 2008 using compost, compost tea, mycorrhizal fungi, humic acids, liquid kelp, and an organic fertilizer. Compared to the control, root growth was two times greater and nitrogen produced was three to four times greater. Yet they were able to mow 50% less, presumably because there wasn't such a big hit of nitrogen and other chemical fertilizers all at once which often produces green grass and fast growth, but eventually causes problems. They cut water use by 30% and that was expected to increase to 50% for a savings of two million gallons a year. Apparently, all 16 acres at Harvard are now organic.

I've had great success with compost tea in my own gardens and the gardens of clients. I've controlled diseases such as mildew and insects such as spider mites. It can't be marketed as a pesticide and people have found themselves in legal trouble for doing so, but of course it can help to control some plant predators because that's what beneficial microbes do. In some gardens, one application of compost tea has cleared out plant predators overnight, and perked the plants up as if it was exactly what they needed. In other gardens, a few applications have been necessary, and in other gardens, not much changed was noticed. Sometimes, an inadequate soil food web is the problem, and sometimes it's something else.

Making Compost Tea

To make a good tea, you need to get a lot of factors right — air pressure, water quantity, size of the air bubbles, amount and types of compost and microbes foods, and on and on. That means you either need to purchase a quality brewer that has been thoroughly tested and has the data to support that, or build your own and test and tweak it until you get it right. The first option may cost you at least a couple hundred dollars for a five-gallon brewer, but that's actually cheaper than the testing that needs to be done to properly build your own. I use an excellent brewer made by Keep It Simple, and there are other great brewers out there, too.

You can also buy a microscope and learn to test compost tea yourself — not cheap, but lots of fun. You can learn more about how to brew good tea from Dr. Elaine Ingham's *Compost Tea Brewing Manual*. There's plenty of advice out there about how to build your own brewer for as little as $25. This can be a lot of fun and you might make a decent tea, but it generally works out that most homemade brewers don't make a good tea until they've been tested and tweaked. There are just too many variables. You probably won't do any harm, though, if you use good compost and if the resulting tea smells good, so it's a great way to start experimenting. If you use a cheap aquarium pump, I recommend using only one gallon of water in the bucket in order to ensure you have sufficient oxygen.

Whether you buy a brewer or make your own, here's how it works. You start with a small amount of exceptionally good, aerobic, fully finished compost. A mixture of two or three different composts is even better. Using different composts will bring more microbial diversity, and you can even throw in a small amount of healthy soil. If you want to promote a fungal tea, perhaps in order to establish an orchard or shrub garden or strawberries, use compost that was made with a lot of woody material and still contains a small amount of woody material. Even better, mix some oatmeal or oat bran into the compost a few days before you brew at three tablespoons per cup of compost. Keep this moist, dark and warm at 75F (25C) to promote fungal growth. For a bacterial tea, go for a less woody compost.

You can put this compost first into a mesh bag or directly into a bucket of clean, room temperature water. By clean, I mean it can't have chlorine in it. If you use city water, you need to let that bucket of water sit out for 24 hours for the chlorine to dissipate, or you can turn your air pump on for 20 minutes instead and that also does the trick. If your city uses chloramine to disinfect the water, you need to tie it up by adding ascorbic acid (vitamin C) or humic acids. I use no more than half a tablespoon of my particular brand of humate in a five-gallon brew.

Your pump will blow air through tubes that are in the bottom of the bucket, the tubes attached with waterproof tape or weighed down somehow. The air goes through the water and compost, keeping the environment aerobic to favor the aerobic microbes, and physically pulling them off the compost. In the old method, those microbes would mostly stay attached to the compost with the sticky substances they manufacture, and wouldn't have enough air to multiply. The new method gives them the right amount of air, plus we add the foods they need to multiply.

Examples of good microbe foods include molasses, kelp, fish, humic acids and rock dust. Obviously, these products should not have preservatives in them, because preservatives are designed to kill microbes. Molasses, other sugars, fruit juice and kelp promote more bacteria growth. Fish, seed meals, humic acids, yucca and rock dust promote more fungal growth. Other than yucca, which is added at the end, these are all added at the beginning of the brewing process. Mycorrhizal fungi can be added at the end of the brewing process if you're doing a soil application.

Here's a recipe I have adapted and evolved for a five-gallon homemade brewer. This takes one to five days to make. I don't really know when it's done if I'm not testing it, but two to three days is a good time frame to start. The mix is: 4-8 cups compost, 6 teaspoons unsulfured blackstrap molasses, 6 teaspoons liquid kelp, and 3 teaspoons liquid fish. If you use a purchased brewer, they often use less compost. You may be able to buy excellent compost from the brewer manufacturer

Phil's Compost Tea Recipe

4-8 cups of finished compost
6 tsp unsulfured blackstrap molasses
6 tsp liquid kelp
3 tsp liquid fish
5 gallons clean water (room temperature)
Brew up to 5 days

and a mixture of the microbe foods too.

As I said, this generally doesn't produce a tea that gives much protection from disease or a big boost in nutrition, unless you get into using a better air pump and doing some testing to make sure you get all of the variables right. The main ingredient variables are water quality and temperature, compost quality and microbe diversity, and the mix of extra microbe foods you use. The main brewer variables are the oxygen level that is maintained in the water, the speed, size and placement of the bubbles, and the buildup of anaerobic pockets. Then there's the question of how long the brewer should be left on.

It's of critical importance to clean the brewer and all of the tubing from the air bubbler very thoroughly right after a brew is done. You don't want any biofilm residues left over, as they promote anaerobic conditions.

Using Compost Tea

Compost tea needs to be used as soon as possible after you make it, because not long after that pump goes off, the oxygen in the water drops rapidly. It can be used with eight hours, but the sooner the better. When possible, I use mine within one hour of its being ready. If used in farming or for other commercial purposes, you'll want to do some testing to make sure you're making a good tea. Use it in the morning or the evening because many of the microbes don't like UV rays.

My method of applying it is to strain it through nylon or cheese-cloth into a quality backpack sprayer, such as those made by Solo. This allows me to spray a mist at 60 psi and thoroughly coat both sides of the leaves of all of my plants. A watering can will suffice for soil applications, but some kind of spray is best.

A hose-end sprayer would work, but that water coming through the hose often has chlorine in it and it's very cold. I'd rather not shock my microbes like that. I add EM and biostimulants in with the tea, even if I already added a small amount to the brew. Commercial growers and wineries might spray weekly during disease season. Home gardeners might spray anywhere from once a month to once or twice a year.

Using a spray is best because research by Elaine Ingham says that we want our leaves at least 60-70% covered by microbes in order to prevent and even cure some diseases. For foliar applications, which is the main method of application you'll do, you'll generally spray compost tea undiluted at 1 pint per 1,000 square feet, which means a good quality five-gallon brew can do about an acre. It doesn't hurt to do more than that, though. You could spray your five gallons on a few thousand square feet and that's just fine.

Of course, if you have tall trees, you'll need more. The rule is 1 pint per 1,000 square feet for each six feet of tree height you have. If your trees are 12 feet tall, you need one quart. We don't dilute the foliar sprays because we want the maximum number of microbes on the leaf surface as possible. It can also be applied to the soil at 1-4 pints per 1,000 square feet. This can actually be diluted with clean, dechlorinated water in order to provide sufficient coverage. When planting, you can drench each new seedling with one to two pints of compost tea.

There are other uses, too. Hydroponic systems use compost tea at 1 gallon per 40 gallons of water. It's applied to ponds at as little as 1 gallon per acre foot. That means if you have a pond that is an acre big and one foot deep, use 1 gallon of compost tea. In a small backyard pond the size of a king-sized bed and four feet deep, that would be 1 tablespoon of compost tea. You also need to apply sufficient aeration throughout the pond so the aerobes can actually live there.

Summary

- Compost tea is a great way to revive the soil food web when there's not enough compost to go around, and to establish beneficial aerobic microbes on the leaves of our plants, as well.
- It's made by pumping air through water that contains a small amount of compost along with foods for aerobic microbes to multiply.
- It's usually applied through a sprayer of some kind, to the leaves of plants undiluted at 1 pint per 1,000 square feet, and to soil at one to four pints per 1,000 square feet, potentially diluted.

Chapter 14
Effective Microorganisms

Dr. Teruo Higa started studying microorganisms in the 1960s and 1970s, mostly at Ryukyus University in Okinawa, Japan. By the early 1980s, he was perfecting his liquid culture of specific facultative anaerobic microbes that provide amazing benefits when combined together in specific proportions. Facultative anaerobic means microbes that can live both in air with oxygen, and also in low oxygen conditions. They're also called fermenting microbes and some of them are responsible for making your bread, beer, wine and yogurt.

Now facultative anaerobic products have various brand names. Effective Microorganisms, or EM, is actually trademarked by one company. Other companies have given it other names. You can buy any brand, as long as it's manufactured based on the research of Dr. Higa, with the microbe species in the correct proportion to one another. It would not be nearly as useful, for example, to buy a product that only contains lactic acid bacteria. I will refer to it as EM here, but I'm not affiliated with any of the companies that make it, and my directions on how to use the product may differ from theirs.

There are up to 20 different microbes in the inoculant from all over the world, but when we put them together, the magic begins. It's not something you can do at home, but you can buy the inoculant from a manufacturer with the equipment and knowledge to put them together in exactly the right proportions and under the right environmental conditions. The three groups are lactic acid bacteria, yeast and photosynthetic bacteria, plus some other wild microbes that will be let into the brew.

Not that it's particularly important to us gardeners, but here's how the three different classes work together. I'm sure it's more complex than this, but here are the basics. The lactic acid bacteria make up the majority of the population. They protect the other two groups by producing acids that control harmful microbes and enhance organic matter breakdown. They can even help fungi to break down difficult-to-digest lignins and cellulose.

The yeasts produce hormones, enzymes, vitamins, and antimicrobial substances that manipulate their environment and protect the photosynthetic bacteria, also known as phototrophic bacteria.

The photosynthetic bacteria can, yes, photosynthesize. They can actually fix both nitrogen and carbon from the atmosphere. While all of the microbes in EM are important, these guys are considered by Dr. Higa to be the "heart of effectiveness" of the group. They supply amino acids, nucleic acids, sugars, and other bioactive substances, some of which they feed to the others. They break down lignins and even decompose toxins and convert them into nutrients.

More important than all of this is how they work together and provide for each other to contribute a host of benefits to our gardens. They create an abundance of antioxidants, controlled breakdown of organic matter, and according to some people, an extremely positive energy force. Really, I think of them as providing all of the same benefits as the other beneficial microbes I hope to house in my garden, but they just happen to be exceptionally good at it when they get together. Take any of them out or even change the proportions in the mix too much, and you no longer have EM or the same benefits.

EM was originally developed and used in agriculture where it was found to improve compost and soil organic matter breakdown. It was even found to have a beneficial effect on other microbes in the soil, coaxing them to get to work. It isn't as well known in the United States or Canada yet, but it's used in over 150 other countries and there have been thousands of trials showing its effectiveness.

After its value was seen in soil and composting, EM started to be used in other areas with astounding results. It has helped plants beat diseases such as Botrytis, insects such as weevils and other stressors. Like compost tea, it's not a pesticide and can't be marketed as such. It simply creates health in the plant and helps to outcompete predators. It also helps crops achieve higher brix and longer storage. One study sticks in my mind because a 50% increase in yield was obtained just with EM.

It's also been found to have uses with animals. Initially with livestock, they found it helps to control odors, diseases and insects when sprayed in the air and on the animals in barns. It also acts as a probiotic for animals as part of their water and feed.

It cleans polluted water and can actually make dirty water drinkable. It has been used to clean up part of the ocean in a bay in Japan. If you go on the Internet, you can find pictures of groups of Japanese people standing by rivers, all dumping their EM into the river to clean it up. It is also used to clean septic systems and sewers, where it reduces odors, toxic gases, sludge, pathogens, nitrates and phosphates and ties up heavy metals. If you have a pond, you should spray it with EM to get the microbes in there and even control mosquitoes.

Of course, it wasn't long before humans tried drinking it. In my opinion, it's probably one of the best probiotics in the world. Not only have I been using it myself for many years, but when I used to sell it, I had many clients get amazing health benefits from taking it — even people with irritable bowel syndrome and other digestive issues.

Plus, it's often much cheaper than many of these other products. I used to sell a one quart food-grade version mixed with organic herbs for about $50. I've read stories of some health practitioners charging hundreds of dollars for a bottle because it works so well. While I certainly can't tell you to do this, I just drink the regular stuff that's brewed for horticulture. That costs half as much, or if "activated" first, the cost goes down to a couple of dollars per quart. You'll learn how to activate EM shortly.

People have found many other uses for it, too, as a deodorant, toothpaste, in skin care products, and for cuts and sores. In fact, some people have miraculously cured eczema and other skin problems by externally applying EM. It's used to wash fruits and vegetables, as an additive in the laundry, and for general odor control. It even does a decent job of removing rust. I know all of these things work because I've been doing them for years. EM is now starting to be used in garbage dumps, for disaster relief, for soil remediation, to clean hospitals, and has the potential to help out when the next petroleum company spews oil all over our oceans.

Now of course, EM is not a magic bullet and results vary depending on many environmental factors, but I have found it can work some miracles, sometimes very quickly and sometimes only when used consistently over a number of months.

Making Activated EM

You can't make EM yourself unless you want to spend tens or hundreds of thousands of dollars to set up a lab and get the proper strains of microbes, but you can buy an existing mother culture from a supplier and multiply that, much like you would make yogurt. The process is called "activating." Unlike yogurt, which you can keep going forever, EM can only reliably be activated once, maybe twice, and then you need to get a new mother culture. This is because the microbes need to be in specific proportions, and will move away from this with each activation.

You can definitely do it once, making five gallons of good activated EM from one quart of mother culture. This is done both to save money and to wake up the microbes that may be dormant if the mother culture has been around for awhile. Dechlorinated water is actually not necessary, but definitely beneficial because chlorine kills microorganisms. Tap water can be dechlorinated by letting it sit out for 24 hours, unless your city uses chloramines, in which case humic acids or ascorbic acid should be added.

Activating EM

Ingredients (per 1 quart)

8-12 tsp EM (1-1.5 parts)

8 tsp unsulfured blackstrap molasses (1 part)

3 1/4 cups water, not distilled or reverse osmosis (20 parts)

1 quart clean, airtight bottle, generally plastic with screw-on lid

pH paper to determine if your batch is good

Optional (but optimal) ingredients to add (per 1 quart):

1/8 tsp EM ceramic powder to structure water (more is okay)

1/8 tsp sea salt/sea minerals to improve process/quality

1/2 Tbsp rock dust for minerals

1/2 tsp liquid kelp for many good things

Directions

1. Heat the water to 115-125F, and pour approximately half into your container to dissolve the molasses.

2. Mix in any of the optional ingredients and then the EM, adding the remaining water last and stirring and/or shaking very well. There should be an air space equivalent to about 10% of the bottle on top.

3. Some people like to leave the lid off for the first 24 hours to encourage some air exchange. Then tighten the lid and keep the bottle warm for at least two weeks, preferably longer. The optimum temperature is 95-110F. It can be kept warm in an oven with the oven light on, kept in a picnic cooler with a terrarium heater or some other heat source, or

---

kept warm many other ways. The whole process can be done at 70F, but it will take six to eight weeks at the lower temperature, and the odds of failure are higher. Even keeping it warm for just the first few days is helpful.

4. After the first few days, the container needs to be burped every day or two simply by opening and closing the lid, because gases are formed that will pressurize and expand the bottle. Some people like to stir and/or shake daily for the first two to three weeks, too, in order to keep everything mixed well and introduce some air. Even though fermentation is an anaerobic process, allowing some air in for the first two to three weeks seems to be beneficial.

5. The pH will drop as it ferments. It can be used as soon as the pH is below 3.9, but preferably it should be below 3.7. It should also have a sweet smell. It may smell a bit when you initially take off the cap, but if that persists for more than 10 minutes of the cap being off, or if the pH is 3.9 or over, it should not be used. The pH may drop below 3.7 within a few days, but it's better left to ferment for at least four weeks for highest benefits.

The following measurements are for one quart of water, but you can multiply it and use bigger containers such as a five gallon size.

Activating EM isn't an exact science. Although it isn't difficult and usually works very well, the occasional batch may fail to drop in pH to an appropriate level. You can try adding more EM, or you may decide to throw it into the compost and start again. Some of the most common reasons for failure are:

• Inappropriate containers (previously containing chemicals, putrefied food, previous bad batches)

- Poor water quality (distilled, reverse osmosis, polluted, very high in chlorine)

- Filling the container too full during initial fermentation stages (should be only 90% full)

- Not optimal temperature (too hot or too cold)

- Not burping and stirring/shaking daily

- Trying to cheat by using more molasses than EM or too much molasses in relation to water

EM mother culture stores for 6-24 months, or potentially a few years, whereas activated EM usually only stores for one to six months. Still, a really good activated EM batch can potentially store for two or more years. After fermentation is complete, cooler room temperatures between 50 and 70F will keep it longer. Store it out of direct sunlight with the lid tight. Indirect sunlight is beneficial. When you begin to use a bottle of activated EM, it's best to use it all within a couple of months, as the air space at the top of the container will shorten the storage time. If you activated it yourself using a basic recipe without ancillary ingredients and without following all of the steps such as keeping it warm for two weeks, it will be most beneficial to use it all during the first month.

While it's good to brew it with a bit of air space and stir/shake it daily during the first three weeks of brewing, it's best to store it without any oxygen after that if you want to keep it stored for more than a month. The odds are, if you're brewing it for long-term storage, you're probably brewing several bottles at once. When the brewing is complete after two to five weeks, one of the bottles can be used to top off the rest so there's no air space, and then the remainder in that bottle can be used first.

Using EM

EM is preferably applied in smaller doses, more often. Like compost tea, it could be daily, weekly, monthly, or seasonally. Application rates are the same for EM and activated EM, the most common suggested rate for agriculture being 1 to 10 gallons per acre per year, which is approximately 6 tablespoons to 2 quarts per 1,000 square feet per year, spread out over as many applications as are feasible.

For some reason, the application rate given for gardens is 1 gallon per 1,000 square feet per year, which is nearly 44 gallons per acre per year, and the suggestion is generally 1 pint per application. I've done a lot of research and never figured out why this discrepancy exists. It may be that it's just more economically feasible to apply it at a higher rate for small areas, whereas it would get expensive on a big farm. It may be because a garden is considered a higher-value landscape, or it may be just a marketing thing.

After extensive research into studies that have been done in agriculture, I go for the high end of the agriculture rate and use 10 gallons per acre per year, which is close to 2 pints per 1,000 square feet per year. More importantly, I generally spread this out into ⅓ cup per 1,000 square feet per month from early spring through late fall. I may not get to the 2 pint total, but it's more important to me not to use too much EM and to achieve a sufficient dilution. If you only want to spray three times each year, I still recommend you go for this ⅓ cup per 1,000 square feet rate.

Please keep in mind that more is definitely not always better. Several research trials have found that 2 teaspoons per 1,000 square feet to be more effective than higher doses. Another study found powdery mildew control at 0.4 teaspoon per 1,000 square feet. If too much EM is applied, studies have found that organic matter may break down too quickly and the soil may become compacted. For all of these reasons, I believe one pint per 1,000 square feet is too high for one application in many gardens.

I usually end up diluting it 1:200 with water, or at a bare minimum 1:100, which would be one to two teaspoons of EM per quart of water. It's technically supposed to be 1:500 or even 1:1,000, but that's a lot of water and pretty much impossible with a backpack sprayer. Despite the cold water not being the greatest for the microbes, a hose-end sprayer works really well for this because you can just set the ratio on the dial and spray.

This ratio also depends on the frequency of application and the area you're trying to cover. For example, daily use through irrigation systems often use very diluted ratios such as 1:10,000. Use on turf and in gardens might be more like 1:100, basically to provide adequate coverage, and then watered in with a sprinkler. Some sources say not to apply it directly to flowers or newly seeded areas, as this could potentially ferment the flowers or seeds. I've rarely found this to be a problem, but it is something to watch out for.

Once your EM or activated EM has been diluted in water — often referred to as "extending" the EM — and mixed with any optional biostimulants, it should be used within a few hours. It's generally recommended to mix it again with equal parts unsulfured molasses, even though this was also done during the activation stage. This gives the microbes some sugar to work with when they get into the garden.

I also apply it with the biostimulants discussed in an upcoming chapter, most commonly some mixture of sea minerals, kelp, fish and humic acids. A recipe is coming up in the final chapter that can be applied to both the soil and directly onto the plants. EM can also be sprayed on compost, ponds, and buildings, and even on pets and livestock. It's entirely safe for people and animals to enter the areas after spraying.

You can see that EM provides many of the same benefits as compost tea, but it's different. It's a mixture of only a handful of species of mostly facultative anaerobic microbes, but they just happen to be very important species, especially when mixed together in the right proportions. The shelf life is quite long and the quality of the product is fairly consistent.

With compost tea, on the other hand, we're going for maximum diversity, with as many different species of aerobic and facultative anaerobic microbes as possible. The shelf life is very short and the finished product more variable. Incidentally, I always put some EM in my compost tea when I'm brewing, at two tablespoons per five gallons. This is not only to make sure those microbes are there, but more to hopefully fill up any anaerobic pockets with these facultative anaerobes that can live there.

I generally recommend EM over compost tea as a starting point for most gardeners because it's much less expensive and easier to get started. I use both and the serious gardener may eventually want to, as well.

Summary

- EM is a liquid mixture of relatively few mostly facultative anaerobic microbes in specific proportions.
- EM is used for soil, composting, plants, water, buildings, animals and people.
- EM can be "activated" kind of like yogurt by fermenting it with molasses, water and optional other ingredients, making over 5 gallons from 1 quart of mother culture.
- EM is mixed with 100-1,000 parts water and applied to plants and soil at a rate of ½ teaspoon to 1 pint per 1,000 square feet, weekly, monthly or seasonally, often mixed with biostimulants (I use ⅓ cup of EM monthly).

Chapter 15

Supplementing Nutrients

STEP 4

The next step is fertilization. Microbes and plants need nutrients. We can supply most of these nutrients through good mulches and well-made compost, but not only do we need the nutrients, we need them in specific amounts in relation to each other. That's were a small amount of specific fertilizers come in, to move towards these ratios. Organic matter generally can't do it alone, so this is a vital step.

There are several definitions of the word *fertilizer*. In many countries, in order to be considered a fertilizer, a product must have a certain amount of total nitrogen, available phosphate and soluble potash, often written as NPK.

Notice that it's *available* phosphate and *soluble* potash, not total. This has an unfortunate consequence for organic fertilizers. Nutrients in organic fertilizers are wrapped up in various organic compounds that need to be broken down by microbes before they become available to plants, as nature intended. This means an organic fertilizer will not qualify as a fertilizer and will look like poor value when compared to the high numbers of a chemical fertilizer. It will be sold as a soil amendment or perhaps a specialty fertilizer.

Further, the law says a "complete fertilizer" only has to supply the three nutrients listed above. We know, of course, that plants need many dozens of nutrients, so it makes no sense to apply only three. In fact, applying any of these three indiscriminately often causes more problems than benefits.

Also, fertilizers don't have to list how much salt they have in them, or how much chlorine, or how much of any other nutrient we may not want. For example, muriate of potash, also known as 0-0-60, contains almost as much chlorine as potassium. It's one of the most common fertilizers worldwide, is used in many NPK fertilizers, and may have caused more damage to our soils than any other fertilizer. Additionally, chemical fertilizers often include a slew of heavy metals, sewage sludge and toxic waste that don't have to be listed on the label. This is a great way for industry to get rid of its toxins — right in your backyard, and you even get to pay them for the privilege.

There are many definitions of the word organic, too. In chemistry, it basically means "containing carbon." I would be using this definition if I were teaching you about chemical pesticides because *organic* pesticides are simply pesticides that contain carbon and include some of our most poisonous synthetic pesticides used today. In biology, organic basically means "derived from living organisms." We use this definition when we talk about organic matter in the soil.

Most of the time, however, when we use the word organic we're referring to more of a cultural definition, which not only means avoiding the use of all chemicals, but also focusing on improving the soil and soil food web, increasing biodiversity, cleaning up the air and water, using sustainable materials, and so on. When I refer to an organic fertilizer, therefore, what I mean is a fertilizer that would be allowed on an organic farm or garden under standards such as those put out by the International Federation of Organic Agricultural Movements (IFOAM) and the Society For Organic Land Care (SOUL), not necessarily one that is derived from living organisms. Calcitic limestone, for example, is a rock we often use.

Also, the organic label has become so misused that you shouldn't buy your fertilizers based on the word organic alone. For example, I would absolutely never buy anything from certain large international garden product manufacturers, even if it was labeled organic. I know from their track record that the health of the planet is not a priority for them, and from looking at their organic products, that quality is not high on their list of priorities.

An organic-based label is even less helpful because it only has to contain 15% organic materials. There are many other potentially misleading terms such as natural, environmentally friendly and balanced. What I do is either look for organic certification on the label, such as OMRI (Organic Materials Review Institute), or I read the ingredients. Most of the products I use have only one "ingredient," such as kelp, lime, sea minerals or rock phosphate, and I try to avoid additives for the most part. Also, keep in mind that just because a product is certified organic doesn't necessarily mean it's good for your situation, only that it's made with allowed ingredients.

So organic fertilizers, chemical fertilizers, mineral fertilizers, and soil amendments come with different definitions. I'm just going to refer to everything as a fertilizer to indicate that it's something we buy in a bag or bottle to apply to our soil and plants.

With all fertilizers, applying more is not necessarily better. In fact, it's usually much worse. An excess of one nutrient results in a deficiency of another. Too much nitrogen can bring a deficiency of copper and potassium. Too much phosphorus can bring a deficiency of zinc and sulfur. Too much potassium can bring a deficiency of manganese and boron. Too much calcium or magnesium can bring a deficiency of many nutrients. There are thousands of relationships like this between nutrients in the soil.

What's important here is seeing why the application of NPK fertilizers and dolomite lime "for good measure" will cause problems more often than not. In the long run, you'll get higher yields by applying less fertilizer. You just need to apply the right fertilizers, and that's why a soil test is so crucial as one of the tools that helps you decide which fertilizer to apply.

I use a small number of mineral fertilizers that are mined naturally without the use of chemicals, and other fertilizers that come from plants and the sea. While these next few chapters don't cover absolutely all of the fertilizers available to gardeners, they do cover all of the ones I use, so you can consider using this as your guide.

Note that while this list may look rather long, you'll probably only need a handful of these fertilizers. The goal is not to use fertilizers indefinitely. The majority of our fertility can be provided by mulch, compost and cover crops. I want to reiterate that point, because we can't sustainably bring in external inputs forever, but they are helpful to get the system working much more quickly and optimally.

Mineral Fertilizers

Naturally mined mineral products such as calcitic lime and glacial rock dust can be incredibly beneficial for the garden. There are a couple of important points to note. We generally should only use natural products, not those that have been altered or mixed with chemicals, so be sure to check the label and ask first.

Even for most of the mineral products we do use, an annual application (for good measure) is mostly unnecessary and potentially harmful. We should use them only when we know we need them, and as the landscape moves into balance, we'll need them less and less, especially if we're focusing on organic matter. Organic matter should still be the main focus, but it's usually not enough on its own for optimal health.

Fortunately, there are products that can greatly help us bring our ecosystems into balance more quickly. Many of the products out there, even organic fertilizers, bring in large amounts of minerals that are often expensive, unnecessary, and are potentially harmful if they aren't needed. Other than rock dust, most mineral products are composed primarily of just one or two minerals, such as calcium and phosphorus.

Generally, they should not be applied in much quantity without both a soil test and often visual verification of certain conditions in the garden.

Let me give an example of why we need to look at both the soil test and the garden. Occasionally, a soil test may indicate you have plenty of phosphorus, but your lawn might be riddled with broadleaf weeds, a sure sign of a phosphate to potash ratio that is too narrow. In that case, regardless of what the soil test says, I would probably bring in a source of phosphorus and more importantly, use several techniques to stimulate the biology in the soil. Soil tests are great, but we need to remember to look at our gardens, too. Conversely, sometimes a soil test will show you things you cannot see in the garden.

When it comes time to fertilize, it used to be that some of the earlier rock fertilizer proponents recommended applying only one at a time to avoid having them interact, but now many people advocate applying them at the same time. For example, it's now common practice for soil labs to recommend calcitic lime, soft rock phosphate and gypsum together. Any of these are best applied in spring or fall. Try to find products that are suitable for organic use, which means they may be labeled organic, but more likely you have to find out what's in them. If possible, it's best to avoid inappropriate additives such as binding agents.

Some gardening books go into great detail on the role of each of the nutrients in plant growth. I'm not going to do too much of that. Not that it isn't interesting, but most nutrients have many different purposes in plant growth and to list them all becomes overwhelming. I will list a few points that are most interesting.

Likewise, I won't spend much time on diagnosing plant nutrient deficiencies through visual inspection because I feel this is much more complicated than it's often made out to be. For example, a phosphorus deficiency shows up as reddish or purplish color on the underside of leaves, but magnesium deficiency can also cause this. Nitrogen deficiency shows up as yellowing leaves, starting with the lower leaves, but this can also be caused by moisture issues, cold weather, disease, and other nutrient imbalances such as a sulfur deficiency. That being said, some people use visual cues successfully along with other tools such as testing, so perhaps I just haven't tried hard enough.

Fertilizers Derived from Plants and Animals

Many of the natural products organic gardeners used in the past are now unavailable to us because of their environmental consequences. For example, here are the meals we probably shouldn't use anymore: blood meal, bone meal, alfalfa meal, canola meal, corn gluten meal, cotton meal and soy meal, just to name the main ones. Let's look at them in order.

Blood and bone meal were great. Blood meal had the nitrogen and trace minerals and bone meal had the phosphorus and some calcium. But now there is the risk of spreading mad cow disease. Some scientists don't think this is an issue, but some do. There is also potential for heavy metal contamination in bone meal.

Plant meals are mostly genetically modified now. Corn gluten meal is a good pre-emergent weed killer for certain weeds, but most corn is genetically modified. In the U.S., it might be possible to find a non-GMO source, but I suspect not for long due to cross-pollination. Canola, cotton, and soy are all genetically modified. Alfalfa meal is loaded with nutrients, although the USDA has recently approved it for genetic modification, too. We definitely don't want to introduce genetically modified DNA into our soil.

Kelp, molasses and humic acids are still good organic fertilizers. Sea minerals and fish fertilizers are others that come from the ocean. We'll look at all of these in the biostimulants chapter.

Blended Fertilizers

In garden centers, you can find blended fertilizers, and you can find recipes online for how to blend together your own. Either way, these will usually include many of the following ingredients: calcitic lime, dolomite lime, gypsum, rock phosphate, bone meal, guano, greensand, kelp meal, fish meal, and seed meals such as soy meal.

When I first got into organic gardening, I was really excited about making my own organic blend. I think there is something very appealing to us as gardeners about this idea. We get excited thinking about feeding this mix to our plants. Then I learned more and gained more experience and realized none of my mentors did this, at least not with these ingredients.

The reason is that we don't know if our garden needs all of these things without a soil test. It may very well be that we are pushing the nutrient ratios further apart by adding all of this. I can see how adding a very small amount might stimulate microbial activity and provide some energy to the garden, but it would be much better to apply just the things we need. We can certainly take the rock dust and kelp meal and apply them without a soil test as well as other biostimulants, but for the mineral fertilizers, we should use them only when we know we need them.

Dry Versus Liquid Fertilizers

Many of our fertilizers are dry, such as crushed or ground-up rock. Examples are rock dust, calcitic lime and rock phosphate. They're applied in the garden with a spreader or even by hand, or best of all, mixed thoroughly into the compost pile first. They're generally broken down slowly by microbes throughout the year or over multiple years.

Along with organic matter and microbes, these dry fertilizers are often the basis of a soil management program. I use them mostly for long-term soil building, although some of them are available to microbes and plants in the short term, too. A fine ground product is better than a coarse grind because it is more quickly available. Some consultants don't mind a coarser product, but the fact is it can take decades for the nutrients to become available from it.

Liquid fertilizers can be fast and efficient at improving overall plant health and correcting specific nutrient deficiencies when sprayed directly onto plants, called foliar fertilizing or foliar feeding. One study found them to be 8 to 20 times more efficient. They can help a plant deal with stress, give it some energy, and move it from vegetative growth to fruiting. Sometimes they're sprayed directly on the soil, too.

They're especially important during the transition to a healthy organic garden, when the plants can't yet get everything they need from the poor soil. Paradoxically, they work best in a mineral-balanced and biologically active soil and don't work as well as a rescue spray. You absolutely need sufficient calcium in your soil for them to work well.

When I think of liquid fertilizers, I tend to think of broad-spectrum biostimulants such as liquid fish, kelp and sea minerals, all of which will be covered in the biostimulants chapter. But more recently, liquids that provide just one mineral are being used more and more to correct specific soil nutrient deficiencies. Liquid calcium is the main one that comes to mind. Not only does this save money, but drastically curtails the environmental consequences of mining and shipping large amounts of dry rock products such as lime.

Liquid products aren't a magic bullet to fix all nutrition problems, but they do give the soil and plant a kick to get to work. Sometimes they're used to "untie" minerals such as calcium or phosphorus in the soil. You may have enough calcium on a base saturation test, for example, but a liquid calcium will often help make it available. A well-made liquid fertilizer directly feeds microbes and stimulates their activity to start working.

Liquids can be applied through an inexpensive hose-end sprayer. A backpack or pump sprayer is even better because you can use rainwater at a warmer temperature than cold, potentially chlorinated, well or city water. The idea is to create a mist that thoroughly coats both sides of all leaves, although if you're using microbial products, you need the openings on the sprayer to be big enough to allow all of the microbes through, so the mist shouldn't be too fine. Fungal mycelium can be broken up if the filter is too fine.

Foliar fertilizers are especially effective when applied to young plants, which are adept at taking up foliar nutrients. Liquids are also used during high stress times, such as transplanting and disease-prone times of year. An advanced technique you'll learn in an upcoming chapter is to use them mid-season with specific fruit-promoting fertilizers to switch a plant's focus from growing to fruiting. Many biostimulants can also be used as often as weekly throughout the growing season, and sometimes even in the winter.

Foliar fertilizers are best sprayed in the morning or evening when the sun isn't as hot or bright, and relative humidity is higher than in the afternoon. They work best when the pH of the final mix is close to 6.4, so an advanced technique is to move the mix toward that level. If you have a means of measuring pH, you can bring your mixture down with household or apple cider vinegar, or bring it up with baking soda. I don't do this often in my sprays because baking soda and vinegar kill some microbes, and I almost always include microbial inoculants in my sprays.

Where to Find Fertilizers

Some fertilizers can be difficult to find. You won't find all of the ones I recommend at your local garden center. You'll do a little better if you go to a farm supply store or a store that supplies the landscaping industry. You may also need to take your search online. Many of the liquid products are economical to buy online and ship, but this isn't the case with the mineral fertilizers. For them, you can still use the Internet to locate a local source.

Many mineral fertilizers will have come from a quarry on the other side of the country, or occasionally from another continent. Many of us question the sustainability and environmental consequences both of transporting these materials and in digging up the earth to get the minerals. I certainly don't feel 100% comfortable with it, but I don't know of a better option.

Some rocks such as limestone are mined all over the world, so we should obviously go for a source that is relatively close to us. Other minerals will have to come from further away. We need to mine these minerals thoughtfully. Some say we can even restore the quarries to be more environmentally beneficial than they were when we started.

Yet a good argument can be made that some of this won't be sustainable. Neither is our health if we keep eating nutrient-poor food. Certainly, the goal is not to keep using these fertilizers indefinitely in such large amounts, but rather as an interim measure to transition to a more balanced ecosystem that largely takes care of itself. Still, perhaps the long-term solution is to use more concentrated liquid fertilizers and homeopathic doses of nutrients. This is not only more sustainable, but more affordable. We're on our way and as you'll see, people are already doing it successfully.

How to Apply Fertilizers

Traditionally, the best time to apply the soil-building mineral fertilizers is in spring or fall. Many soil consultants have a preference for fall, but if it's spring right now and you have a soil test showing you what you need to do, start now. It can take three or more years to correct nutrient imbalances in the soil, so I like to get going right away.

Other fertilizers are applied regularly throughout the year, especially liquid fertilizers and biostimulants that keep a crop growing. On a farm, the soil-building mineral fertilizers might be applied all at once because it can become uneconomical to make too many passes over the field. In a small garden, I prefer to split my fertilizer up into two to four applications per year. For example, instead of applying 40 pounds of calcitic lime all at once in the fall, I might apply 20 pounds in the fall and 20 pounds the following spring.

When it comes to determining how much to apply, the soil lab will tell you that. For those who like math, here's a brief explanation of one way they might figure it out if they're using the base saturation numbers. It's not as confusing as it initially looks, but it's also not necessary for us to worry about this because they will do it. If the calculations don't interest you, skip ahead to the next chapter. The main reason I'm including them here is so you can see the logic behind fertilizer recommendations. This works for each major nutrient and the equation is as follows:

CEC x saturation lbs./acre x saturation deficit / raw material nutrient

Let's use the same test as we did in the soil nutrient testing chapter to go through the equation.

Soil Test Sample

Nutrient	Units	Ideal	Actual
K	%	2-5	2.2
Ca	%	60-70	36.6
Mg	%	10-20	11.6
Na	%	0.5-3	0.2
CEC	mEq/100g		7.7

The soil test gives us a CEC number. A sandy soil will usually have a CEC of between 0-10, while a clay soil will often be from 20-50. You can see from the equation that a lower CEC soil is going to require a smaller application of fertilizer. This makes sense because a sandier soil can't hold as much nutrient, so if we add too much it will just leach through. The value from our soil test is 7.7.

Let's break down the rest of the equation using calcium as an example. We would need 400 pounds per acre of calcium to occupy 100% of the cation exchange sites in a soil with a CEC of 1. That number never changes. The math that went into determining this number is beyond the scope of this book, but it involves looking at the weight of the soil and the weight and molecular structure of the calcium ion. The second number in our equation, therefore, is 400.

To do this part of the calculation for the other main cations, we would use 240 pounds for magnesium, 780 pounds for potassium and 460 pounds for sodium. The phosphorus to potassium ratio should be 1:1 in most soils, so phosphorus is 780 pounds. The sulfur number is often put at half of phosphorus, so 390 pounds. You don't have to memorize these numbers, as they're right here.

Next we can easily determine our base saturation deficit. If we're trying to get a calcium base saturation of 68%, which is often considered ideal with a proper Albrecht test, and if our current base saturation of calcium from the above soil test is 37%, then our deficit is 31% (68-37=31). You can see that the bigger the deficit, the more fertilizer you'll need to add.

Last, we need to know how much of the required nutrient is in the raw material we'll be using. Let's say in this case that we're using calcitic lime as our calcium source, with a calcium content of 35%. If it was only 25% calcium, we would have to use more of it.

Plugging the numbers back into the equation looks like this:

$$7.7 \times 400 \times 0.31 / 0.35 = 2,728 \text{ pounds per acre}$$

The soil lab may still round up to 3,000 pounds, or we can just work with the 2,728, which is 62 pounds per 1,000 square feet. That's how much calcitic lime we theoretically need to add to bring the calcium level up to 68%. Of course, there is margin for error in all parts of the equation, so it's not exact. Also, the soil is highly complex and certainly does not represent perfect lab conditions, so things will definitely work out differently than we plan, but this is a good start.

I would split this into four applications throughout the year, which works out to 17 pounds each application. Personally, I would bring it down to 10 pounds per application. The more I learn, the more I feel we should make fertility changes slowly and see if we can partially improve soil fertility levels by also improving the health of the soil food web.

This calcitic lime is going to supply perhaps 4% magnesium, so that should be taken into account, too. Don't worry if these numbers are a bit much. As you can see, this can get rather complicated, so you can just let the soil lab do it for you. They can also factor in the Reams test and other wisdom. I wanted to show you how to do it so you can understand the factors that affect fertilizer recommendations.

Summary

- Mostly, we want to use fertilizers derived from naturally mined rock and from plants, although many of the plant fertilizers we used in the past are now from genetically modified crops.
- We can use a mix of dry and liquid fertilizers to achieve short and long-term goals, applied throughout the growing season, with spring and fall being the most important.
- It's generally best to stay away from using purchased blends of fertilizers, because some of the ingredients will supply nutrients that actually throw our soil out of balance, and some may be from genetically modified plants.
- We may have to do a bit of searching to find the fertilizers we need, but in the end it's definitely worth the effort.

Chapter 16
Calcium & Phosphorus

Calcium and phosphorus are two of the most important nutrients for plants. Conventional gardening and farming largely ignores these, especially calcium, in favor of short-term remedies. Organic gardeners often ignore them, too, in favor of organic matter. We need organic matter, but we need the minerals, too. These foundational minerals build the optimum environment which soil biology needs in order to flourish.

Calcium

Calcium is one of the most important minerals for both plants and microbes, probably *the* most important. Yet we know there's really no such thing as one mineral being the most important, because they're all important. Interestingly, it *is* the most needed element by weight and volume for plants, and without sufficient calcium, nothing works. While nitrogen and potassium get a lot of attention, more and more focus is being put on calcium, particularly in organic horticulture.

Calcium helps plant cells communicate with each other by physically moving between cell membranes. Not only is it integral in the basic structure of plants, with a deficiency often showing up as thick, woody stems, it's largely responsible for the availability of nutrients in plants and has a strong influence on microbial activity. In the book *Mainline Farming For Century 21*, Dan Skow says "calcium is essential energy creation potential in the soil to release the other elements cause a plant to grow."

With enough calcium, roots and fine root hairs proliferate, stimuting soil microbes and building humus. This means that without enough calcium in the soil plants can't access or utilize nutrients very well. Likewise, foliar fertilizers and microbial inoculants will have little effect if there's a major calcium deficiency. You can waste a lot of time and money on fertilization if you don't have sufficient calcium.

We're looking for 60-75% calcium on a base saturation test, and a 10:1 calcium to magnesium ratio with a minimum of 2,000 pounds per acre of available calcium on a Reams test. This goes down to 60% and 7:1 for grasses/grains and very sandy soil. If your calcium is less than 60% on a base saturation test or 2,000 pounds per acre on a Reams test, there's a good chance your soil will be compacted and riddled with grassy weeds, your soil food web will be unhealthy, your plants will be sick, and your fruit will be weak and easily bruised. This can happen even if you have enough total calcium, but your calcium to magnesium ratio is less than 7:1 on a Reams test. In fact, the list of things that fall into place when the calcium to magnesium ratio is in line is really too long to put down here.

Microbes need this ratio to be in line in order to create a soil that is free of compaction. The microbes need to be there in order for the calcium to be available, too. You can pile on bags and bags of calcium and you won't get anywhere if you don't have the humus and microbes to make use of it.

A calcium shortage needs to be improved before other nutrient ratios will be fixed. For example, adding sulfur in the form of gypsum or ammonium sulfate can bind with excess magnesium and leach it, but you need sufficient calcium for this to happen efficiently. Calcium is associated with nitrogen fixation and amino acid formation, so low calcium means the nitrogen cycle in the soil will also be less efficient and nitrogen will more easily leach.

Some gardeners and farmers are so in love with calcium they think

you can't have too much, so they may apply it annually without much thought. This is a bad idea, because if you use too much calcium, other nutrients will become much less available or even get leached out of the soil. Too much calcium can also create so much air space in the soil that it's difficult to keep it wet. Let's look at the main calcium sources we could bring in if a soil test and garden observations tell us we need it.

Liquid Calcium and Micronized Calcium

The most common calcium sources are to follow, but first I wanted to mention liquid calcium because I believe it's the most important. Liquid calcium is becoming more and more popular in ecological agriculture as part of foliar spray mixtures and soil applications. There are many forms, but the most common is generally from liquefied calcium nitrate, which is 9-0-0 with 11% calcium. It's not technically considered organic, but it's one of the rare synthetic products that's worth using. There are organic versions available, too, such as one from calcium lignosulfonate and others from micronized calcium carbonate. There are also inferior versions such as liquid lime and calcium chloride that I avoid.

Liquid calcium products are applied in very small doses because they're so readily available to be used by microbes and plants, and can be spread out so evenly that not much is needed. Often, ⅓-⅔ cup per 1,000 square feet is all that's used (or even less). These products can be difficult to find, but if you need calcium, I recommend you take some time to try to find one. The price is often $20-$30 for a quart.

They should be mixed with sugar (such as molasses), microbial inoculants, and some of the biostimulants you'll be reading about soon, especially liquid fish or sea minerals, and fulvic acid. Some products have some of these ingredients included already. Don't mix it in the same sprayer with humic acid, chemical phosphorus or very hard water, as you can get some unhelpful reactions. Liquid calcium is useful in spring and especially in fall, to stimulate bacteria that break down organic matter residue.

Calcitic Lime
(30% Calcium and 4% Magnesium — Varies)

Calcitic lime, also known as high-calcium lime or calcium carbonate — or aragonite, which is actually ground sea shells — is the main rock fertilizer used to increase calcium levels, especially when the base saturation test is low. As mentioned, some people are moving to liquid calcium as the first choice, but be forewarned it's not always able to bring calcium levels up high enough.

Calcitic lime is not to be confused with hydrated lime or quick lime, which aren't approved in organic gardening standards. They can be beneficial, but they can burn crops, as well as your skin. Calcitic lime contains approximately 25-35% calcium and a few percentage points of magnesium. Some soil labs may recommend 45 pounds per 1,000 square feet, while some soil scientists like Dr. Arden Andersen, author of *Science in Agriculture*, advocate starting out by using less, such as 10 pounds, perhaps applied more often.

Neal Kinsey of Kinsey Agricultural Services recommends calcitic lime as high as 180 pounds. Personally, I stick to the lower end of the scale because every time we add any fertilizer, we impact the soil environment and the soil food web. As I've already mentioned, I prefer to use fertilizers slowly and work on the soil food web for further stimulating fertility.

I'll use 10-45 pounds per 1,000 square feet in my garden in one year, and some people would advocate even less. Actually, I follow both of these pieces of advice by keeping the application rates low and spreading them out during the course of the year. I apply 10 pounds per 1,000 square feet, as often as twice in the spring about four weeks apart and twice in the fall.

There's one circumstance in which I may apply calcitic lime without a soil test — when I see an explosion of weeds that indicate a calcium deficiency, such as dandelions and crabgrass. I'd almost always take a soil test anyway. In North America, calcitic lime should be between $7 and $20 for a 50 pound bag, so it's definitely not too expensive for a typical residential garden. The price depends whether you buy it from a wholesale farm supplier or from a retailer, as follows the range of the other prices in the next few chapters.

Sometimes, the base saturation is okay, but the Reams test is low. This means we may have sufficient calcium in the soil, but our plants just can't get enough of it. We may still add some calcitic lime, but there are probably more important things to do. Why isn't that calcium available? Perhaps we need to throw a bit of a party for our microbes to coax them to get excited about getting to work on the calcium. Liquid calcium is often used for this.

Also, aerobic microbes need sufficient air in the soil and the right amount of moisture. They like humic acids, compost and leaves. They like sugar, especially molasses. So, the easiest first steps are to make sure you're irrigating properly and adding enough organic matter. Then you can bring in some EM and/or compost tea, some humic acids and molasses, and perhaps some liquid calcium.

Dolomite Lime
(22% Calcium and 12% Magnesium — Varies)

I don't know how dolomite lime has come to be used by so many gardeners. Maybe it's just because the dolomite industry has done a wonderful marketing job. Maybe it's because it was promoted by some of the early organic proponents who have had a big influence on the rest of us. It's in the same price range as calcitic lime, but personally, I almost never use it.

It's approximately 22% calcium and 12% magnesium, a 1.8:1 calcium to magnesium ratio, whereas calcitic lime is approximately 30% calcium and 4% magnesium, a 7.5:1 ratio. Actually, magnesium has 1.7

times more exchange capacity than an equal amount of calcium, so we use correspondingly less magnesium when we're trying to raise magnesium levels. This was shown in the last chapter when we looked at how we would need 400 pounds per acre of calcium to occupy 100% of the cation exchange sites in a soil with a CEC of 1, but only 240 pounds of magnesium. In a way, that makes the effective calcium to magnesium ratio of dolomite less than 1:1, and more like 4.5:1 for calcitic lime.

Too much magnesium in the soil can cause nitrogen to volatize into the air and soil to compact. Dolomite generally brings in too much magnesium for what we need. If you had a soil with extremely low magnesium in relation to calcium, such as a 12:1 calcium to magnesium ratio, then it might make sense to use dolomite.

Gypsum (22% Calcium and 17% Sulfur)

Gypsum is calcium sulfate. I'm not referring to drywall, which contains ingredients that are toxic to plants, nor the chemical version of calcium sulfate, which also shouldn't be used. Gypsum is a sedimentary rock that is fairly common and is mined in many places. It's in the same price range as calcitic lime.

The sulfur is in the sulfate form containing one sulfur molecule and four oxygens, readily available to plants. I use it for the sulfur when I need it. And I use it very often as a calcium source along with calcitic lime and soft rock phosphate. It helps bring more oxygen into an anaerobic soil, so it's even used when calcium is adequate.

Phosphorus

Phosphorus is the other most important mineral. It's generally present in the soil, but is often unavailable in soils with a low organic matter content and a poor soil food web. Having active biology in the soil is probably the most important factor in getting phosphorus into plants. Carey Reams taught that calcium and phosphorus are two of the most limiting elements in soils.

Phosphorus is the element P on the periodic table. Fertilizers show phosphate rather than phosphorus on their labels. Phosphate is the main form of phosphorus that plants use. Actually, fertilizers show *available* phosphate, which is the phosphate that is more readily available to plants, not tied up. Available phosphate is P_2O_5, two atoms of phosphorus attached to five atoms of oxygen. In NPK fertilizers, for example, the middle number represents available phosphate as a percentage of the weight of the bag. Multiplying that by 0.44 gives us the amount of phosphorus. If the middle number is 10, the phosphorus is 4.4% of the weight of the bag. Soil tests may give you the phosphorus number or the phosphate number. The nutrient testing chapter showed how to tell which is which.

Along with magnesium, phosphorus is necessary for photosynthesis. It's in every living cell. It's the major catalyst in all living systems, which means its presence is vital for many other reactions to take place in the plant, and for many other nutrients to get utilized. For example, it promotes more photosynthesis and higher brix. The phosphates not only help produce the sugar, but also bring it to the roots where it's excreted to soil microbes. Then, the microbes make more nutrients that become available to the plant, so the plant can make more sugar.

It also circulates throughout the plant, up and down, carrying other nutrients to where they're needed. For example, calcium bonds with phosphorus to create phosphate of calcium. The phosphate brings the calcium through the plant and drops it where it belongs. It transports all nutrients throughout the plant with the exception of nitrogen. Phosphorus is also needed in order for carbon and nitrogen to be made into all of the things they're made into — amino acids, proteins, enzymes, vitamins and all of the things that are the basis for plant health and the health of every living thing on earth.

A conventional soil test doesn't tell us much about phosphorus availability, as the number given is relatively inaccurate. A Reams test gives better information on phosphorus availability, and for this, the ideal number would be 400 pounds per acre. For either test, the ratio of phosphate to potash would ideally be 2:1 in general, not 1:2 as many labs recommend. It should be more like 4:1 for grasses and leaf crops, such as lettuce and greens. When it gets lower than this, plants will suffer and be more prone to insect and disease damage, and there will be more broadleaf weeds such as plantain. The only way to maintain adequate available phosphorus levels is to have a biologically active soil. Fungi are the main harvesters of phosphorus from the soil environment.

Most forms of phosphorus are not soluble in water, so it's mostly not found floating around in the soil solution. It's an anion, so it can attach to positive charges on organic matter. More often, it binds with calcium to form calcium phosphate, or with other cations like magnesium and iron. Because phosphorus doesn't move down into the soil, it's nice to incorporate phosphorus fertilizers into the top few inches.

A big problem is that there's not a whole lot of phosphorus left in the world. Like oil, it has peaked, perhaps about 20 years ago. Should we be using what's left? I don't know. Someday, we'll all have to become biodynamic gardeners so we can use the energies we have on site and use homeopathic doses for our gardens and farms. We should start that now.

At the same time, there are two other methods of maintaining phosphorus levels and availability in the soil. The first is that we need to learn to make high-quality compost that will supply phosphorus and microbes that make phosphorus available. We should even be composting human manure to recycle that phosphorus, among other nutrients. The second is that we need to promote mycorrhizal fungi in our soil and bacteria that specialize in moving phosphorus. The fungi are one of the most important pieces of the puzzle in most of our soils when it comes to getting phosphorus into the plant.

Bone meal has been a main phosphorus source of gardeners for a long time. I don't use it anymore due to the potential of spreading the prions associated with mad cow disease. Many ecological gardeners are still recommending it, though. Another one I use is molasses. If a conventional soil test indicates there's a lot of phosphorus in the soil, but a Reams test indicates there isn't enough available phosphorus, molasses can be applied to the soil at ⅔ cup per 1,000 square feet, mixed with as much water as you need, to help "loosen" the phosphorus.

Rock Phosphate (Mainly Phosphorus and Calcium)

There are two main sources of phosphate we use in organic gardening. Both of them come from the same parent material, which is ancient animal bones. They contain a lot of both phosphorus and calcium, although the amounts can vary greatly depending on the source. They are called hard rock phosphate and soft rock phosphate, and they cost $20 to $40 for 50 pounds, twice as much as many of the calcium sources. They can be difficult to source, but some farm supply stores have them. I wish the most important products were more readily available, but I'm sorry to say that's not always the case. I still have to recommend them because they're the most effective. Unfortunately, it may be a bit of work for you to find a couple of them. It's work for me, too.

Hard rock phosphate is the more commonly available of the two, containing approximately 30% phosphorus and 30% calcium. It's mostly tricalcium phosphate and is difficult for plants to get out of the soil because the phosphorus is bound tightly with the calcium. The calcium will become available over time, but we don't use it to rapidly change the ratio of calcium on the cation exchange sites.

The phosphorus is only 3% available and takes many years to become available to plants. It's often ground to a find dust and granulated with chelators that are supposed to make it more available to plants, but it's still not the best. I'll use it in a pinch, though, in order to build up long-term phosphorus reserves. In my experience, it won't give as effective a result as soft rock phosphate. If you do use it, be sure you're also focusing on coaxing together the most active, healthy soil food web you possibly can. Of course, it's a good idea to do this anyway.

Hard rock phosphate is also treated with acids to create chemical fertilizers like superphosphate (0-20-0) and triple superphosphate (0-46-0). These are more available to plants, but 85-90% of the application will be leached, wasting money and polluting the environment, not to mention the other soil problems these fertilizers can cause.

Soft rock phosphate, on the other hand, is a by-product of hard rock phosphate mining. It's so much better than hard rock phosphate that I've driven hours just to go get a couple hundred pounds. It can be difficult to find. Traditionally separated from the hard rock as an impurity and trucked away to holding ponds, it's now considered superior to the hard rock form because it's colloidal, meaning it's in a form that won't leach and doesn't tie up as tightly as hard rock phosphate.

Like hard rock phosphate, it may only be listed as 3% available, but over a few years, it's 100% available to plants. It does combine with calcium, but not in the unbreakable bond that hard rock creates. It's also a good source of silicon and many trace minerals.

In addition to the colloidal type, there's reactive soft rock phosphate. There's a myth that this type is not as good, and that it ties up calcium, but neither of these are true. In reality, it may actually be more available to soil microbes and contain less heavy metals. I say go with what you can get, colloidal or reactive. Either will help loosen up your soil like a loaf of bread rising in the oven. Like calcitic lime, it's often recommended at 10-45 pounds per 1,000 square feet. I like to spread this out into at least two applications throughout the year or add some of it to the compost.

You can get a powder form and sometimes a granular form. The best products come from Idaho, North Carolina and Tennessee. I really like the powder, although it's a bit tricky to spread. Pick a calm day. In the book, *The Non-Toxic Farming Handbook*, Phil Wheeler and Ron Ward advise to lay colloidal phosphate and then calcitic lime in order to create an energy that kills surface weed seeds.

Summary

- Calcium and phosphorus are two of the most important soil nutrients. One of our first goals should be balancing the calcium to magnesium and phosphate to potash ratios.
- Liquid calcium, calcitic lime and gypsum are three of the best sources of calcium, while soft rock phosphate is the best source of phosphorus.
- Dolomite lime, in my view, is usually inappropriate as a fertilizer.

Chapter 17

Other Major Nutrients

While calcium and phosphorus are often considered the most important minerals among organic and biological gardeners and farmers, we know it's not that simple. All nutrients need to be there in sufficient quantities and proper ratios for optimal health. Still, there are only a handful we focus on as being the foundational nutrients, with the rest supplied mostly through things like compost, sea minerals and rock dust. In this chapter I'll look at some of the fertilizers that supply the other main nutrients.

Rock Dust

Rock dust is one product everyone can use without a soil test. In my opinion, a good quality dust is one of the most important mineral soil amendments. The best dusts contain an abundance of major and minor minerals that can be applied to the soil and used by microbes and plants. You may be able to find a good dust locally from a quarry for a very low cost, or you may have to buy it at a garden centre or other fertilizer supply store where the cost is $20 to $40 for 50 pounds.

Minerals from land slowly make their way into rivers, lakes, and eventually, the oceans. Periods of glaciation, volcanoes and other natural events contribute to the process called remineralization. In the last century, our agricultural practices and general intervention in the planet's natural systems has greatly accelerated the loss of minerals to the point where our soils are depleted. We can do the same work of a glacier in order to get some minerals back in the soil by using rock dust.

Rock dust is a fine powder, the best type coming from glacial or volcanic rocks such as basalt and granite. Research on its benefits has been done for at least 60 years. The dust often contains a wide array of minerals, particularly if it's from a glacial source that has a mixture of many different kinds of rocks. Rock dusts have produced amazing results, such as doubling yield and vastly increasing nutrition in vegetables. Vegetables grown with rock dust are bigger, tastier, and much more nutritious. In one experiment, iodine in spinach was 1,600 parts per billion on conventional soil, versus 640,000 on soil that had been remineralized with rock dust.

Remineralize the Earth is an organization doing a lot of research. They recommend between 150 and 500 pounds per 1,000 square feet. Still, good results have been seen with less than five pounds per 1,000 square feet with certain dusts. It can be applied in any way that gets it onto the ground, whether it be by hand, with a shovel, or with a spreader.

Incidentally, if you're composting, it's even better to put the rock dust in there rather than straight onto the ground because it will have a chance to get integrated and chelated with the organic matter. When composting, Phil Callahan, author of *Paramagnetism* and *Tuning In To Nature* recommends 40 to 50 pounds per cubic yard, while Remineralize The Earth recommends using 2 to 20 pounds. More important than how you use it is *that* you use it.

Magnesium

Magnesium helps give structure to soil. That's why we need a little more of it on sandy soils as compared to clay soils, to help that sand glue together a little better. Too much magnesium in relation to calcium causes soil compaction, a common occurrence.

Magnesium also regulates nitrogen in the plant and helps transport phosphorus, so deficiencies in these nutrients may have to do with excess magnesium. See how intertwined all of these nutrients are! It's difficult to isolate them as each having their own tasks because they all work together.

Magnesium is at the center of the chlorophyll molecule, which is responsible for photosynthesis. Interestingly, the chlorophyll molecule is almost the same as the molecule that makes up our red blood cells, except that blood cells have iron at the center instead of magnesium. Magnesium is important for plant health, but often, when we need magnesium, we need calcium, too, which is why I use calcitic lime much more often than dolomite.

We're looking for 7-15% magnesium on a base saturation test, and a 10:1 calcium to magnesium ratio on a Reams test. This goes up to 20% magnesium and down to a 7:1 ratio for grasses and sandy soil. The plant won't take up enough magnesium if there's too little *or* too much in the soil. Most of our soils have too much magnesium, which means the plant won't take up enough, which may be why our food is so deficient in magnesium. I like to keep magnesium on the low side because magnesium ties up nitrogen, and I don't apply much nitrogen. That being said, some people have success keeping magnesium levels higher. If your calcium to magnesium ratio is low, though, you're probably going to have nitrogen deficiency problems, compaction, and grassy weeds.

Langbeinite is approximately 27% sulfur, 22% potassium and 11% magnesium. It's also known as sul-po-mag or K-mag, and is a good, natural product that is useful if a soil test indicates you need sulfur, potassium and magnesium. It's a bit pricey at $30 to $40 for 50 pounds, but Dr. Reams liked it a lot and wanted it to be applied in mid to late summer. It can be difficult to find and most people will look at you like you just zoomed in from Mars if you ask for langbeinite. They may have heard of sul-po-mag or K-mag, but they may substitute a synthetic version so be sure to ask for organic.

Another source of magnesium is epsom salts, also known as magnesium sulfate. It contains approximately 16% magnesium and 14% sulfur, and costs about $10 for a few pounds. It can be used as a foliar spray or on the ground, when you know you need magnesium and sulfur.

Potassium

Potassium is involved in many plant processes, but extra potassium is not needed in the soil of most home or market gardeners who are using compost and mulch. Everywhere I've lived, I've had to worry more about getting the phosphorus up in relation to potassium, so I haven't wanted to add too much extra potassium. It is important, though for determining the caliber of the stalk and leaves and the size and set of the fruit, among other things. Compost made with lots of green matter and a bit of manure generally provides plenty of potassium.

Traditionally, we go for 2-5% potassium on a base saturation test and a 2:1 phosphate to potash ratio on a Reams test, up to 4:1 for grasses and greens. More recently, some consultants advocate the upper end of the 2-5% range in order to ensure we have more potassium than nitrogen in a plant tissue test. Of course, most of us don't do plant tissue testing, but just knowing that we should try to move the potassium towards 5% and not over-apply nitrogen is helpful. On the other hand, too much potassium compacts the soil.

Langbeinite supplies potassium and was mentioned in the magnesium section. If my soil had a potassium deficiency, I might also use some seaweed if I could get my hands on it, as well as granite dust and ash. Granite dust is 3-5% potassium, while wood ash can have a potassium content as high as 10%.

Greensand (5-7% Potassium)

Greensand is a sandstone with approximately 7% potash and a fair amount of iron and silica, as well as a very broad spectrum of trace elements. Although the potassium is tightly held and slowly released,

I like greensand because of the benefit of the silica and trace minerals that come with it, although it is a bit pricey at $25-$40 for 50 pounds. It's high in iron, so you don't want to use it if a soil test says you already have too much iron. You must have an active soil food web to make available the potassium in greensand, and in granite dust and ash for that matter. Greensand is seen in many organic fertilizer blends and is a common suggestion for homemade fertilizers, but I feel it's not something that should be added indiscriminately, because you probably don't want the additional potassium.

Potassium Sulfate 0-0-50
(50% Potassium and 17% Sulfur)

Potassium sulfate is white salt. It's expensive, but you only need two pounds per 1,000 square feet when potassium is low on a soil test, unless you're growing a big crop of plants with high potassium needs, like potatoes or pumpkins, in which case you might double or triple that. A 50 pound bag costs $40-$50, but you might be able to find five pounds for $15 or less.

I don't recommend the chemical potassium sulfate that's made by reacting potassium chloride with sulfuric acid. Also, don't get this confused with muriate of potash (potassium chloride, 0-0-60) which is mostly potassium and chlorine, and is one of the most detrimental fertilizers in use today. We don't ever want to be adding this much chlorine to our soil because it kills soil life.

Sulfur

Sulfur is important, and lacking in many soils, which is one reason why gypsum is often recommended along with calcitic lime. Like nitrogen, sulfur is a major component of protein, and its presence helps nitrogen to be used more efficiently. Sulfate can enhance calcium availability and is used by plants in several ways.

Gypsum, discussed in the calcium section of the last chapter, is the way to go for organics. I don't tend to use elemental sulfur because it can create sulfuric acid, tie up calcium and cause your fruit to rot at maturity, but some people use it successfully. Langbeinite, potassium sulfate and epsom salts, all discussed previously, contain sulfur, too. We're looking for a 1:1 potash to sulfate ratio on a Reams test.

Sulfur bonds to excess cations and leaches them, provided there is sufficient calcium. It will bind with calcium, magnesium, potassium and sodium, and then water will leach some of it down. I use an appropriate form of sulfur when a soil test indicates I have too much of one of the cations. Using the right form of sulfur helps to kick the calcium, magnesium, potassium and sodium toward their appropriate numbers.

The form of sulfur you add depends on which cation is in excess. If calcium is low and magnesium is high, gypsum (calcium sulfate) is often included in a fertility program, often at 10 pounds per 1,000 square feet. If calcium is high and magnesium is low, epsom salts (magnesium sulfate) would be added. If calcium or magnesium is high and potassium is low, potassium sulfate would be added. If sodium is high, choose the best for your situation from any of the above.

Sodium

Sodium is needed in small amounts, between 20-70 ppm. Below this, there may not be enough energy in the soil to grow a good plant. Above this, there's too much energy, which also causes problems. Also, sodium above 70 ppm will generally cause soil compaction, even if the calcium to magnesium ratio is perfect.

Gypsum is often used when sodium is too high, to bring it down. I've heard of table salt, which is sodium chloride, being used to raise sodium when it's low, although too much chlorine has negative effects on the soil. I prefer sea minerals, discussed in the upcoming biostimulants chapter. Manure contains sodium, too.

Nitrogen

Lastly, we come to nitrogen. It's the basis for all amino acids and proteins in our bodies and the bodies of all living things. Interestingly, while the air is 78% nitrogen, we can't get nitrogen directly from the air and neither can plants. Luckily, certain microbes can. While rainfall and lightning bring some of this nitrogen down into the soil, nitrogen-fixing bacteria and actinomycetes provide most of it. As we've seen, they take nitrogen out of the air and convert it into other forms of nitrogen they can use and plants can use.

Nitrogen exists in many different molecules, generally combined with hydrogen or oxygen. While plants take up complex nitrogenous proteins and amino acids, the two main forms they use are the relatively simple ammonium (NH_4^+) and nitrate (NO_3^-). Most food plants use ammonium in small amounts, especially towards the fruiting and flowering stage. It's mainly produced when microbes decompose organic matter such as leaves. Since ammonium has a positive charge, it's held on cation exchange sites, although relatively weakly.

Some of the soil ammonium is converted to nitrite (NO_2^-) and then nitrate (NO_3^-) by different groups of bacteria. The hydrogen coming out of this process kicks cations off the exchange sites. We don't want too much of that to happen at once, so we don't want to add too much nitrogen at once.

If the soil is dominated by fungi, much of this ammonium won't get converted to nitrate. This is great if you're trying to grow perennials, trees and shrubs, which prefer more ammonium. If you're trying to grow annual vegetables and grasses, they mostly want a soil dominated by bacteria, and consequently more nitrate.

Nitrate is the main form most crop plants use and this is what certain microbes manufacture from other forms of nitrogen. Most of this work happens during the growing season as temperatures get warmer, just when plants need more nitrogen. This is good because nitrate would leach away very quickly if the microbes made too much. A lot of nitrate nitrogen leaches away after application of chemical nitrogen, or also with the application of too much fresh manure. Nature knows the right amount to make available, but to get the best crop, it's often necessary to supplement some nitrogen.

But chemical nitrogen fertilizers are overused in conventional gardening and agriculture, especially early in spring before the microbes are ready to use the nitrogen. This is when it leaches down through the soil to pollute the ground water and consequently isn't available for the last few weeks before fall harvest. While nitrogen fertilizers are often overused, it doesn't mean we shouldn't be thinking about how to supply sufficient nitrogen to the soil and microbes.

Nitrogen in the soil is like the electrolyte in a battery. We need enough to provide energy to the soil to get everything else working. Like phosphate, nitrogen also transports nutrients throughout the plant, especially when phosphate is short. Liquid fish is a good nitrogen source that we'll look at in the biostimulants chapter. It doesn't provide a huge amount of nitrogen, but it's good quality and definitely helps build proteins and amino acids.

As discussed in the cover crops chapter, most legumes contribute nitrogen to the soil. I use as many as 25% leguminous plants in a new garden design in order to ensure the nitrogen needs of the soil food web and plants. You probably need to inoculate your legumes with Rhizobia, and your soil has to be healthy enough to support them. Otherwise, they won't hang around, so be sure to work on the nutrient levels, too.

To follow are some other sources of nitrogen.

Manure and Compost

As we've seen in the composting chapter, manure should be composted first. It's great to get different sources, but rabbit, chicken and horse manure are the highest in nitrogen.

Compost also supplies nitrogen. It's the manure, food scraps and fresh plant residue that contribute most of this to the pile. Applying ½ yard (⅙ inch) of compost per 1,000 square feet each year will give you a lot of nitrogen as well as phosphorus and potassium, slowly released by microbes. You really need look no further than good compost for much of your nitrogen needs.

Dean Craine of AgriEnergy Resources in Princeton, Illinois says an increase in soil organic matter of 1% to a depth of 40 inches brings 45 pounds of nitrogen per thousand square feet. I'm not sure how he did his math, but it's a good example of how important it is for us to focus on our organic matter. This kind of nitrogen doesn't all show up on a soil test because it's bound up in organic molecules, not free in the soil as nitrate and ammonium.

Chilean Nitrate

My understanding of Chilean nitrate is that it's sodium nitrate, derived from bat manure (guano) deposits in Chile. It's allowed under some organic standards in the U.S. and Chile, but isn't allowed in Canada and most other countries partially because of environmental degradation associated with mining the product and also because of concerns over the leaching of the soluble nitrate into the groundwater.

Some organic proponents endorse it and others don't, but it is OMRI listed. It's rather expensive, and high in nitrogen (16%) and sodium (26%), so it can negatively impact the soil food web and waterways. I've never used it and so can't comment much, but I wanted to include it here because you may hear of it.

OMRI - Organic Materials Review Institute

Summary

- A good quality rock dust is one of the best fertilizers because it contains a broad range of minerals that will slowly become available over a number of years.
- It's generally more important to increase calcium than magnesium, but the latter can be supplied by dolomite lime, langbeinite and epsom salts in order to get at least a 7:1 calcium to magnesium ratio.
- If we're composting, we should have enough potassium, which can also be supplied by greensand and potassium sulfate to aim for a 2:1 phosphate to potash ratio.
- The potash to sulfate ratio should be 1:1 and sulfur can be supplied with gypsum, langbeinite, potassium sulfate and epsom salts.
- Nitrogen is easily supplied with compost, legume cover crops and fish fertilizer.

Chapter 18

Synthetic Products

Pesticides, genetically modifed plants and fertilizers, and chemical fertilizers can cause tremendous damage to plants and soil. These products are often harmful to soil life, they acidify the soil and deplete it of nutrients, cause compaction, burn up organic matter, pollute our water, and cause plants to grow in such a way that they invite predator damage and can't properly mature food.

Pesticides

I'm not going to get into detail about the health consequences of pesticide use because that would take us too far off track. Many of them cause cancer, neurological damage and other diseases. Pesticides have traveled to all corners of the world, even into the tissues of penguins on the south pole. The list of negatives goes on and on. What I do want to outline briefly are a few of their negative effects on the garden, and specifically on the soil.

When I was younger, I spent the better part of a decade maintaining a 9-hole, par-3 golf course owned by my parents. You can bet I sprayed pesticides. The enemy on the course greens was a fungus called dollar spot. The main pesticide ingredient was chlorothalonil, a polychlorinated aromatic that killed the fungus really well for about seven days until I had to come back and spray more. So yes, I've used pesticides.

Pesticides kill living things. "Cide" means to kill. Herbicides are specifically made to kill plants, but we're not talented enough to create these poisons to kill only their target kingdom, so herbicides often kill or at least hurt animals, bacteria and fungi, too. Of course, bactericides and fungicides and insecticides kill or hurt animals and plants, as well. For example, the fungicide I sprayed on the golf course greens was deadly toxic to fish, too. While these various forms of pesticide work differently, we really can talk about pesticides as a whole.

The pesticide manufacturers tell us these poisons will be broken down by the microorganisms in the soil. This may be true if we have a healthy, diverse soil food web, but every time we or our neighbors spray, even those neighbors many miles away, we decrease the number of healthy, happy microbes until eventually, there are very few of them left to perform this important function. Even when it rains, we get unbelievably high doses of pesticides from thousands of miles away.

Many pesticides have indeed done a great job of killing all insects, diseases and weeds for awhile, sometimes even for decades. Eventually, the predators figure it out and come back with a vengeance. This time the chemicals don't work as well or at all. In the meantime, the pesticides have done a dandy job of terrorizing the soil environment, ensuring that weeds are the only plants that will grow there and that plant predators are the organisms that flourish. Using a herbicide just prolongs weed problems. It does not do any of the other soil improving steps we'll be looking at — in fact, it does the opposite.

We've already seen how microbes are vital to the very existence of the garden, so we know we don't want to kill them. Plants are also hurt by pesticides to the point where protein synthesis stops, soluble nitrogen and sugars increase, and predators are invited to dine. Animals — our fertilizers, our seed dispersers, our pollinators, birds, bees, butterflies and everyone else — are hurt, too. We know that certain pesticides contribute to colony collapse disorder in bees.

Nearly 100% of rivers in North America and probably the world have pesticides in them and the majority of wells do, too. Many lakes and rivers are unfishable and undrinkable. It would be a good idea to stop using pesticides in our gardens. In my view, there's never a good enough reason to warrant using them in a garden.

Genetically Modified Organisms (GMOs)

GMOs are made by taking a gene from one organism and firing it into the DNA of another organism along with a virus or bacteria to help the gene infect that DNA. The genes from the giver and receiver organisms can come from entirely different domains — bacteria, viruses, plants and animals. For example, trials are underway with human genes being inserted into corn and rice, spider genes into goats, and jellyfish into pigs. Obviously, it's nothing like the benign grafting and hybridizing that horticulturists have been practicing for many years, although adherents regularly equate them.

Even though the biotech industry likes to promote the idea that their main goal is to create more food for the starving masses, the kinds of genetic modifications they're making suggest otherwise. The two main reasons genetic engineering is done in plants are to give them the ability to produce their own pesticides and to make them resistant to herbicides. Many people don't realize that GMOs make up the vast majority of corn, soy, cotton, and canola, and that our processed foods contain a lot of ingredients derived from these crops. Alfalfa will be on this list soon, as the USDA recently approved it against recommendations of its own committee. Also, farm animals feed on GMO plants, and even honeybees feed on GMO pollen. At least 60% of foods in the U.S., therefore contain GMOs.

All of this is quite scary when almost all studies and some real-world experiences are showing that GMOs can cause major health problems in animals, including humans. GMOs are toxins, allergens and carcinogens that will promote new diseases and nutritional problems.

But here, I'm going to touch on a topic that is discussed somewhat less — the effect of GMOs on the environment. For example, *Bacillus thuringiensis* (Bt) is a bacterium that produces a substance toxic to some insects, such as caterpillars. It has been used as a biological insecticide since the 1920s, and is now used to make Bt cotton, Bt corn, and Bt potatoes, which are genetically modified crops.

The DNA of these plants is altered with a gene from the bacteria that gives the plants the ability to produce the toxin themselves. Research shows soil microbial life and beneficial enzymes decrease when Bt crops are planted. One study concluded that soil life could be entirely dead after 10 years under a Bt crop. Another study found the gene in GM corn was passed to various soil organisms. We don't know exactly what happens in that situation, but it seems that gene transfer from GM organisms to other organisms is commonplace. Other plants are genetically engineered by companies to resist the herbicides they sell, such as Roundup Ready soy. This allows farmers to spray their fields with Roundup, killing the weeds but not the crops, making it easier for farmers to use herbicides, thereby increasing the use of herbicides.

The list of other potential problems is long. Altered genes get into our waterways where they may affect aquatic life. They may impact beneficial insects in our garden. Because genes can and do jump from one organism to another, they contribute to herbicide-resistant weeds. The general consensus among organic gardeners and most environmental and health advocacy organizations is that we should avoid using any GMOs in our garden because we don't know the long-term effects, and because there is absolutely no reason we need to use them in the first place. This means not only that we don't plant GMO seeds, but we don't use alfalfa meal, canola meal, corn gluten meal, cotton meal, soy meal or any other plant fertilizers unless we're absolutely sure they are non-GMO.

Personally, I see no good reason for us to be pursuing the use of GMOs. You may have a different viewpoint, but what we must agree on is that planting them all across the world before we know all of the side effects is probably not a smart idea. Fortunately, most parts of the world are rejecting GMOs, but unfortunately, it may be too late to stop them from spreading, especially as government regulatory decisions in the U.S. and Canada continue to reflect the desires of the companies producing and selling these seeds over the desires of the general public. What we can do is let more people know about them and get more support for banning them. You can read Jeffrey Smith's books, *Seeds Of Deception* and *Genetic Roulette* to learn more about GMOs.

Chemical Fertilizers

It's important to note that many chemical fertilizers are potentially just as damaging to the soil as pesticides. Chemical fertilizers undergo chemical reactions in the soil that can produce acids with a pH lower than 1.2 or bases with a pH above 11, both of which are extremely toxic to pretty much any living being. Even the fertilizers themselves, which are salts, either destroy or interfere with the cell walls of microbes, hurting or killing them. These fertilizers contain a lot of hydrogen, which kicks minerals out of the soil, depleting the soil of nutrients with repeated use. Plants and microbes use hydrogen for this purpose, too, but in a much more controlled fashion.

Oxygen is created during this chemical reaction and organic matter is burned up. Some fertilizers even include or form formaldehyde, which does the same thing in the soil that it did in your high school biology class when you used it to preserve specimens.

Chemical fertilizers are mostly nitrogen, phosphorus and potassium. Consistent applications of these nutrients at the expense of the dozens of others that are needed creates an imbalanced soil environment, not to mention the sewage sludge and toxic metals and all kinds of other garbage that are often included in the fertilizers as filler. Most of the nitrogen — and some of the phosphorus and potassium — leaches into our waterways causing all kinds of problems to the greater environment. Manufacturers eventually started coating the fertilizer with nutrients such as chemical sulfur to decrease this problem by making the fertilizer more "slow-release." This sounds like a great fix on the surface, except when heavy doses of sulfur combine with water to produce sulfuric acid and kill soil life.

We must definitely stop using the traditional chemical fertilizers such as urea (46-0-0), triple superphosphate (0-46-0) and potassium chloride (0-0-60, including 40-50% chloride). These are what make up many of the conventional nitrogen-phosphorus-potassium (NPK) fertilizers, such as 10-10-10, and they are extremely toxic.

Urea is consumed by bacteria that convert it to toxic anhydrous ammonia. It also reacts with water to produce toxic ammonium hydroxide with a pH of 11.6, killing microbes and harming seeds. If it's coated with sulfur, the sulfur reacts with water to form toxic sulfuric acid with a pH of less than 1. Triple superphosphate is very acidic and binds with calcium in the soil, making both unavailable, until eventually maybe 10-20% of the phosphorus can become available with microbial breakdown. Potassium chloride often increases chloride levels to 50-200 ppm in the soil, when 2 ppm of chlorine is often sufficient to sterilize drinking water. Adding one pound of potassium chloride is like applying one gallon of bleach. Too much potassium disintegrates clay and compacts the soil.

These products are harmful to soil life, acidify the soil and deplete it of nutrients, cause compaction, burn up organic matter, pollute our water, and grow plants that invite predator damage and can't properly mature food. The fertilizer industry would have us believe that plants prefer taking up their chemicals in ionic form, which means as molecules or elements with a positive or negative charge, such as calcium as Ca^{2+} or sulfate as SO_4^{2-}. Plants certainly take up ionic chemicals, but they also take up complex organic molecules and prefer natural sources of vitamins and other substances to synthetic sources, just as our bodies do. Plants prefer molasses or seaweed, for example, over an iron sulfate chemical fertilizer.

There are many pesticide-ban laws coming in around the world, but they are not addressing chemical fertilizers. Since chemical fertilizers exacerbate many predator problems, we will have some major issues until the laws catch up. For the most part, if you don't use pesticides, make sure you don't use chemical fertilizers, either, especially the NPK brands from your local garden center.

Occasionally, however, some people may choose to use specific chemical fertilizers if their goal is optimal garden health. I don't mean the usual NPK fertilizers like 21-7-7 and 10-10-10 that I used to broadcast on the golf course. I'm referring to a different set of fertilizers. Let me explain why I have used these different ones, and let me first say that when I initially got into organics, I swore off all synthetic products as if they were all toxic. I looked down upon people who used them, until I did more research and gained more experience. If you're in that mindset, I've been there.

In fact, I've been there in other areas than just gardening. When I became a vegetarian, I noticed after a short while that I was feeling superior to, and more ethical than, my meat-eating friends. It didn't take long to realize how dumb that was. I had eaten meat for most of my life and I don't think I was an unethical person during this time. Of course, when I started following a vegan diet, vegetarianism was no longer good enough, until I came to the same realization.

So if you currently believe all chemical fertilizers are evil, I'll ask you to open your mind while you read the rest of this chapter, or skip it, which is absolutely okay by me. I had my reservations about including this information in a book about organic gardening because I sympathize with those who want to be 100% organic. In the end, I chose to include this information nonetheless because it's important.

Still, you don't need to use any of these chemicals to make healthy soil and I'm not going to try to convince you to do so. It's rare that I use them myself, and the majority of the products in this book are organic. I do want to mention a couple of synthetic fertilizers, though, because you may see them listed as recommendations on a soil test from one of the labs I previously recommended, and you may actually agree with the reasons for using them and want to use them yourself.

My ultimate goal is to grow the healthiest food and ornamental plants possible. I can certainly grow healthy plants with organic products, but in order to get optimally healthy plants, a couple of chemical fertilizers can be helpful. There is a philosophy one step away from the organic movement that some people call "biological," and like organics, the goal of this movement is to grow the healthiest food possible while improving the health of the environment.

It turns out there are certain chemical fertilizers that can help us grow food that has even more nutrition than organic food. These aren't the chemicals used by conventional farming and gardening today, but they're still chemicals that can hurt soil life if used improperly. When used consciously, however, in very small amounts based on soils tests, they can be very helpful in getting more nutrition out of a crop — particularly while we're in the process of transitioning a garden to one that is more balanced and self-sustaining.

These fertilizers are used primarily to provide energy to a crop and soil that organic products can't provide. In your garden, for example, you might apply a couple of pounds of 11-52-0 to give the push a crop needs to go from say, 8 to 12 brix. I've listed several of the main ones below, but you may get a couple of others recommended on a soil test, particularly nitrogen sources such as ammonium nitrate 34-0-0, or 28-32% urea-ammonium nitrate, or even potassium nitrate when you're low in potassium.

Calcium Nitrate 15-0-0 (with 19% Calcium)

Most calcium nitrate comes from Norway, where they make nitric acid from atmospheric nitrogen and then react it with limestone. The process may sound harmless enough, but it isn't allowed under organic standards. It certainly is a big hit of nitrogen all at once, although interestingly, in conventional farming, it's considered low in nitrogen.

That goes to show how much nitrogen they normally use.

I don't tend to use calcium nitrate much because there are many natural forms of calcium that have worked for me, but it's quite useful when applied at only a few pounds per 1,000 square feet, especially on leafy greens and members of the broccoli family. It's even used at as little as a half pound per 1,000 square feet to make nitrogen more available. The liquid calcium version that I mentioned in the calcium chapter does this, too.

The product is coated in wax in order to keep it from getting too moist in the bag, or you can get a crystal version that you run through a drip line or turn into a foliar spray. I've seen 20 pounds of calcium nitrate selling for $20-$30.

Monoammonium Phosphate (MAP) 11-52-0

Monoammonium phosphate (MAP) contains a lot of phosphate and a fair amount of ammonium, too. I've used this one in regions where I couldn't find any soft rock phosphate, or to "loosen" existing phosphate, when I seemed to have plenty on a conventional soil test, but not much available on a Reams test. I've also used it for this purpose at the same time as applying soft rock. Diammonium phosphate (DAP) has a very high pH and ties up tightly with calcium, so it isn't recommended.

I would only use MAP if nitrogen and phosphorus are both low, at 1 to 4 pounds per 1,000 square feet, combined with molasses, while focusing on soft rock phosphate in the long term. Phosphoric acid prices have skyrocketed around the world, so MAP is quite expensive right now for farmers, but it's not so bad on a garden scale. I've purchased 50 pounds for less than $30. Of all the chemicals, this is probably the first one I would recommend if you can't find soft rock phosphate because it's just so important to get some available phosphate in there, but it's also one of the most difficult to find.

Phosphoric Acid (75-85% Phosphoric Acid)

Food-grade 75-85% phosphoric acid is useful in a foliar program. This is the stuff they put in soft drinks, and in my opinion, we should not be ingesting it at all. Spraying two to four teaspoons, however, with some fish and kelp and two quarts of water per 1,000 square feet every couple of weeks during the growing season can be very helpful in keeping the phosphorus, and therefore the brix, at appropriate levels. If you're in the dry season and the humidity is low, keep it at two teaspoons maximum in order to not burn the leaves.

Phosphoric acid isn't a quick fix, but gradually helps throughout the season. It should cost less than $20 for a quart. It's corrosive, so be extremely careful with it. Don't use it unless you have some knowledge and comfort working with this kind of thing. Don't mix it with liquid calcium or you may get a jelly consistency in your sprayer.

Ammonium Sulfate 21-0-0 (24% Sulfur)

In the long term, the focus should be on compost and cover crops for nitrogen, but this product can be helpful during the transition. It's especially useful on farms where it's difficult to make or buy enough compost, but if you're composting at home, you should be okay for nitrogen. Remember, plants will pass up chemically produced nitrogen in favor of amino acid or protein-based nitrogen any time they're available, so our focus is still on organic matter.

The sulfur in ammonium sulfate does a better job than gypsum to counteract an imbalanced soil by leaching excessive cations, and can make the calcium more available. The ammonium is also slower to release than nitrate fertilizers, which is great, but you need to have sufficient calcium in the soil in order for ammonium sulfate to work.

The best kind to use is the dark gray colored form, a by-product of the nylon industry. Since sulfur works right along with nitrogen to form proteins and makes nitrogen use more efficient, this is a pretty good match. One of the other most important uses is to raise the energy of the soil, the ERGS, which we'll look at in the energy chapter. This product is one of the best for raising the ERGS mid-season when you want to promote fruiting in the plant. The cost is $0.20-$3.00 per pound, and this product is easier to find than the others mentioned in this chapter.

Of course, you should only use extremely small amounts. Otherwise, it reacts with water to create sulfuric acid, depletes too many cations, and oxidizes the organic matter. Personally, I don't use it often, but both of my soil labs often recommend it at low doses, not at the high amounts that conventional farming uses. The rate is two to four pounds per 1,000 square feet on the lawn and in the garden. I use only the lower end of this recommendation. This low amount should not leach and cause problems, especially if you're working on building organic matter.

Growth Versus Fruiting

This is more of an advanced topic, but very interesting. Cationic nutrients like calcium, magnesium and potassium, as well as the anions chlorine and nitrate nitrogen, tend to help a plant with vegetative growth. Anionic nutrients like phosphorus and sulfur, as well as the cation ammonium, tend to push a plant towards reproduction, producing seeds and fruit. Of course, all of the nutrients are involved in both processes, but certain nutrients are needed for the plant to switch from growth to fruiting.

The nutrients just mentioned that promote growth I will call "sweet," while those that promote fruiting I think of as "sour." If you're growing a big crop and are serious about getting the best response, you can consider the implications for your fertilizer program. This is often where certain beneficial chemical fertilizers come in because of the energy they bring to the table, but organic products can help here, too.

You may apply small amounts of materials at certain times to provide energy to a crop. For the first month or two after plant emergence, you can focus more on "sweet" fertilizers that provide more quickly available calcium, such as organic liquid calcium, or synthetic calcium nitrate. After that, or whenever you see buds, you can focus on "sour" fertilizers to promote fruiting, such as soft rock phosphate, or synthetic 11-52-0 and ammonium sulfate. Foliar fertilizers are especially useful for promoting growth or fruiting because the response is faster.

For the most part, this means the "sweet" fertilizers are applied in spring and the "sour" fertilizers in the summer. If you're growing greens and herbs, you're not concerned about fruiting, so you'll always stick with "sweet" fertilizers. If you're growing fruit trees, they begin the fruiting process in the spring and the growing process in mid- to late-summer, so the timing is reversed.

I tend to apply a bit of soft rock phosphate when I'm ready to promote fruiting, and I have used 11-52-0 in the past. I don't often use any of the other chemicals for this because I don't have them sitting around. I actually apply a simple recipe to promote fruiting that I learned from Dan Skow: four tablespoons of apple cider vinegar and two tablespoons of ammonia in two quarts of water per 1,000 square feet. Ammonia can be difficult to find anymore, but I found some at a hardware store recently.

Boron helps with fruiting, too. If I have it, I might instead spray three tablespoons liquid calcium mixed with two to four teaspoons boron, along with seven tablespoons liquid fish hydrolysate, four teaspoons kelp and one to two tablespoons of apple cider vinegar, in 1¼ gallon of water per 1,000 square feet. For either of these recipes, you need sufficient calcium in the soil for them to work, and you'll probably want to do them several more times through the remainder of the season in order to keep up that fruiting energy.

Summary

- Pesticides are toxic to all life and fail to solve the root cause of the problem, which is unhealthy soil and plants.
- We don't know the long-term consequences of GMOs, but what we know so far tells us they have no place in our gardens. This means no GMO seeds and no organic fertilizers that could have come from GMO plants, such as alfalfa meal, canola meal, corn gluten meal, cotton meal, or soy meal.
- Like pesticides, most chemical fertilizers cause many problems to soil and the soil food web, so we absolutely must stop using most of them, too.
- A select few chemical fertilizers can be intelligently used to improve the health of the soil and plants beyond that of organic products.
- My top chemical fertilizer is MAP (11-52-0) for phosphorus, especially when I can't find soft rock phosphate.
- Soft rock phosphate, ammonium sulfate and MAP can help a plant to begin fruiting when used before or early on in the initial reproductive stages of the plant, as can the recipes listed at the end of this chapter.

Chapter 19

Biostimulants & Micronutrients

STEP 5

In 2008, I started The Organic Gardener's Pantry to sell microbial inoculants and most of the fascinating products outlined in this chapter. I moved in 2010, but my friend Christina still has the business going strong. One of the bonuses of getting these products out into the world was that I was able to see how effective they could be since I had hundreds of clients using them.

There are more than 80 elements, many of which are important in small amounts as part of coenzymes, which help chemical reactions take place in the soil and plants. These are called trace minerals or micronutrients, and examples are iron, manganese, copper, molybdenum and selenium. Our food supply is tremendously lacking in most of these, and our health is suffering as a result. A very well-made compost with many different raw materials can supply many of these nutrients, but we can go a little further to make sure they're there and available to microbes and plants.

Farmers and market gardeners may benefit from analyzing some of these nutrients in the soil and plants, and then taking action to supply one or a few of them with specific products. This can be beneficial, but I have thus far relied on compost, rock dust and microbes to do the work, plus biostimulants. Sea minerals, kelp and fish fertilizer all supply most or all of these micronutrients.

There are many organic and synthetic micronutrient blends on the market, some of which are good. I don't tend to use them because there are plenty of "whole food" options available. What I mean is that I would rather get my own nutrients from food than from a multivitamin as much as possible, and I would rather get my soil's trace minerals from kelp and ocean water than from a synthetic or even an organic formula. In fact, one of the main reasons it's recommended that we take a multivitamin is because these trace minerals are lacking in our food supply. Our goal here is to bring them back into the food we grow.

Biostimulants often contain many trace minerals, but they also stimulate biological processes in more ways than just through nutrients. Their use can result in healthier microorganisms, better soil, and improved plant growth, even when applied in small quantities. While they may contain vitamins and minerals, the benefits they bring are often attributed to non-nutritional means — natural hormones, amino acids, and other bioactive substances. Still, since many biostimulants are also good sources of trace minerals, I've put them into the same chapter.

The many benefits of biostimulants seem to partially result from their influence on hormonal activity in plants and probably microbes. Hormones control how a plant grows. Biostimulants can also supply a lot of antioxidants that help plants deal with stressors such as drought and heat. Plants with high levels of antioxidants are much healthier, for their own sake, and healthier for us when we eat them.

Biostimulants bring many different benefits to the garden. They can increase photosynthesis and respiration in plants, increase yields, and increase brix and nutrition in food, making it taste better and store longer. Depending on conditions, they have a bigger effect at some times than at others. They almost always have a bigger effect when used regularly, rather than just once or twice. Growth stimulation is usually best after four to six weeks of treatment, so it's good to start at the beginning of the season.

Of course, they don't replace the need for organic matter and balancing other nutrients. Some people think of them as being ineffective, mainly because a lot of the marketing of them has been exaggerated hype, but that doesn't mean the good products out there aren't helpful. The term biostimulants may not be the best, because when you think about it, there are many things that "stimulate biological processes" that we tend to categorize in groups other than biostimulants, such as compost and even microbial inoculants. Also, some of the products in the biostimulant category could be listed in the mineral category, and vice versa.

The term itself isn't that important. The products in this chapter are what I call biostimulants, but what's more important is what they do and how to use them. If you don't want to bring in too many external inputs because you don't want to spend the money or just want to be more self-sufficient, that's okay. These products can be very helpful, but they're not always required. Also, you don't need them all. If I was on a budget, I would start with sea minerals and that would be all.

Let's have a look at the best products. Note that some of them may come mixed with chemicals, so for the most part, be sure to find something that is certified organic, or that has only organic ingredients.

Sea Minerals (Ocean Water)

To me, this is the most important broad-spectrum micronutrient source available. It provides a broader range of micronutrients than any rock dusts I've seen and the crop response from sea minerals is often very impressive. This is probably the most important product in this chapter.

Maynard Murray did many of the first scientific experiments with ocean water, along with his associates and many followers. He was a medical doctor who became fascinated when he discovered there was very little disease in many of the animals in the sea — not much cancer, heart disease, arthritis, or anything else. In some respects, elderly whales had the same level of health as baby whales. Ocean trout lived many times longer than lake trout and didn't develop cancer, whereas lake trout mostly did get cancer of the liver after only a few years.

Murray reasoned that the high nutrient content in the oceans was responsible for this, and his subsequent research on the use of sea minerals in horticulture spanned more than four decades. He found that plants grown with sea minerals benefited in numerous ways, from increased yields and more nutritious food to healthier, pest-resistant and stress-tolerant plants. Of course, these are all related. If you're interested in his amazing research, read more in his book, *Sea Energy Agriculture*.

Bounty from the Sea

Sea energy agriculture, which is growing foods with sea solids as fertilizer, provides a means for improving our chemical intake without sacrificing our eating habits. Our meats, vegetables, fruits and cereals would all be adequately balanced with the essential elements simply by growing all crops with sea salt technology.

It has been shown by agronomists that soil may contain a large amount of one particular combination of elements, yet the plants cannot absorb them. The complex molecules of living tissue in plants and animals are made possible by the carbon atom. The linking up process is made possible by the various elements in combinations called catalysts and these catalysts invariably have a critical minor element or "trace element" that apparently serves as the key to their function. The presence or absence of a trace element can be the deciding factor in determining whether a necessary element is absorbed into the plant's root system. The balance of elements must be right in the soil for plants to synthesize their complete chemistry.

Tomatoes serve as an example of the need for this balance. There may be a few individuals who know as much about raising tomatoes as I do, but there's nobody who knows more. Tomato growers know that potassium is a macro element, or an element with a major function in the plant's growth. Potassium is added to the soil in quantity by tomato growers. Yet the tomato itself has only a minor amount of potassium in the mature product. My hydroponic experiments proved conclusively that only a small amount of potassium, as found in its proper balance in sea water, was needed to grow outstanding crops of unusually healthy tomatoes. My point is that it is unnecessary to fertilize heavily with one element or another if an adequate balance of elements can be made available for the plant's use.

— Maynard Murray, M.D. in *Sea Energy Agriculture*

While some of Murray's early research was with plain ocean water and he saw many benefits from this, he eventually moved to more concentrated forms of ocean water, as transporting railroad cars full of water was not economically feasible. If you live near the ocean, you can apply it at one cup per square foot of soil.

Nowadays, there are also very concentrated liquid sea mineral products on the market. They contain over 80 natural source minerals and active organic substances from ocean water. Many gallons of seawater are processed to produce a single gallon of these products. This has become one of my favorite biostimulants, perhaps even more than the ever-present kelp. The clear color and lack of odor may not be as impressive as the lovely green of kelp, but the results are incredible.

The price of the brand I use is about $60 for a gallon or $20-$25 for a quart if you can find it in that smaller size. Some people even take a teaspoon of this every day in some water or juice as a source of minerals, but of course the horticultural versions of these products aren't marketed or sold for that purpose as the regulatory agencies would have a hissy fit. There are food-grade versions available, though.

Now, using concentrated ocean water in the garden is a strange one to most people. The most common question I get is, "Isn't it too salty?" Interestingly, it's not too salty. The sodium is buffered by the other 80+ minerals present in the water. In fact, the mineral makeup of sea minerals is strikingly close to our blood.

Other questions people have are whether the water from the ocean is polluted, and why we should pay money for something that is so abundant. The latter question often comes from people on the coast and it's a good one. All I can say is that over fifty years of research says it would be an excellent idea to pay for ocean water if you want healthy soil and crops. As for pollution, yes, the ocean is extremely polluted in some places and not so bad in others. The good products come from relatively pristine waters. You probably wouldn't want to take water from too close to a major center, although depending on the circumstances, the minerals might be worth the associated toxins.

The book, *Fertility from the Ocean Deep* by Charles Walters chronicles the life of Maynard Murray and discusses many of the hundreds of experiments that were done over the years. I won't go into those studies here, but the yield and size increases of food plants are impressive.

There is also improved resistance to plant predators, improved stress tolerance, better taste and longer storage life. The list goes on and on, and this doesn't apply only to food crops. A lawn isn't really all that different than a vegetable garden. They're all plants and all need nutrients. Note that sea minerals and fish fertilizer may be better applied separately, as there's some evidence that their effectiveness is reduced when they are mixed together.

Sea Solids

When major elements are in relative balance, it still proves much cheaper to supply trace nutrients in a broad-spectrum way with ocean solids rather than to deal with zinc, iron, manganese, etc. A starter supply of nutrients around the seeds should guarantee the nutritional needs of essential elements throughout the life of the plant. The harvest of 10 to 20 percent more seed from the use of even one sea solids treatment is now a matter of record. Competent farmers have come to obtain such yields on acres too numerous to be considered a test plot.

Often, poor soil cannot be balanced in a single year. It is precisely such a condition that ratified the use of ocean solids. As biologically correct fertilizer, ocean solids can make up for the imbalance and limitations and produce better crops while soil conditions are repaired. It does not seem possible for a hostile environment to complex the nutrient load contained in ocean solids. These nutrients are always available to start the germinating plant with more vigor, vitality and more complete natural absorption capacity. The cell wall structure can be more efficient for the intake of nutrition.

It will undoubtedly be a requirement for farmers to know as much about the soil as they do about the science of agriculture. He or she will have to let the soil tell what is right as well as what is wrong, the way an old-time physician looked to signs and symptoms rather than laboratory results.

— Charles Walters in *Fertility from the Ocean Deep*

Kelp

Kelp contains over 70 minerals, vitamins, chelating agents and amino acids. Perhaps more importantly, it's an excellent source of cytokinins and auxins, both natural plant growth hormones. The cytokinins are said to improve soil tilth, regulate cell division and cell wall formation, increase photosynthesis and chlorophyll production, improve root and shoot growth, and extend the growth season in the fall. The auxins are said to regulate cell elongation, stimulate rooting, and promote fruit development.

This is one of the least expensive, yet most highly beneficial products out there. Certain varieties of kelp can be sustainably harvested because they grow as much as two feet per day and get well over 100 feet long. Recently, however, I heard Arden Andersen say that there's a worldwide shortage due to overharvesting, so I'm just starting to rethink my use of kelp. What follows is still my glowing account of the benefits.

For the best quality, kelp should be processed quickly at cool temperatures to preserve all of the benefits kelp has to offer. Kelp meals are less processed than powders. Kelp is a staple in any foliar feed and is often applied with microbial inoculants and other biostimulants. Definitely pick this one up if you're applying a microbial product such as EM. It's also great for starting seeds.

In the soil, the benefit of using kelp meal and fresh kelp from the beach is that you get a huge amount of nutrients, ready to be used by plants and microbes. Using kelp meal as a micronutrient fertilizer, we apply 3-10 pounds per 1,000 square feet. A 50-pound bag costs between $50-$80, while you can find 10 pounds for $20-$30. Kelp from the beach can go on the soil as a mulch layer where it will disappear quickly, or it can go into the compost. Either way, there's no need to wash off the salt.

Liquid kelp has the same nutrients, but we use it for its natural plant growth hormones, those cytokinins and auxins that stimulate many processes in plants. It's used as a foliar spray, where we apply perhaps only four teaspoons per 1,000 square feet. Although the nutrients are beneficial, at this small amount it's really all about the hormones. They have the final say as to how your plants will grow, reproduce and die. It's $10-$25 for a quart, which is all most people need.

Fish

Fish fertilizers come in different forms and qualities. According to the book *Food Power from the Sea,* fish was used as a fertilizer in Europe as far back as the Middle Ages. The technology has changed — we now have liquid products that are easier to apply and more efficient — but the principles are the same.

A fish emulsion is a liquid that's cooked to kill putrefying bacteria, filtered and stabilized with sulfuric or phosphoric acid. The important oils, amino acids, vitamins, hormones, and enzymes have either been separated for use in different products or denatured in the high temperature manufacturing process. Some people prefer an emulsion over a hydrolysate. My view is that it's often a lower quality product, but is still beneficial to use.

A hydrolysate is a liquid often made with by-catch, which is all of the unwanted fish that were caught in the process of catching other more desirable fish. The whole fish is used in this process. Instead of cooking, it's digested with enzymes at cooler temperatures, ground up and liquefied. Phosphoric acid is used here, too, as a preservative. Many of the oils, amino acids, vitamins, hormones, and enzymes remain in the product. The result is a nutrient-rich product that has many trace minerals, is less prone to leaching than soluble fertilizers, and is wonderful microbe food.

It's $20-$30 for a gallon of quality emulsion or hydrolysate. The application rates vary widely, from approximately 1½ cups per 1,000 square feet for my hydrolysate to three quarts per 1,000 square feet for some of the emulsions I've seen.

You can occasionally find either of these liquids without phosphoric acid as a preservative, which is okay as long as you use it before it spoils (or explodes). I don't mind the small amount because it's a good source of phosphorus. It's still allowed in organics if it's under a certain threshold.

Fish meals contain 5-12% nitrogen. The oils are removed to increase the nitrogen content and prevent it from spoiling. They're applied to the soil or mixed in a foliar spray. I don't use them because I've always stuck to a really good hydrolysate I found early on, but they are another option. It's $45-$70 for 50 pounds, which covers 500-1,500 square feet.

Fish fertilizers can be mixed with EM and water, and optional humic acids, and left to sit for a few hours before application to decrease the odor of the fish. I had one client complain that the fish attracted cougars, but mixing it with EM should cut that odor down tremendously. Many people swear by this as a foliar feed. There's a golf course in the U.S. that uses this as their only source of nitrogen.

Fish brings in many nutrients like the sea minerals, but it's particularly high in nitrogen, available phosphorus and potassium. These natural, quite available forms of nitrogen and phosphorus are especially useful when you don't have enough humus yet. Fish hydrolysate also has proteins, carbohydrates, enzymes and other substances. It's been combined with kelp in the same foliar mix for many decades, as they complement each other very well.

I've done a fair bit of research on the sustainability of these products. Ninety percent of the big fish in the ocean are gone, so we need to take drastic measures to reduce this trend. Some fish products are better than others depending on how they're caught and other factors, but I still tend to opt for sea minerals instead, even though it doesn't contain much nitrogen. We are running out of fish, but ocean water will be plentiful for much longer. Whether or not the ocean becomes completely toxic, like many fish, remains to be seen.

Unsulfured Molasses and Other Sugars

Molasses provides some nutrients, but is mostly just a great source of carbohydrates, which are food for microbes. It's a very good idea to apply it with most microorganism products because it gives them instant food to begin working with. It's essential to apply with nitrogen fertilizers to give the microbes a carbon source they can use in order to effectively work with the nitrogen. It should also be applied with phosphorus. We often hear that nitrogen is a building block of amino acids and protein, but so is carbon. Carbon is also a major part of DNA.

The unsulfured variety is preferred because the form of sulfur used in most molasses is there to kill microbes. Molasses is also sticky and helps everything stick to the plant leaves. Blackstrap molasses is used in the fermentation process to make EM, and in brewing compost tea.

In organic agriculture, a mixture of ⅔ cup molasses and ⅔ cup liquid calcium mixed in two quarts of water per 1,000 square feet is often sprayed on the soil right after planting to suppress weed germination, with success rates often equaling the old toxic chemical programs. This mixture is also used to "release" calcium and phosphorus in the soil, when a conventional test shows plenty of calcium and phosphorus, but a Reams test shows that not much is available. The molasses works on the phosphorus part of this equation, probably by stimulating mycorrhizal fungi and other microbes. It costs $10 for a quart of organic blackstrap molasses in the grocery store, or you can get it much cheaper in bulk from a bulk food store or farm supply store.

Sometimes it's just the simple things that our garden needs. Microbes need sugar. Our soil may very well be lacking in this sugar, especially if we don't have a functioning ecosystem with nutrient cycling and humus formation occurring, and especially if we're removing the grass clippings or neglecting to keep a quality mulch layer in the garden. Molasses is a relatively inexpensive tool to use as we transition to an ecosystem that is more alive.

GALLON · BLACKSTRAP = 11.7 POUNDS /

Just for fun, try this. Next time you're starting seeds or you get some new, young houseplants, water half of them with just water and the other half with two tablespoons of molasses per gallon of water. See which plant gets bigger when you do this over time.

Some kind of sugar source should be used in nearly every foliar spray. It's often molasses, but other sugars can be used instead. While white sugar is generally not good for us because we don't need more sugar, especially stripped of the accompanying fiber and minerals, on the other hand in the soil, sugar may be the limiting factor, so white sugar can actually be helpful.

Dextrose or corn syrup are often used at two to four ounces per 1,000 square feet or only one ounce in a foliar spray, but they are derived from corn which is mostly genetically modified, so I don't use them. Even a can of soda is a cheap source that can be beneficial. Again, I don't drink the stuff or even have it in my home, but on a practical level, if that's what you have, it will work. I mean the real stuff, with sugar, not artificial sweeteners. It will also give you some carbon and phosphoric acid. Even two tablespoons of vinegar and a can of soda mixed in enough water to cover 1,000 square feet can stimulate microbes and plants.

Humates

Humic and fulvic acids are present in compost and humus. It's extremely beneficial to build them up in our soil. It can also be useful to buy them as a product that is derived from leonardite, a soft brown coal, or other kinds of shale or humate deposits. Humic and fulvic acids are very similar, the main difference being that fulvic acids are smaller, which means they are more soluble in water. They're both important in the soil, though.

The dry products are messy, dark powders that get into everything, so it's better to mix it outside and not even bring it inside. Some people prefer to use a liquid product because it's easier to work with and the humic acids are more quickly available, although it's more expensive. I used to sell one for close to $50 for one quart, which covered 10,000-15,000 square feet. The quality varies drastically from product to product for both dry and liquid, so it's a good idea to buy it from someone you trust and learn a little bit about where good sources come from and how they're processed. It's nice to find a product that has been processed naturally instead of with harsh chemicals.

I use humates mostly in liquid foliar applications. The main benefit here is that the plant will be able to take up and utilize the other nutrients in the solution many times more effectively because of how the humic acids combine with the nutrients, a process called chelation. Make sure to mix it thoroughly in the spray tank.

Humic and fulvic acids are also important chelators in the soil, combining minerals into organic compounds that are more available to plants. They also tie up toxins, making them less available to plants. They will already be present in good soils with a lot of organic matter. Otherwise, they'll be lacking so it will be beneficial to bring them in while also focusing on increasing the organic matter content of the soil.

It's a great idea to mix humates in with calcitic lime before you apply the lime, especially in a soil with low organic matter. The lime wants to sink out of the root zone and the humates want to rise to the surface, so they help keep the lime up where you want it. I do this at two tablespoons of dry humates per ten pounds of lime.

Humates also increase the water infiltration and water-holding capacity of the soil, increase plant root growth and metabolism, enhance seed germination, and help plants deal with environmental stresses. They remove odors in slurry and compost piles, and keep irrigation lines clean. They are mostly used in such tiny amounts that you can purchase a pound and it can last a long time in a typical residential garden.

Soil Conditioner

Soil conditioner can mean many things and can include some of the above products. When I say soil conditioner, I mean a product with concentrated ammonium laureth sulfate as the main ingredient, sometimes with some proprietary secret ingredients, although I tend to stay away from the ones where I'm not allowed to know all of the ingredients. My understanding is that ammonium laureth sulfate is not toxic to the microbes, unlike sodium laureth sulfate which has a bad reputation.

Both of them are used in shampoos and soaps. The former is quickly biodegradable and functions as a soil aerator, allowing water and air to more easily get into the soil. When mixed with other products at around ½ teaspoon per 1,000 square feet, it can also act to help those other products get into the soil and stay on plant leaves. It's $25 for a quart.

Yucca

Yucca extract is sometimes used in compost tea brewing and foliar sprays to help plants deal with stress and to help the spray stick to plant leaves. It's also used to clean out irrigation emitters. Other than some experimentation, I haven't bothered using it much because I don't think it's as important as the above biostimulants and it's manufactured so far away from me. I have heard good things, though. It foams heavily when added to a tank that is being agitated or a compost tea bucket that is brewing, so it's added at the end. I've used ¼ cup per 1,000 square feet, and it sells for $20-$40 for a quart.

Hydrogen Peroxide

Hydrogen peroxide is water with an extra oxygen molecule, H_2O_2. Our body makes it to control microbes and so do plants. It may kill microbes when used full strength, but is occasionally used diluted in the garden to improve plant health and control fungi. It's an unstable molecule that quickly breaks down to one water molecule and one oxygen molecule. It's applied at ⅓ to ¾ teaspoon of 35% food grade hydrogen peroxide in two quarts of water per 1,000 square feet. It's $10-$15 for a quart. I would tend to apply some EM the day after applying this.

Enzymes and Vitamins

Various enzymes and vitamins are being marketed for plants. Most of them aren't useful for home gardeners, but some are excellent and are likely to be especially beneficial under certain environmental conditions. Some of the soil labs make specific vitamin recommendations for a quick fix, and these can be beneficial. Vitamin B12, for example, can help to loosen up calcium from the soil, by coaxing the microbes into action. While microbes can make their own B12 if they have the right nutritional and environmental conditions, supplementation can be very helpful in the meantime. In my opinion, this is a fun area in which to experiment, as long as you've already taken care of the basics.

Specific Micronutrients

Specific micronutrient formulas are used by some farmers to correct deficiencies. Most home gardeners needn't get into them and should instead focus on the other aspects of this book. When the basics are covered and the main nutrient ratios are in line, micronutrient deficiencies aren't as big of an issue.

Some of the micronutrient fertilizers are synthetic, but you can find many organic sources, too. The chelated forms are the best quality and most biologically available. The sulfate forms are second best, but the oxide forms are not as good. Individual micronutrients should mostly be used under the guidance of a good soil lab or consultant. When you get your soil test done, they may recommend something for you and you're welcome to do it, but be sure to focus first on the major nutrients.

That being said, here are a few examples of how micronutrients are used. I should mention again that plants need phosphate in order to take up and properly use these micronutrients. Micronutrients are also often sprayed along with liquid calcium, because plants need sufficient calcium in order to take up and use other nutrients.

Calcium also needs boron to be present in order to start a series of events that allow calcium to move in the plant. If your soil is highly deficient in boron, therefore, you might as well be deficient in calcium. Boron is needed to help transport water and nutrients up and down the plant, and is integral to forming fruit. Most boron products are mined from sodium borate and can be used in organics. Spraying three tablespoons liquid calcium, two to four teaspoons boron, ⅓ cup liquid fish hydrolysate, four teaspoons kelp and one to two tablespoons of apple cider vinegar in five quarts of water per 1,000 square feet can help fruit and seed set if sprayed just before or early on in the initial reproductive stages of the plants. We want a maximum of two to three ppm of boron in the soil, so not too much.

The vast majority of soils and plants are lacking boron, which is why I recommend you use the above recipe if your soil test confirms you need it. Most soils also have less than optimal levels of other micronutrients which is why you might consider using many of the micronutrient-biostimulants listed in this chapter.

Manganese is a nutrient that goes to work early in the process of seed germination, and is responsible for drawing water in to the seed and producing the first roots and shoots. There are other micronutrients that are needed at various levels between 5 and 20 ppm. Iron can be brought in on its own, but it also comes in greensand and some rock dusts. Zinc and copper are vital and often lacking. Even chlorine is needed at one to two ppm, but we don't have to worry about adding it, as deficiencies are rare.

How to Apply

Most of the products in this chapter are combined in water and sprayed onto plants, with some going onto the soil and perhaps being lightly incorporated into the top few inches. The water should be as clean as possible, and ideally not too cold. This spraying is preferably done in the morning or evening. I use a backpack sprayer for this, although a hose-end sprayer or irrigation system works, too. You can experiment with the products that sound good to you. You certainly don't have to use them all.

I generally use a base mixture of ⅓ cup of EM or another microbial product, either 1 cup of sea minerals or 1 cup of liquid fish hydrolysate, with 4 teaspoons of liquid kelp and ⅓ cup of molasses all together in 4 gallons of water. This covers 1,000 square feet. The mixture could be allowed to sit for a few hours before spraying in order for the microbes to start breaking down the other ingredients. The measurements will be different for the brand of each product you buy, so be sure to check the label.

Optionally, you can include any or all of the following: 2 cups compost tea or more, ½ teaspoon humic acids, ½ teaspoon soil conditioner, ¼ cup yucca extract, ½-1 mg of vitamin B12 or even a full vitamin B complex, ⅔ cup liquid calcium and any specific micronutrients you're using. Never mix phosphoric acid with liquid calcium, as you may get jelly, although the phosphoric acid is okay in small quantities as part of liquid fish or soda.

Specific micronutrients may be toxic to the microbial inoculants, so you may want to apply them separately, but EM is so inexpensive that it doesn't hurt to include it anyway. A powder form of mycorrhizal fungi that goes through a sprayer can also be used in this mixture if you're doing a soil drench, but there's no use in applying it to leaves.

When you're mixing this together, start with the water, add any chemical fertilizers and micronutrients you're using, followed by molasses and biostimulants and then microbial inoculants and vitamins. It helps to first dissolve the molasses in warm water.

Summary

- Some of our best whole food sources of micronutrients and biostimulants come from the ocean in the form of sea minerals, kelp and fish fertilizers, and they make up the basis of my organic foliar fertilizer program.
- Some form of carbohydrate, such as molasses, should be used in every foliar spray to feed the microbes.
- There are many other products with which you can experiment if you wish, such as humic acids, soil conditioners, yucca, hydrogen peroxide, enzymes and vitamins.
- Advanced gardeners and farmers may wish to use specific micronutrients to correct deficiencies found on a test, after taking care of the basics.
- Most of these products can be mixed together with microbial inoculants and water and sprayed directly onto plant foliage, preferably in the morning or evening.

Chapter 20

Energy

STEP 6

I have an acquaintance who practices a method of energetic healing called Quantum Touch. She has helped me, my dad, and even my dog with various health issues. She did this by manipulating our energy, over the phone, from thousands of miles away. It's the kind of thing you have to experience to believe, so if you're skeptical, I understand. The topic of energy is much misunderstood and just the word "energy" can make some of us a little bit suspicious and even defensive.

Take biological transmutation as an example. For at least 200 years, we've known that microbes, and even plants and animals, can combine certain elements together to form other elements, such as combining sodium and oxygen to form potassium, or potassium and hydrogen to form calcium. French scientist Louis Kervran was nominated for a Nobel Prize for his work on the subject, and U.S. Army Scientists have also verified the phenomenon.

This information is still considered controversial, and is largely ignored by science. I mentioned it once to a friend who was studying chemistry, and she said it was impossible, that the energy required to complete such a feat would be too vast. That's what the textbooks say about it. My goal here is not to convince you of this, nor do I claim to understand how it all works, but if you're interested, check out

Kervran's book, *Biological Transmutations.*

I just want to point it out, because the main implication I see for us is that we want to promote a healthy, diverse soil food web, and hope the right microbes and plants are in there to transmute certain elements that are lacking in our system. Heide Hermary of Gaia College points out it's yet another reason to look to the native plant communities in our region when we're designing our gardens and use not just one or two of these native species, but a whole selection of plants that naturally grow together because those plants may be transmuting nutrients for each other.

Why We Need Energy in the Soil

It takes various forms of energy transfer for rock to become soil, for plants to grow and for birds to fly. A plant is an antenna. It receives and broadcasts energy. It has millions of tiny hairs that act as tiny antennas, capturing energy from the sun. A plant can also get a lot of its nutrition from the air. In order for a plant to do these things and reach its full potential, it needs all of the things we've looked at so far, plus various forms of energy in order to do the receiving and broadcasting.

In the soil, this energy comes from microbes and animals, water, air, plant roots, and nutrients, and from the interactions of all of these things. It also comes from fertilizers. We can measure one form of energy in the soil with an electrical conductivity meter. Soluble fertilizers have the biggest impact on this form of energy, especially nitrogen.

Energy is one of the main reasons biological soil consultants recommend some chemical fertilizers. These products have a large amount of energy potential. This energy helps the microbes to break down and rearrange other nutrients in the soil. Not only that, but certain fertilizers seem to attract or magnify energy. Putting a tiny amount of the right fertilizer on in the fall can result in a seemingly impossible increase in the availability of certain nutrients in the spring, as confirmed by a soil test. The recipes at the end of the chemical fertilizers chapter are used to provide an energy boost to plants. Biostimulants provide energy, too. Even plain old sugar and molasses give energy to microbes, as does the vinegar and soda recipe from the biostimulants chapter.

Organic gardeners need to learn to create energy in order to get higher brix, healthier crops and better yields. If I start gardening on good, virgin soil, or on soil that has just been cleared or burned, that soil may have a lot of energy already — a mineralized soil doesn't need a lot of fertilizer inputs. The not-so-great soil that most of us start with, however, does need some help.

Chemical fertilizers are only one way of doing that. It can be done naturally, albeit a bit more slowly, with naturally mined minerals and manure and compost and all of the things we've been over. Fish fertilizer can be very high in energy. There are some other ways, too, and that is what this chapter is all about.

In fact, by working on adding organic matter, improving the soil food web and balancing the foundational minerals plus the micronutrients, we're going a long way in creating good energy in the soil. We can go even further by increasing paramagnetism, spraying or broadcasting biodynamic preparations, and using radionics.

An even easier way to manipulate energy is to start playing classical or Indian music in the garden, or even better, get your hands on some Veges low-frequency sound tapes or CDs that have produced amazing results in the field. These play sounds in the low frequency range that for some reason stimulate an increase of nutrient uptake in plants. But I'm getting ahead of myself. Let's look at how we can measure energy.

Energy Released per Gram of Soil (ERGS)

ERGS, energy released per gram of soil is another Reams term. It's measured with an electrical conductivity meter, which gives the electrical current flow of soluble salts in the soil. Basically, it measures how much energy is available to plants and microbes.

We want ERGS to be between 200 and 800 microSiemens (µS) above a reading taken of a wild corner of your property that isn't gardened. If you don't have a wild corner, you can just use your garden very early in the spring as the starting point, before the soil food web has come to life. If that sample is 100 µS, for example, you're looking for at least 300 µS (100+200=300) in the spring and higher in the summer and towards fruiting. If your ERGS is too low, your plants won't grow very much. If it's too high, microbes and plants may suffer, roots may burn, and nematodes may infest. "Too high" is relative, as some people do well at 2,000 µS, but mostly 800 µS and below is what we are looking for.

Much of this energy balancing is accomplished by reaching our other goals of balancing nutrient ratios, particularly calcium to magnesium and phosphate to potash, and building humus in the soil. In the short term, however, it can be difficult to get enough energy into the soil. Even one to three tablespoons of table salt per 1,000 square feet can help, assuming you're low in sodium. Liquid calcium can help, as can using the soil conditioner product I mentioned in the last chapter, or tilling to dry out the soil, all of which increase energy.

Low energy is one of the main reasons biological labs may recommend chemical fertilizers, such as aluminum sulfate mixed with liquid calcium. In conventional farming, chemical fertilizers are the main or only input brought into the soil. In biological farming, minerals and organic matter are the main elements brought in, with the chemicals used only in tiny amounts to supply energy to the system.

Too much rain or not enough air can also bring down ERGS. We can use irrigation to do this on purpose if the ERGS is too high. Lack of sodium, nitrogen and other nutrients can also bring down ERGS. Like a pH test, ERGS doesn't tell you what you need to add, but just gives an indication as to what might be going on, and how your management practices are working throughout the year. As such, it's not something you need to rush out and start measuring right now, as soil tests allow you to make more educated soil management decisions.

Paramagnetism

Soil is paramagnetic. It isn't magnetic, but is mildly attracted by a magnet, and partially aligns with the earth's magnetic field. Some soils are attracted more than others, and generally, the more paramagnetic your soil is, the better. This is because highly paramagnetic soils are more energetically aligned with the earth and even the universe, and actually invite energy into them.

Increased paramagnetism brings increased water retention, earthworm and microbial action in the soil. Plants experience better nutrient utilization, seed germination, resistance to predators, and resistance to environmental stresses. Plants are diamagnetic, which means they're repelled by a magnet. I imagine it's a good thing, too, because it gives the soil and plants a kind of yin-yang relationship. The energy from a highly paramagnetic soil flows into plants, vastly improving their growth. This energy also improves microbial growth.

Many soils are relatively low on the paramagnetism scale. In these soils, it will always be a struggle to raise healthy plants and nutrient-dense food. You can measure yours with a PC soil meter, named after Dr. Phil Callahan, who spent decades studying paramagnetism in soils and rocks around the world. He discovered the most productive soils are highly paramagnetic. I've had an opportunity to play with the meter and it's fascinating, but costs about $500, so for most home gardeners it just makes sense to assume our soil could use a little more paramagnetism. His book *Paramagnetism* is a very interesting read if you want more information.

Moving the calcium to magnesium ratio towards ideal will increase the paramagnetism, and soils with more organic matter and an abundant soil food web are often higher, too. The way to increase it even more, though, is by adding paramagnetic rock, generally from volcanic, granite or basalt sources.

If you were thinking of adding rock dust anyway, you can get both the mineral benefits and energy benefits by using one that is paramagnetic. Most rock is paramagnetic, but you need one that is highly paramagnetic. Even then, sometimes you get a big boost, sometimes not, but it's worth just going ahead and trying it in a small garden. It can be somewhat difficult to find paramagnetic rock dust in some areas, but if you're growing a lot of food, it's worth it. There are many brands on the market. Application rates are the same as for any rock dust, generally between 50 and 500 pounds per 1,000 square feet.

Biodynamics

I want to include a brief section on biodynamic farming and gardening because it's potentially the most important method of gardening. I hope everyone will be doing it some day. This section can't even be considered an introduction to the topic because I don't have enough experience in it yet. I'm not a biodynamic gardener and I don't like talking much about things I haven't done myself. I've incorporated some of the biodynamic ideas into my gardening, and that is all I wish to show here.

The original ideas behind biodynamic gardening came from Rudolf Steiner and were first described in a series of eight lectures in 1924. To most people, myself included, many of these ideas seem complicated. His thoughts on how plants grow are very different from what you would find in a modern botany textbook.

The goals of biodynamics are very similar to organic, with perhaps even more emphasis on working with nature and the sun, moon, planets and stars. The soil and soil food web are seen as the basis for plant health, but there is more emphasis on energy. Everything is energy. Even this idea has crossed over into organic soil management, where we think of fertilizers not only as suppliers of minerals, but as sources of energy, or as increasing the energy in the soil.

Biodynamic farmers often plant by the phases of the moon. They weren't the first to do this — there are actually other cultures that use the moon even more for their gardening schedule, but biodynamic practitioners have developed their own system.

The basics are as follows. According to biodynamic thought, the full moon helps to draw water into plants, so the best time to plant seed is in the second quarter, just before the full moon. That's when the moon is facing left, waxing crescent (with the right side visible). The best time to plant root crops and do transplanting is when maximum root growth occurs, in the third quarter, when the moon is facing right, waning crescent (with the left side visible). Nothing is planted in the fourth quarter. Following these rules can make a big difference in the health of your plants.

My first time putting a biodynamic practice to work was actually when I did my Permaculture Design Certificate. We made and applied a tree paste of manure, clay, sand and a biodynamic preparation that we then rubbed onto the trunk of some fruit trees. The goal was to strengthen the bark, control disease and even improve fertility.

The biodynamic preparations get a lot of attention. They require a bit of a leap of faith for most people before they'll try using them. They are a series of nine remedies for the garden, used in homeopathic doses. While conventional gardening tends to frown upon them, there is much experiential evidence that they work.

For example, prep 500 is one of the main preparations. It's made by taking cow manure, packing it into a cow horn and burying it in the ground over winter. This is said to concentrate the earthly growth forces in the manure. It promotes roots, encourages lush growth, and aids germination — all most important in the early stages of plant growth.

Finely ground quartz is packed in a cow horn and buried over summer for prep 501. This enhances plant maturation. It promotes flowers and fruits, flavor, color and storage — more important in the later stages of plant growth.

To create a remedy for spraying on the garden, the material in these preparations is stirred into water, changing directions to make a vortex in one direction and then in the other, back and forth, for an hour. There are also six preparations to be used in compost and one herbal preparation of horsetail to prevent fungus and help toughen plants, due to the high silica in the horsetail. You can learn to make all of these preparations, but for most gardeners, it may be better to buy them.

There are other non-biodynamic products called "energizers" which also often work using very dilute doses. Examples I've used successfully are Penergetic products to improve compost, water quality and plant health, and GSR Calcium to provide small, yet powerful doses of calcium into the garden.

Though some people think the biodynamic movement has ignored mineralization and balancing soil nutrient ratios just as much as the organic movement has, I believe biodynamics will be an important part of our gardening future. The great news is that we can draw on all of these different disciplines that people have put together to form a holistic approach that integrates the best of them. Two of my favorite books that look at biodynamics and energy are *Secrets Of The Soil* by Peter Tompkins and Christopher Bird and *A Biodynamic Farm* by Hugh Lovel.

Radionics

Dr. Carey Reams stressed that plants grow from energy, not from fertilizers. Calcitic lime from one source may have a much higher energy than from another source, even if they look exactly the same chemically. We can actually measure this energy in order to choose the best product using an electronic scanner, a type of spectrometer used by a small number of farmers and soil consultants.

Comparing two different sources of lime isn't its only use. The vitality of a plant can be measured, as can the vitality of a weed. The vitality of a plant can be measured after it's been treated with a certain foliar fertilizer, in order to see if the vitality raises and you are therefore using the right fertilizer for the job. The same can be done to see what will lower a weed's vitality. You may find that you have an excellent fertilizer, but it just doesn't match the needs of the plant today. We do the same thing with a refractometer for brix readings, but the scanner can be more accurate in the hands of the right person. It can get quite detailed, for example determining if you should use sugar, dextrose or molasses in a foliar spray.

Interestingly, weeds are often strengthened by some of our most common chemical fertilizers and pesticides, while food plants are often weakened. Conversely, plants are often strengthened and weeds weakened by many of the organic and biological products we've been looking at so far. Yet, it depends on many conditions, and the scanner — in the hands of a skillful operator — eliminates the guesswork. Not just anyone can use a scanner. It requires learning and practice.

Once an appropriate fertilizer mixture is found, the "energy" of that fertilizer can be broadcast into the field rather than having to broadcast the fertilizer. I think of this as being kind of like homeopathic medicine, where the "information" contained in a substance is more important than the substance itself. Of course, I know this will be a little too out there for some readers, and that is just fine. I'm just presenting what works for other people and letting you decide about what makes sense to you.

Summary

- One form of energy in the soil is the soluble salts, which are measured with an electrical conductivity meter and manipulated using organic matter, microbes, fertilizers, water and air.
- Paramagnetism is another form of energy that can be increased by the same methods, but even moreso by applying paramagnetic rock dust from volcanic, granite or basalt sources.
- One day, we may all garden simply by manipulating the energy patterns in our soil and plants, which has been done successfully with biodynamics since the 1920s, and more recently with homeopathic energizers and radionics.

Garden Action Strategies

Now it's time to put it all together. Next, we will see how all of the strategies outlined thus far work to drastically decrease pests and weeds. Then we'll learn how to work with soil, and finally, I'll outline a garden health management plan.

Chapter 21
Plant Predators
& Weeds

What kind of food does an aphid like? What about a disease such as powdery mildew? In what kind of soil does a dandelion grow? To stop these things from being a problem, we need to delve into a topic that most gardening books brush over — why they're there in the first place. This is relevant in a book about soil because soil health is directly linked with plant predators and weeds.

Why don't we start with what *we* look for in food. Humans and other animals prefer plants that are healthy and full of nutrients. Sure, most of us seem to have lost a lot of our ability to differentiate between a healthy plant and a not-so-healthy plant, but animals are still very good at it and they choose the healthy stuff. Even farm animals will choose healthy feed over the pesticide-laced, imbalanced feed that makes up the majority of what is being fed to them. But why do insects and diseases eat our plants? It all comes down to the same reason.

We tend to think insects and diseases are making our plants unhealthy, but actually, they are there *because* our plants are unhealthy. This is one of the biggest shifts we need to make in our thinking when moving to organic gardening practices, and to me it's absolutely fascinating. While animals prefer healthy plants, insects and diseases prefer the opposite. They choose plants that have a nutritional imbalance of one or more nutrients. They literally do not possess the enzymes necessary to digest healthy plants.

In *Healthy Crops*, Francis Chaboussou pulled together various research concluding that this imbalance shows up as an excess of soluble nitrogen and sugars in the plant. This excess can be caused by many things: soil imbalances, an excess of soil nitrogen, the use of pesticides and chemical fertilizers, water problems, physical damage, or anything that would make a plant sick. For us, the most important concept to understand is that an optimally healthy plant will not be attacked by predators. It's simply not possible. A lawn with a balanced soil will not be overtaken by weeds. They could never compete with the grass.

Many of us are learning that human health follows the same rules, that a healthy diet along with exercise and happiness prevent almost all of the diseases inflicting us. We need to make this connection with the garden more. Sir Albert Howard figured this out during decades of experiments at the beginning of the 20th century, stating that "healthy, well-fed animals reacted towards the disease exactly as improved and properly cultivated crops did to insects and fungi — no infection occurred."

If you can grasp this concept, you will be ahead of most of the big institutions doing agriculture and horticulture research in North America, even the organic institutions. I still receive newsletters and read books where they are researching so-called organic pest control products to substitute for chemicals. They still don't understand the most basic truth that our problem is not a lack of pesticides — it's a lack of health. They are still trying to manage pests instead of managing health. This is one of the most important concepts I learned from Heide Hermary, founder of Gaia College. Our goal is health management, not pest management.

In fact, we mostly try to use the word "predator" instead of "pest." An aphid feeding on a rose is a plant predator just like a lion feeding on a zebra is an animal predator. We use the word pest because it is a pest to us. This is accurate enough, but to me, it implies that the offending insect or disease has no place on this planet. Further, it serves to blame the insect or disease for the problem, rather than the lack of plant or ecosystem health. It's just a terminology thing, but I think predator is more accurate much of the time.

The step up from managing predators is allowing plants to use their own methods of protecting themselves, as long as they are healthy enough to put those methods in place. That is an important step, but I see one more. Perhaps it's not much further than the last step and perhaps they're very much intertwined, but the final step is optimal health in the plant to a point where predators can't digest the plant and hardly bother trying, so that the plants don't even have to devote much energy defending themselves.

Insects

Insects sense their surroundings with their antennae. That's how they find a mate and how they find their food. These antennae interpret electromagnetic frequencies in the infrared spectrum, which is right beside the visual light spectrum we can see.

For example, a female moth emits pheromones in the infrared spectrum that a male interprets as a suitable "mate" for them. The males don't go chasing the females around for miles and miles with their eyes. They follow these pheromones and home in on them like I used to do as an airplane pilot following the signal from a radar beacon.

Plants also emit pheromones that insects interpret as "food" for them. Not all plants emit these pheromones, though. It turns out that only *sick* plants emit them in such a manner as to be seen as food! This finding has the most amazing implications for organic gardeners and farmers. Healthy plants simply don't emit these signals, so insects don't see healthy plants as a food source. Even if they do land on a healthy plant, for the most part, they don't have the enzymes to digest it.

Why do sick plants invite predators to eat them? I don't think we know for sure. Some people think the plants don't want to survive since it would be a detriment to their species. If sick plants were to continually reproduce, the species wouldn't be as strong and would have a much more difficult time surviving, so they "take one for the team," so to speak. All I know for sure is that insects eat sick plants.

As you may have noticed, most insects don't go around eating any plant species in their path. They usually have just a few species or perhaps a family of plants that are their food and they don't — they can't — eat anything else. That's why plant predator books are often organized by plant, because when you know the plant that's being eaten, it narrows down the potential predators to just a handful. Each insect antennae are shaped in such a way to collect only the frequencies from certain plants.

I think of insects as being like the cholesterol in our bodies — not all bad. Cholesterol has come to be regarded as an enemy in human health, but the truth is that it's vital to our health. It does all kinds of important things in our bodies. When it gets too high, we are told to stop eating things like eggs because they are high in cholesterol (which makes very little sense, but that's for another book). We find a way to blame the cholesterol, when it is just a symptom of a bigger problem. The same goes for plant predators. Their presence tells us our plants are sick. It's not the predators fault.

Diseases

The same goes for disease. Disease refers to bacteria, viruses, fungi and other microbes that eat plants or animals. They don't have the big antennae that insects have, and to be honest, I have no idea how they find the plant they're going to eat. But like insects, each microbe generally has only a few species of plants it eats, and they eat sick plants. In fact, fungal diseases seem to go for plant tissue that is already dying.

Weeds

Weeds come with definitions such as "a plant growing where it is not desired" or "any plant that crowds out cultivated plants." A strawberry plant in a formal rose garden might be considered a weed. Of course, when most of us think of weeds, we think of the common ones that come into the garden and are not as apparently useful as a strawberry.

I like to define weeds as "beautiful, resilient plants that are doing everything in their power to improve our imbalanced soil conditions." And yet for some reason we have it in our mind that we need to get rid of them. In fact, perhaps half of "weeds" have actually been used as medicinal plants and many of them are exceptionally tasty. As for the other half, perhaps we just haven't figured out how to use them, but they offer benefits to more than just human health.

The Weed Connection with Soil

The best weed manual in the world can only hint at solutions to the many problems related to weeds. Unfortunately, those who have taken the weed situation by the nape of the neck and the seat of the pants over the past fifty years have done little more than shake out poisons, not results.

There are many mansions in the house of weeds. For example, there are swamp weeds, the cattails and the rushes. There are desert weeds. There are weeds that grow in sand and weeds that grow in silt, and there are weeds that grow in gumbo so tight it resembles modeling clay. Foxtails grow in gumbo, but they also grow in sand when such soils are out of balance and the electrical tension on soil particles is so tight that even sand can build clods and restrict air in the soil enough to set free the hormone process that wakes up foxtail seeds.

There are subsoil weeds. There are weeds that grow in acid conditions and — in the West — there are weeds that like alkaline conditions. Up in Wisconsin and Minnesota there is a weed called devil's paint brush by the locals. This one joins the daisy in having a love affair with sour soils. Almost always, such soils have an excess of iron and flush out a lot of trace minerals and rock minerals that support the hormone processes that give permission to live for these weed species.

— Charles Walters in *Weeds, Control Without Poisons*

Weeds heal the soil. Each weed can grow in different imbalanced soil conditions and work to bring the soil into balance. It is a common myth that weeds and more desirable plants like the same soil conditions. In *Science in Agriculture*, Arden Andersen says, "the belief that healthy soil grows weeds equally as well as the desired crop is based on the misconception that the soil in question is healthy." In reality, most of the really pesky weeds get sick in balanced soil conditions. Like insects, they thrive on imbalance. Here are just a few ways weeds help out.

Weeds:

- Bring minerals and water up from deep in the soil and down from the air, and subsequently make them available to microbes and plants.
- Break up hardpans and compaction and control erosion.
- Increase the organic matter content of the soil as they continually grow and die.
- Tell us a tremendous amount about the nutritional condition of our soil through their presence and growth habit.
- Fix nutritional imbalances, vastly improving soils in as little as a couple of years, or sometimes decades or centuries. That's the role of weeds in nature.
- Provide homes and food for microbes and animals.

So why do weeds grow in the first place? Weeds are there because they are the most suitable plant for the job, more suitable than what we're trying to grow. Most weeds grow in very specific soil, nutrient and climate conditions. In fact, you can tell a lot about the conditions of soil just by the weeds there. They are as useful as a soil nutrient test for diagnosing certain fertility issues.

Of course, we don't really want weeds to be there because we're trying to grow something else. To a certain extent, they can make a crop healthier, but they can also compete with our plants for nutrients and water, especially if they get too big. The other main reason for not wanting weeds — that they are "ugly" — is debatable when you think about it, but understandable. At some point in our history, we started applying an aesthetic order to our gardens that is reminiscent of the order inside our houses. I'm okay with that. I prefer a weed-free bed, too.

So a weed is simply a plant growing in an inconvenient spot, working to fix our soil. It can be clover growing in a lawn, or wildflowers growing in a corn field. In another garden, they might be desirable plants. Weeds persist despite our efforts to get rid of them. They're able to outcompete other vegetation when that vegetation is sick, growing in the wrong spot or poor soil conditions. When fertility, soil texture and soil structure are altered, the weed population will also change; and importantly, when these factors are improved, the desirable plants will outcompete the weeds.

A plant of some kind will almost always grow where there's bare soil, because it has the light and space needed for seeds to germinate. Good examples are thin or short turf, shrub beds without ground cover and mulch, bare soil in vegetable beds, and gravel pathways. In fact, some weed seeds remain dormant and viable in the soil for decades, even centuries, just waiting for the right conditions to germinate, and many weeds produce a lot of seeds.

Another way that weeds can proliferate is through growth strategies. Some annual weeds have several life cycles per year. For example, a plant like common chickweed or pepper cress produces seeds, which germinate quickly, producing more seeds, and the cycle continues. Many perennial weeds have deep and extensive root systems which might regenerate several new plants when damaged. And many weeds, such as dandelions and purslanes, can mature their seeds even after they have been pulled.

So weeds have some pretty decent skills when it comes to surviving, which is actually good for us because of all the benefits they bring to the table. We'll never entirely get rid of them and it is foolish to think we can or even should, but we can vastly decrease their presence if we feel the need. There are many ways to do this. Let's just touch on one of them for now — nutrient ratios.

Our most common pesky weeds proliferate in an imbalanced soil. A balanced soil favors the plants we want to grow, and the weeds simply do not want to grow there. If you do a really good job of balancing the soil, plant-feeding insects will leave your plants and move over to the weeds, as the weeds actually become sick in healthy soil. To me, this is just so fascinating. I've had the privilege of seeing this happen several times.

While it's a good idea to avoid bringing new weeds onto our property via lawn mowers, soil and plants from the nursery, the seeds aren't the root cause of the problem. Weed seeds fly into our yard all the time, from many miles away. The availability of weed seeds isn't the real reason you might have a lot of weeds in your garden. The root cause is the nutritional imbalances and an unhealthy soil food web. In fact, if you and your neighbor's lawn are both covered in dandelions and you correct the soil, the dandelions will magically disappear from your lawn even as the weed seeds from your neighbor continue to visit.

There are three interesting nutritional insights for you to remember about weeds. These three points have shown up as a theme throughout this book:

1. Grassy weeds like quackgrass indicate a calcium deficiency. You may not have enough calcium in the soil, or it could be the calcium just isn't available.

2. Broadleaf weeds like plantain indicate a deficiency of phosphate in relation to potash. This can be fixed with supplements and microbes.

3. Succulent weeds like purslane indicate a biologically active carbon deficiency and poor water-holding capacity. Carbohydrates and enzymes can wake up the microbes.

Then there are even more details we've learned about specific weeds. There are weeds for every situation: too wet or dry, poor drainage, not enough air, compaction, improper decay of organic matter, improper nutrient exchange, and so on.

Ragweed, for example, grows late in the season in very dry soils. This isn't so much because the soil is dry, but because the dry soil causes the microbes to grind to a halt. This causes potassium to be unavailable or improperly processed. Arden Andersen says ragweed growth indicates a copper deficiency, and that people who are allergic to ragweed have a copper deficiency in their mucous membranes.

Morning glories and bindweeds grow via underground stems called rhizomes in sick, eroded soils with poor decay of organic matter. Perhaps there was too much organic matter piled on at once and there is insufficient air and moisture content to properly decay that organic matter, and probably the calcium to magnesium and phosphate to potash ratios are out of whack. When these problems are corrected, the fungi that decay these rhizomes will make quick work of them and the area will be ready to support more desirable plants, which these fungi will leave alone.

When the weeds are healthier than the plants, it can also indicate a lack of mycorrhizal fungi in the soil. Most common weeds are not colonized by mycorrhizal fungi and therefore don't need them in order to be healthy, whereas plants do.

There are lots of weeds that grow in soil where organic matter is not decaying properly, which comes back to improper nutrient ratios and a lacking soil food web. Increasing the diversity and number of microbes in the soil helps with weeds because they create a healthier soil that weeds don't want. They actually move the nutrient ratios towards balance, break down organic matter, relieve compaction and balance air and water.

So we can actually learn a lot about our soil simply from the weeds that are growing there. We generally still want to do a soil test to get more detail, but weeds are often just as helpful as a soil test at giving us an overall look at the most important nutrient deficiencies and prevailing environmental conditions.

Health Management

This chapter presents a very exciting and important concept — health management. Rather than treating disease, we remove it from the picture by creating health. It must be noted that the garden is a dynamic environment, so even healthy plants are probably always fluctuating in and out of a state of optimal health based on any number of factors.

Even in a fairly healthy soil, we could get a month of dry days in the summer, an early freeze, a loss of soil energy in the fall, or any number of conditions that impact the health of a plant to the point where some predators can come and dine for awhile. But if we can accomplish the goals laid out in this book, healthy and predator-free plants will be the main outcome.

Arden Andersen writes "an organism will survive and thrive only if the proper conditions have been established for it to do so." Everything we've looked at in previous chapters contributes to controlling pests because all of these practices contribute to healthy soil and healthy plants. The most important concept to remember is that weeds proliferate in imbalanced soils, and insects and diseases feed on unhealthy plants. A garden or field full of pests has come to be considered normal, but it's not normal and must be considered a signal of a lack of health.

Once you know that, it's all about implementing the steps in this book. When we provide sufficient water, increase humus and improve the soil food web, balance soil nutrients and ensure there is proper energy in the system, pests go away. Most pest situations can be improved by balancing the calcium to magnesium ratio and the phosphate to potash ratio, which can only be done long-term if all of these steps are taken care of.

Instead of shooting the messenger, the pest, we should actually thank them for telling us something is wrong.

Summary

- Insects and diseases eat unhealthy plants and can't digest healthy plants.
- Weeds colonize imbalanced soils and can't outcompete other plants on healthy soils.
- Our job is to coax the system toward balance, rendering plant predators all but obsolete.

Chapter 22

Weeds: A Primer

Weeds, Control Without Poisons by Charles Walters is a fascinating look at the world of weeds in relation to their environment and strives to inform about how to control these plant pests without the use of chemicals. The following twelve ubiquitous weeds have been excerpted from this reference. The illustrations were created by Regina Hughes and originally published in either *Selected Weeds of the United States* or *Weeds in Kansas*.

Ragweed

Linnaeus named ragweed *Ambrosia elatior*, possibly as a joke because of its offensive odor. It is an annual that reproduces by seeds, sometimes in cultivated fields, sometimes in run-down pastures. This weed is bushy and hairy atop a fibrous root. Leaves alternate in general and are deeply bipinnated, variable and also hairy. Flowers are very small in terminal clusters.

Ragweed

Some few heads at the base have pistillate flowers. The upper flowers are staminate. The fruit is an achene in a woody enclosure, with tubercles straw-colored to brown. Drought and poor moisture reserves in the soil cause a shortfall in the potassium processing system. This signals ragweed to have at it for the season. Cultivation and mowing will annihilate ragweed. It has to be an object of control because of the misery it delivers to human beings. Cattle should be kept from ragweed because it taints milk.

Ragweed out of control can be managed with manganese, copper, vitamins C and B12, calcium, phosphate and sugar in a solution, recipe to be worked out on-scene according to test readings. Potassium chloride, compaction, complexed zinc, low bio-activity, and chemical toxicity usually figure when this weed gets out of hand.

Quackgrass *(a.k.a., couchgrass)*

Quackgrass

Quackgrass, *Agropyron repens*, is a perennial that reproduces by seeds and extensively creeping underground rhizomes. In fact, seeds are relatively unimportant for reproduction much of the time. Examination of ears often reveals seeds to be nonexistent or sterile.

Although considered a noxious weed in the United States, rhizomes from this plant have herbal qualities and are used as extracts in treating urinary disorders. Rhizome propagation makes clean tillage hazardous. Each little broken piece of root or stem promptly becomes another thriving plant when moisture conditions so decree. Dealing with this weed means structuring a proper decay system in the soil, one that invites actinomycetes and several other species of molds, acidiomycetes included. In order to endure, these beneficial molds must have a well-aerated soil and adequate calcium.

No one seems to have trouble identifying quackgrass. Spikelets are pendulous, glumes smooth, lemmata with stiff brown hairs at the base. Copper, manganese, soft rock phosphate, vitamin B12, calcium, molasses, soil aeration and use of sulfates in some areas will reduce or eliminate this weed, the recipe to be determined by scanner. Potassium chloride, sterile soil conditions and compaction help this weed proliferate.

Purslane (a.k.a., pursley, pussley, common purslane, pursley duckweed, wild portulaca)

Purslane, *Portulaca oleracea*, is an annual that reproduces by seed. It is sometimes used for greens. Pigs and chickens love it as a succulent. Purslane grows down close in a mat about a foot in diameter from a shallow fibrous root system.

Smooth leaves cluster, are simple and broadest near the apex. Small, yellow flowers are in the axils. Fruit is a capsule.

Control is simple during the early stages, but even physical removal serves up a phenomenon — the plant continuing to live and mature seeds after being uprooted. Seeds cannot endure and set new plants if cation balance is achieved and pH

Purslane

is properly structured with calcium, magnesium and potassium in an Albrecht equilibrium. Even more important is regular introduction of air into the soil.

Cation balances are sometimes difficult to achieve because purslane soils have high potassium and magnesium levels. High iron and copper releases also figure when this weed declares the kingdom for the season. Calcium and phosphate levels are always low in purslane territory. Aerobes go off duty under low porosity and low moisture conditions, hence acid soil release of iron and copper. Horse purslane is much the same weed, with round leaves and diced prominent veins.

Hedge Bindweed (a.k.a., *creeping bindweed, morning glory, climbing false buckwheat*)

This perennial, *Convolvulus sepium*, reproduces from both seeds and shallow creeping roots. It is a blood brother to field bindweed or morning glory, *Convolvulus arvensis*. The *C. sepium* brother is also known as climbing false buckwheat. It grows almost everywhere, even on eroded hillsides that are well drained.

Hedge bindweed

Bindweed is a typical reflector of an improper decay of organic matter and excess accumulation of heavy soil metals. It may be that a bale of hay broke open in an area, and was left there. It may be that cattle were fed, and much organic matter was stomped into the ground.

Morning glories function best in the presence of ample humus materials and an antagonistic decay system. Bindweeds tend to flourish more in an eroded low humus soil, which cannot support corrective decay systems for soil restoration. Low calcium, phosphorus, potassium and pH are benchmarks. Crusting and sticky soil are also consequences. Most creeping-vine-type weeds have extensive and fast growing rhizomes that develop to completely entrap the soil nutrient system in and around all the clusters of organic residues. The biological energies contained in these foul, rotting residues support numerous dominating hormone enzyme systems that are "just right" for the vine weed families, and "not just right" for other species of soil and plant life. Such conditions can occur within soils of high exchange capacity (clay) or low exchange capacity (sandy) — with low or high organic material content — always in soils that impose limitations on ferment and breakdown of organic residue in the desired direction. Such soils are unable to govern the humus system. They also lack the capacity to support the right kind of nutrition needed for better plant and animal food, chiefly because of the imbalanced hormone-enzyme system that is sustained by improper decay.

Field bindweed, morning glory, creeping bindweed all dominate the plant kingdom because of a short circuit in the energy release of fouled decay systems. These limits are generated by an accumulation of dry-dead organic substances either under dry fall conditions, or in wet spring soil — with compaction, sedimentation, and improper tillage timing figuring in the equation.

Cultural practices that relate to stress systems are greatly influenced by the pH character of the colloidal system involved and by the effect of drainage and air capacity of the decay medium. Correct these soil limitations through pH management and the bindweed-morning glory syndrome becomes completely dispersed. No herbicide chemical or fertilizer material can replace good soil management. Roots that go down four feet in the first year can't be chased by phenoxy herbicides.

Hedge bindweed is easy to identify. High twining with smooth leaves that alternate, are simple, long-petioled, triangular ovate, the plant has white to pink to almost reddish flowers. The fruit is glabrous and covered with bracts and calyx.

Lambsquarters *(a.k.a., white goosefoot, pitseed goosefoot, mealweed, baconweed, wild spinach, white pigweed, fat hen, frostbite, chou grass, muckweed, dungweed)*

Lambsquarters, *Chenopodium album*, is not a serious weed, yet very common. Hogs and chickens love the plant in its succulent stage. It is an annual that reproduces from seed and generally indicates a rich, fertile soil. Potato acres in particular become infested with lambsquarters once the potato plant's specific requirements become unavailable. Otherwise the massive root structure of potatoes prevents lambsquarters growth.

Pithy names tell something about how plants grow according to available light, temperature and geography. Lambsquarters sometimes grows five feet tall. It harbors a lot of nutrition for certain insects and stores a high quality of phosphate. It reflects the availability of good nutrition in the soil.

Lambsquarters

Used in silage, it supplies needed nutrients. As a matter of fact, both pigweed and lambsquarters can become excellent silage. Both have a high protein content. Lambsquarters grows in a soil that has an appropriate decay system going, which of course has a direct bearing on release and catalyzing release of a good array of quality mineral nutrients. This weed does not depend on phosphate or potassium from fertilizers. Soil is intended to grow vegetative matter.

Lambsquarters and redroot pigweed stand at the top of the ladder of the phylum of weeds that can grow under different soil conditions. They reflect almost ideal producing functions in an active biological soil system. There is no water insoak problem where lambsquarters and pigweed grow.

Both of these weeds are easy to control. Neither have serious negative effects through auxin emission to growing crops. Indeed, there is a symbiotic relationship between redroot pigweed and lambsquarters and most plants. These weeds are the best possible laboratory analysis for phosphate being available on a daily meal basis. Where lambsquarters grows year after year, there is no need to buy phosphate fertilizers. There is no concern about buying potassium or about raising the levels of potassium, even though a soil audit might suggest that the till is not quite full enough.

Anatomically, lambsquarters is an annual that reproduces by seeds. It grows five to six feet in height from a taproot. Simple leaves alternate, are ovate in shape. This weed has green flowers in irregular spikes clustered in narrow panicles.

Selenium, molybdenum, hydrogen peroxide, calcium, soft rock phosphate, vitamin C, sulfates and sugars — in some areas — put heavy stands of lambsquarters on the run. Potassium chloride, chemical nitrogen and magnesium may be contributing factors in this weed's more than normal proliferation.

Common Burdock

Burdock, *Arctium minus*, is a biennial herb that reproduces by seed only. Its existence on a farm is generally a signal that the soil system is dominated by iron and is in need of calcium, and has a low pH. It is found all over the United States.

Burdock has fantastically enormous roots, big leaves and burs that stick to animals as well as clothes of human beings. Common burdock, *Arctium minus*, is smaller than great burdock, *Arctium lappa*. Gypsum soils frequently exhibit burdock and it can be suggested that burdock is often a signal that soil has been incorrectly limed with magnesium carbonate or subdued with great applications of sulfate of ammonia and lime, giving the effect of calcium sulfate in the soil.

Burdock is a good phosphate feeder. It has to have a good available source of phosphate. In the midwest there are a lot of soils low in calcium and high in magnesium, pH reading being on the low side. Many times farmers apply gypsum or ammonium sulfate on soils reading below pH 6.2. Unfortunately this has the effect of agitating the construction of the pH, driving it down to pH 5.8 or 5.7 in terms of a colloidal position. A colloidal position pH can be lower than the pH in terms of the entire environment, taking both colloidal and soluble form pH ingredients into consideration. Remember that magnesium will raise pH 1.4 times as high as the same amount of calcium. When gypsum, calcium sulfate, is put on soils at pH 6.2 or 6.1 — the resultant pH structure will still be too low to govern the proper release of trace minerals regulated by calcium. At such pH levels there are mineral releases on the surplus side. Often there is a surplus of aluminum. Moreover, there is a

Common Burdock

difference in gypsums, depending on whether and where they are mined, or whether they are byproducts. As a rule byproduct gypsum is more easily broken down to influence the reconstruction of the pH equilibrium. It has a more fluffy particle surface (like a snowflake), which is quite different from the usual product which is textured much like a pearly smooth grain of sand. Many mined gypsums take a decade or more to break down. Heavy acid flushes both trace minerals and heavy metals out of the soil. When calcium levels are low, aluminum is flushed out very easily, as is iron. Burdock can tolerate more iron and aluminum than other weeds and crops, but it is still a good phosphate feeder. It has a capacity for tolerating this inventory of conditions without becoming toxic. By way of contrast, corn and grain crops cannot tolerate the releases of aluminum and iron made mandatory by very low pH systems. Burdock will proliferate in an environment of iron and aluminum that is killing off higher plants. In soils that are low in iron, or do not have a daily release of iron, burdock will not grow. Soils that have a proper decay system going — and this will not happen at low pH — will not give burdock permission for life. If a low pH soil is releasing a full complement of iron, burdock will function. Iron in relationship to manganese is also an important factor. High iron in the presence of low manganese regulates the kind of fungi that can operate in that soil. This iron manganese posture also affects the bacterial processes that can occur, again determining which hormone systems are going to function and allow a weed seed to wake up and grow.

Dandelion (a.k.a., blowball, lion's tooth, puffball, milk witch, yellow gowan, witch gowan, door-head clock, cankerwort, common dandelion)

Dandelion

This weed, *Taraxacum officinale* needs no description. Of all the weeds, this one is most recognized by laymen who know no other weeds. It is a perennial. It is usually a symptom of overgrazing. Lawn aficionados go after the dandelion with a vengeance, as though it offended both the eye and the psyche of mankind. Yet on balance, the dandelion is a friendly weed. Its roots penetrate some three feet deep, transporting calcium and other minerals to the surface. Earthworms like the vicinity of the dandelion. Each time such a plant dies, remaining root channels become a conduit for worm travel and also a colloidal source of worm nutrition.

The dandelion is a monoculture weed, an index of sedimentation, a biography of rain, root webbing, organic material forever in place and unstirred. In every case calcium is colloidally weak or absent. The dandelion simply says organic matter residues are musty and are barricading the warehoused supplies of food. As the season goes along, dry weather usually weakens and subdues the dandelion. But if a quicker remedy is sought, the soil should be treated six to seven inches deep with a supply of high calcium lime. Anyone really desperate will have to replant, but chances are the dandelion won't be back for a long time. It might be added parenthetically that astute lawn managers often regulate the availability of phosphorus to reduce the growth of grass and yet keep it strong in the absence of dandelions.

The object is to restrict photosynthesis capacity of leaves by managing the conversion and release of phosphorus on a diet of "one meal" per day. Actually, we do not want a lot of soluble phosphorus on a lawn. It needs a good supply of zinc regulated by a calcium base, not too much nitrogen — just enough to etch the phosphate needed to grow a day at a time. The phosphorus should be lazy and slow, and at a balanced pH of 6.5. Never apply nitrogen or phosphorus fertilizer. Instead use gypsum and sulfur as needed to have a slow growing, healthy and vigorous lawn and watch neighbors wear out their lawn mowers. A pH range of 6.2-6.6 happens to preside over actinomycete mold balanced activity, mineral release — and as with all other weeds, there has to be a reference back to calcium and its colloidal function.

The dandelion is not very important in crop production, and might be excluded from this roster except for its negative popularity.

Crabgrass

This annual, *Digitaria sanguinalis* reproduces by stems rooting at the nodes and seeds. It usually dies with the first frost. It is tufted, mostly prostrate, and roots at the nodes. The fruit is a caryopsis. It literally blankets the United States, sparing no geographical area, yet is limited to environments that are right.

Crabgrass simply says that the soil is low in calcium and that it cannot support decay starting with actinomycetes molds. It is usually possible to adjust the system in a year or two, putting

Crabgrass

a little calcium lime and sulfur or gypsum on the soil in order to restructure the pH. As this is accomplished, most of the infestation dissipates, virtually rotting away. Usually applications can be computed on the basis of 1,500 pounds of high calcium lime per acre, 30-40 pounds of processed and active sulfur per acre. If ammonium sulfate is used, a little more calcium is required. On certain soils a mixture of calcium lime and gypsum is also good. As calcium exerts its adjusting capacity to correct the soil, a whole new array of rotting and decay organisms start eating at the roots of the crabgrass. Desirable humic acids are made available to release soil nutrients for lawn grasses. These can now begin to fill in eroded patches formerly occupied by crabgrass. *Digitaria ischaemum*, sometimes called smooth crabgrass, and *Digitaria filiformis* are somewhat similar, albeit with shorter and narrower fingers.

Yellow Nutsedge

Found all over the United States in cultivated fields, gardens, grainfields, rich or sandy soils, Yellow nutsedge, *Cyperus esculentus*, is a serious perennial weed. It reproduces by seeds and weak thread-like stolons that end by hard tubers. Stems of this weed are tall, simple and triangular in shape; the pale green leaves are three-ranked, about as long as the stem, with closed sheaths mostly at base. Yellow nutsedge produces

Yellow Nutsedge

spikelets that are yellow to golden-brown, strongly flattened, mostly four-ranked along the wing-angled rachis, blunt, the tip acute to round.

Appearance of nutsedge indicates soils seriously out of sorts with very low levels of calcium and phosphate and very high levels of potassium and magnesium. Iron, sulfate, boron, selenium, salt and aluminum levels are likely to be high. Soils are also likely to have low humus and porosity, high moisture, anaerobic bacteria, and poor drainage and residual decay.

Redroot Pigweed (a.k.a., green pigweed, Chinaman's greens, careless weed, green amaranth, redroot, rough pigweed)

Redroot pigweed is a member of the Amaranth genus, specifically *Amaranthus retroflexus*. It is an annual that reproduces from seeds and can prove quite troublesome in cultivated crops, orchards, vineyards, etc. As with Amaranthus hybridus, *Amaranthus retroflexus* can cause nitrate poisoning of livestock when mature. *Amaranthus retroflexus* stands four to six feet high, and branches freely. The taproot of redroot pigweed is quite red. Flowers are small and green and grouped in spikes. Seeds are black, glossy and lens-shaped or oval. Leaf tips are notched with the midvein reaching the notch with a temporary bristle. *Amaranthus retroflexus* is easy to control. Joe Cocannouer, in *Weeds, Guardians of the Soil*, did not see redroot pigweed as a big nemesis, even though it signals a calcium-potassium ratio out of whack, potassium too high, calcium too low, with a resultant shortfall in humus. The phosphate complex also needs attention when the weed proliferates. Calcium, phosphorus, copper, molybdenum, carbohydrates, humates and vitamin C in some areas will reduce or chase away this weed when it dominates a field. Chemicals and salts in undigested manures, magnesium and potassium chloride often contribute to redroot proliferation.

Redroot Pigweed

Chickweed (a.k.a., common chickweed, starwort, starweed, winterweed, satin flower)

Chickweed is an annual or winter annual. In some cooler areas it survives through summer and behaves like a short-lived perennial. In the manuals they call it *Stellaria media*, but on the lawn it is a bearcat.

It is weakly tufted. It reproduces by seeds and all sorts of creeping stems, rooting at the nodes. As a universal weed, chickweed grows from coast to coast, border to border, seemingly impervious to heat and snow. Once established, it can cover the soil like an army blanket, keeping out air and sunlight and water. Chickweed is the antithesis of crabgrass. Chickweed grows where there is a good amount of working organic matter on the surface of the soil — more so than at great depths. It is frequently a case of too much grass clippings not being consumed, a lot of peat or manure on a garden, with acids coming off organic matter flushing out minerals that become a little too hot for grasses or vegetables. This situation issues an invitation for chickweed to set up shop. Sometimes organic matter on a lawn decays for a week, dries up, gets wet again, and once more dries. With organic matter decaying in a detoured media, chickweed takes off if the pH is right,

Chickweed

that is, not too low or too high. By way of contrast, crabgrass reflects soil that is tight, crusty and sedimentary. Acids from partially decayed organic material influence release of excess amounts of trace minerals that are needed, and it does this in a good colloidal way. It is possible to release the minerals but not have enough colloidal material in the soil to hold those minerals. They become water soluble and disperse, and the next stage of degeneration begins. Chickweed, crabgrass, quackgrass, nettles, plantain, buckhorn, dandelions and others grow the "green flags" of nature's system of limitations.

Chapter 23

Amending Soil

I've shoveled a lot of soil and compost in my time. I quite enjoy it. Moving rocks is no fun, but soil is easy. When I was a professional gardener, I would often bring two to four yards of compost into a backyard for a new garden installation, 10-20 big wheelbarrow loads. This is the best time to amend your soil, *before* you plant a garden. With new ground, you can get compost, fertilizers, and microbial inoculants mixed right down into the root zone. You can do this in an existing vegetable garden in the off-season too if the bed is empty.

When you're planting a tree, you want to amend the soil over a larger area than just the planting hole. You don't want to remove the native soil from the planting hole and replace it with just lush topsoil and compost, because the roots may never want to leave that hole. It's much better to amend a bigger area with compost and minerals than just the planting hole, leaving the native soil intact over the whole area. That's what the roots ultimately have to get used to.

How to Improve Heavy Clay or Sandy Soil

Gardeners often ask how to amend a heavy clay or sandy soil to improve water infiltration and drainage, air content and nutrient-holding capacity. In many gardens, clay doesn't infiltrate and drain fast enough, while sand drains too fast. Clay may have a good cation exchange capacity, but not enough air and increased potential of compaction.

Sandy soil may have plenty of air and resist compaction, but not hold onto nutrients long.

The common advice is to add clay to the sandy soil, or add sand to the clay soil. My experience has been that both of these approaches are generally bad ideas. Before we go into why, we need to take a quick look at how water moves through the soil. After rain or irrigation, water moves both downward to the water table and upward to eventually evaporate from the soil surface. This water flows through the open pores between soil particles. In any soil that isn't dominated too much by sand, silt or clay, roughly half the soil volume is pore space, and water and air share this pore space.

When soil is entirely saturated with water, gravity forces the water to move down quickly through the big pores, but the rest of the time, gravity doesn't play a big role in how water moves through the soil. Most of the time, adhesion and cohesion govern the movement of water. Adhesion is how water molecules tend to stick to other surfaces and cohesion is how water molecules tend to stick together.

We definitely don't want to bring in a layer of topsoil and just spread it on top of the existing soil. Let's look at what would happen if we did that. Say you have a clay or silt loam soil that doesn't infiltrate or drain well. What happens if you add six inches of a coarser soil such as a sandy loam on top of the finer soil? When it rains, it may infiltrate better, but as you might imagine, the water slows down when it hits that fine soil layer, although it does continue to move through the soil. Still, it slows down, which is the opposite of what you were going for.

Let's reverse it and say you have a sandy soil that doesn't hold water. This part is really interesting. What happens if you add six inches of a finer soil on top of coarser soil below, or if the original garden builder brought in some topsoil that was clay based and put it on top of your sandy subsoil? When it rains, you might think the water would speed up when it hits the coarse sandy layer, but in fact, water movement stops until the new soil becomes nearly saturated above. Even more interesting, if the finer soil is on an especially coarse sand or even gravel, the finer soil must become extremely wet before water will move down through the coarse layer. In this case, the overlying soil can hold two or three times as much as it normally would.

These same principles are often used when making golf greens. A layer of gravel is used underneath the sandy soil for the green in order to create a situation where water will stay in the upper, relatively fine layer of sandy soil and be available to the short roots of the grass on the green, rather than draining away. Doing this in a home garden is dangerous because you may create the opposite problem, which is a very waterlogged soil.

The logical solution is to till the two soils together, but it doesn't always work. It can work well if the imported soil has a similar sand, silt and clay content to the existing soil, but if you till the sand into clay or vice versa, the sand often gets embedded in the clay and forms a soil environment that's like concrete. I've heard and read the recommendation to add sand to a clay soil many times, but in my view, it's bad advice.

Besides, there's a much better way to improve clay and sandy soil, and that's organic matter in the form of compost, sheet mulch and cover crops. Work two to three inches of good compost into the top of a clay soil and it will improve infiltration and probably the amount of air and water available to your plants. Wait until the clay isn't too wet or too dry, otherwise you'll make the situation worse. If you don't have compost, other organic matter will work as long as it's finely ground up. Ground corncobs, buckwheat or rice hulls, peanut shells — anything that can be incorporated well will help to improve the clay.

As an aside, for the most part, no amount of organic matter, rototilling and aeration will fix a serious drainage issue such as flooding. That needs to be addressed by installing drainage tiles, swales or ditches, or even better, work with nature and put in a pond. Sometimes this can be fixed by balancing the nutrients in the soil to create a soil that drains better, by using the nutrient ratios previously outlined.

Since we've been learning about how water moves through the soil,

I'd like to mention an interesting side note about patio pots. Gardeners sometimes put a layer of gravel in the bottom of a container to improve drainage, but as we've seen it often does the opposite. The soil on top may have to become very saturated before the water will drain through. This is not necessarily a bad thing if you want the soil to hold more water, but it's important to know how this works.

So, if you need to bring soil into your yard in order to build your garden, I recommend you incorporate it into the existing soil extremely well. If you just drop it on top, you're potentially creating an interface that will slow drainage. Also, try to find a soil that has a similar texture to your existing soil. For example, if your soil is clay, bring in a clay based topsoil rather than a sandy topsoil. Also, use compost for at least 25% of the mixture.

One product that can be useful in some gardens is zeolites, a type of clay. Unlike most clays, which are sheet-like and easily compacted, zeolites have a honeycomb structure that stays intact. Probably their biggest claims to fame in horticulture are their exceptionally high cation exchange capacity and their resistance to the shrinking, swelling and compaction that happens with many clays. There are many additional benefits that zeolites provide, such as providing a high water-holding capacity, supplying minerals, and tying up certain toxins. A study out of Ukraine used zeolites to immobilize lead and zinc, with some success.

All of these qualities make zeolites an excellent addition to sandy soils that will receive a lot of foot traffic, such as golf course greens and soccer fields. Compost is great for this, too, and that's what I use, but zeolites don't break down like organic matter. They are also useful in a compost pile and vermicompost bin at 3-5% of the volume of the other materials to stop some of the nitrogen from leaving the pile, reduce odors and generally speed up and improve the process. If you use zeolites, make sure you get the right type for your use, because there are different kinds.

Making Your Own Potting Mix

There are many ways to make potting mix for starting seeds or container gardening. You'll find various recipes out there that can get rather involved. For some reason many people feel like the more things we add, the better the mix. Here are some of the ingredients you will see suggested: soil, clay, sand, compost, manure, leaf mold, peat, coir, newspaper, kenaf fiber, sawdust, perlite, vermiculite, and organic fertilizers and seed meals.

I'm not an expert on potting mixes, but I've had success by keeping it simple. Whether it be for starting seeds or containers, I use compost, good soil and sand. I mix the three, generally in approximately equal amounts, but with a little less sand than compost and soil. I use coarse sand, although some people prefer sharp sand. If I have leaf mold, I'll use an equal part of that, too. I use mycorrhizal fungi in both of these, along with some form of the liquid fertilizer mixture (that was given at the end of the biostimulants chapter). So in fact, I guess I do end up using a lot of ingredients when the liquid fertilizer is included, but that's more of a bonus. The base is simply compost, soil and sand.

As already discussed, I stay away from peat and coir. I don't use manure, newspaper or sawdust because I prefer to compost those first. If you want to experiment with perlite and vermiculite, they're alright for potting mixes, but not useful in the garden. Perlite doesn't offer much other than an ability to hold water and create air spaces. Vermiculite holds water and has a good CEC. Personally, I rely on good compost instead for these roles.

To Till or Not to Till

Garden tilling, also called cultivating, is often done with a gas-powered rototiller that goes down perhaps six or so inches. Soil can be tilled with a tool such as a pitch fork, too. Either way, you're turning the soil over so some of the lower soil comes up and some of the upper soil goes down. It's kind of like a food processor for your soil, just not as fast.

To till or not to till has been a hot topic for decades and still is to this day. I've researched this extensively and find that arguments on both sides make a lot of sense. I've also found personally that by correctly following a no-till or a low-till method, excellent results can be achieved.

The main reason tilling can be useful is to get organic matter incorporated into the soil of a new garden bed or a fallow vegetable garden. If there are plants in or near the garden, their vital surface roots will be damaged by tilling, so we don't do it in those gardens. If you're preparing a new garden, however, in a soil that is very low in organic matter, you might bring in six or so inches of compost and till it in as deeply as a rototiller will let you. You would do this knowing that it may take a few years for the soil structure to repair and produce a great crop, but it's often worthwhile if the organic matter was low to begin with. It's nice to get that organic matter down in there to create a deeper soil root zone that encourages plant roots to go down.

Double digging is another method you can use if you don't have or want to use a tiller. Remove the weeds, grass and roots in the area where a new bed will go and apply at least a two to three inch layer of compost, along with any fertilizers you need to incorporate based on a soil test. Then start at one end of the bed and dig a trench approximately 12 inches deep, removing the soil and putting it in a wheelbarrow. Next, use a pitch fork to loosen the soil in the bottom of the trench as much as you can, hopefully another 8 to 12 inches below the level of the first layer you removed.

Dig a second 12-inch deep trench right next to the first one, and put that soil in your first trench. Loosen the soil in the bottom of your new trench. Now continue the process all along the bed, filling the last trench with the soil in the wheelbarrow. Some people advocate doing this every few years when the soil gets compacted again. My view is that the soil shouldn't get compacted if the nutrient ratios are in line and the biology is happy. You can find videos online that show the entire double digging process more clearly.

Research shows you can get more carbon and humus formation in a tilled soil. I could especially see this being the case because in traditional no-till farming, which uses chemicals that decimate the soil food web, organic matter left on the surface isn't going to break down. In a soil with an abundant soil food web, however, earthworms, insects and fungi can get up to the surface and work on the organic matter. Another argument for tilling is that it gets the organic matter down into the soil where it can be broken down into humus, whereas if it stays on top, more of the carbon is volatized into the air.

Other research shows that if no-till is used with sufficient existing biomass, both the supply of nutrients and good soil structure can be maintained. This is especially true if you've tilled in compost and green manures for the first couple of years to bring up that biomass.

In the long run, I'm most likely to do just shallow tilling to a couple inches deep, mostly by hand. The main reason you might do this shallow tilling is to lightly incorporate the organic matter from a cover crop or from this year's veggies or compost, as this does hasten decomposition and promotes more humus formation and less volatization of carbon into the air. If you stay shallow, you won't have as detrimental an effect on soil structure, dormant weed seeds, microorganisms, and earthworms. Even so, do this minimally and carefully in order to limit the disturbance. There's generally no need to till in order to prepare the garden for seeding, other than perhaps with a light hoeing.

Sometimes, I sheet mulch to prepare new garden beds. As we've seen, this involves layering organic matter 12 or more inches high right on top of the grass or soil. It takes longer for the organic matter to get down into the soil, but you don't cause drastic soil structure damage. Many people have had great success doing this, but I mostly prefer to do it when I know I have a decent organic matter content in the soil already. Something else I sometimes do for fun is work on half of a garden with the tilling or double digging method, and the other half using the sheet mulching method, to see which does better over the years.

The other main reasons gardeners may till are: 1) to make the soil look fluffy and nice, 2) to allow more air and water into the soil, 3) to reduce weeds, and 4) to relieve compaction. Tilling is generally a short-term solution for all of these. I'll now address each of them in more detail.

1. One reason we can get rid of right away is "to make the soil look fluffy and nice." Not that the goal isn't achieved, but the goal is arguably unreasonable. We've learned to think of bare, fluffy soil as being the most attractive "look" for our gardens. I understand this — and tilling is a good fluffer-upper — but I also think leaf mulch and other natural mulches are attractive. That's what you see in a forest, not bare soil or several inches of bark mulch for that matter.

   As organic gardeners, one of our goals is working with nature. It doesn't mean we need to have a messy garden, but we definitely aren't going for cleanliness like that of a living room floor. If you want to put a wood mulch on to make it look tidy, it would generally be better not to use bark. Preferably a better type of wood mulch would be from hardwoods, not softwoods such as cedar and fir.

2. Another reason a person might till is to allow more air and water into the soil. This does happen in the short term, but the soil will eventually revert to its original structure because soil structure is a function of the soil texture, fertility and biology in the soil. It may even get worse if you burn up too much organic matter and kill all your fungi. A similar reason for tilling is to loosen and warm up the soil for spring planting and seeding. This can be done lightly with a hoe or garden fork if you want, but there's no need to slice and dice everything.

   The long-term solution for improving air and water is balancing the nutrient ratios, increasing organic matter and improving the soil food web. Still, this can take a few years, so tilling during the transition may be worthwhile. It might be even better to do it manually with a garden fork, to avoid the violent soil movement created by a rototiller.

3. Yet another reason to till is to kill weeds. Again, this is a short-term measure because the weeds are killed and new ones come in. In fact, while annual weeds will have been killed, many perennial weeds may have been cut into pieces that will all come back as new weeds. While your vegetable seeds now have perfect conditions in which to germinate, so do all of the weed seeds that were lying dormant lower down in the soil.

   Farmers have developed various plows that are effective at knocking down weeds on the surface, but a rototiller is more muscle than is needed for this purpose. The gardener's version of the farmer's plow is a hoe. The long-term weed management strategy is the same as up above — balancing the nutrient ratios, increasing organic matter and improving the soil food web — plus mulch and cover crops.

4. The last reason for tilling is to relieve compaction. As stated above, soil structure isn't simply a mechanical problem. It's a chemical, physical and biological problem. We need to establish a healthy, diverse population of microorganisms and soil animals, build our humus and balance those nutrient ratios in the soil. A balanced soil acts like a sponge. You can drive across it with a heavy tractor and it won't compact. If the calcium to magnesium ratio is less than 7:1 and/or there are more than 70 ppm sodium, the soil will compact, but if we can get those numbers in line along with the phosphate to potassium ratio, compaction is gone.

You can see how in the short term, the above organic gardening goals are often satisfied by tilling. But other than the important goal of getting organic matter incorporated, tilling can cause more problems than benefits, especially if done often and if done too deeply. Let's look at the problems of tilling.

The main disadvantage is the effect on beneficial microorganisms and earthworms, both of which are absolutely essential to the health of the soil. Upon deeply tilling a garden, some of the microbes that need oxygen are buried, killing many of them. Conversely, some of the microbes that can't live with too much oxygen are brought to the surface, killing many of them. Tilling causes miles and miles of beneficial fungi to be sliced into pieces. Those fungi provided important nutrients to the plants, which no longer happens after tilling. Earthworms are also killed and their tunnels destroyed. Despite what we may have heard as kids, cutting a worm in half doesn't make two worms — it makes one dead worm, or if you're lucky, one injured survivor.

All of these critters had taken a long time to find the perfect spot for themselves in the soil. They worked day and night to build themselves little homes and communities. It can take years for this to happen, and tilling destroys that all very quickly. Perennial flowers, shrubs and trees prefer fungal-dominated soil, so if we're trying to establish a shrub garden or grow trees, it makes sense to leave the mulch on the surface rather than tilling it in. If we till our gardens, we destroy many important fungi, resulting in a bacterial-dominated soil. This is more conducive to growing annual vegetables, but we still want some fungi in these soils, too.

Another potential problem that is often overlooked is the effect on the soil nutrient ratios. When compost and organic matter are left on the surface, they are broken down much more slowly than when they are tilled in, so the effect on soil nutrient levels is not so drastic. When they're tilled in, however, if they are high in certain nutrients such as potassium, they can throw the nutrient ratios off and cause problems.

Another big problem is that soil structure can be decimated if the soil is too wet, especially with clay soil. Tilling your garden when it's wet causes long-term structural damage to the soil that can last for years. It's much better to wait a couple of weeks and plant late, rather than working wet soil.

While the initial influx of air and water after tilling breaks down the organic matter more quickly, and releases nutrients that allow microbes and plants to flourish for a short time, that organic matter is oxidized faster than it is replenished. Annual deep garden tilling without adding more organic matter will cause a decrease in organic matter in the soil. This decreases soil fertility, nutrient-holding capacity and water-holding capacity, and hurts soil structure. If the soil is left bare, it can crust over so that water runs off and causes erosion instead of infiltrating.

So we can see that tilling has advantages and disadvantages. Tilling can be successful in vegetable gardens over the long term if organic matter is brought in at the same time. No-till and sheet mulching can be successful over the long term, especially if the soil had some humus to start with. I think the main reasons people place themselves strictly in one of these camps or the other may be because one theory makes the most sense to them, or because they've had success using one method in their garden.

The bottom line is that one of the methods will work well in your garden, and a combination of the two may even be optimal. I may till in some compost in the beginning if my soil is very low in organic matter, and no-till and sheet mulch later on. I definitely opt for no-till in the long term in order to establish a healthy soil food web. You can experiment to see what works for you.

Summary

- Both clay and sandy soils are best amended with compost, other organic matter and perhaps zeolites, but not more soil.
- My basic potting mix recipe is equal parts compost, soil and sand, with some biostimulants and microbial inoculants for optimal health.
- Tilling can be useful mainly to incorporate organic matter into the soil, while no-till and sheet mulching offer many other advantages. A combination of the two may be best for the garden.

Chapter 24
Garden Health Management Plan

There are now some additional new goals on which to focus: avoid using pesticides, harsh chemicals, and GMOs. We need to build organic matter, humus and the soil food web. We need to remineralize the soil, and more specifically to balance certain nutrient ratios. Using biostimulants to further stimulate the system is beneficial. Also, we need to ensure the soil has enough energy.

Which of these is the limiting factor in plant health? Heide Hermary points out that most of the above goals have been considered limiting factors by different soil scientists over the years. J.I. Rodale and his mentor Sir Albert Howard considered composting and organic matter the primary focus in the garden, but in my view, they didn't place enough emphasis on balancing minerals.

German scientist, Justus von Liebig concluded NPK was what we needed to add. William A. Albrecht emphasized the importance of calcium, while Carey Reams emphasized calcium and phosphorus. Ana Primavesi discovered that micronutrients are a limiting factor. Elaine Ingham has said we have at least some of almost every nutrient in the soil and that a healthy soil food web is the limiting factor. Phil Callahan has put forth the idea that paramagnetism is what is needed, and the biodynamic movement has helped bring our awareness to energy.

In reality, whichever one is lacking the most is the limiting factor in your garden, but the bottom line is that we need to pay attention to all of them.

Where do you start? Start with your own observations. Dig a hole. Check the texture, structure, color and smell, and look for earthworms and other insects. Measure the topsoil level and see if the roots are hitting a hardpan, and if they have fine root hairs that indicate enough oxygen. See if you have a good leaf and twig litter layer, and if your soil has some darkness that indicates organic matter. Compare this to the soil test value for organic matter. Do you need to add compost? It's difficult to grow good crops sustainably without having a good humus level. Microbial inoculants are always a good idea.

If it's mid or late season and you have plants growing, look at them. Obviously, disease and insect damage indicate sick plants, but in addition to that, are the leaves a dark, vibrant color or do they have blotches, streaks or discoloration that indication one or several nutrient imbalances? If your fruit trees only produce fruit every other year, that's an energy or fertility problem. The same goes if your lettuce and other greens bolt to seed early or if your fruits and vegetable don't develop fully.

Soil tests are one tool for figuring out what kinds of problems you might need to address. Cation exchange capacity gives us an indication of the soil's capacity to hold cations. The CEC number should confirm the ribbon and/or sedimentation test you did. A low CEC means sandy soil with little organic matter. It will need to be watered and fertilized more often, but the good news is it's easier to balance the nutrients. Soils with a higher CEC need less irrigation and fertilizer, but are harder to balance because you need a lot more fertilizer to make a change.

Look at your base saturation test and see if you have 60-75% calcium 7-20% magnesium, 2-5% potassium, and 0.5-3% sodium. If anything is low, you need to find materials from the fertilizer chapters that will contribute more of the lacking minerals.

The Reams test gives a better indication as to what was available in your soil right when the test was taken. Comparing it to the base saturation test, look for discrepancies. If any of the cations are plentiful on the base saturation test, but not on the Reams test, adding raw materials may not be as important as doing something to activate the nutrients you already have.

You're aiming for somewhere between a 7:1 and 10:1 calcium to magnesium ratio, with Reams test values of 2,000-6,000 pounds per acre of calcium. You're aiming for somewhere between a 2:1 and 4:1 phosphate to potash ratio, with Reams test values of 400 and 200 pounds per acre, respectively. You're aiming for a potash to sulfate ratio of 1:1. I tend to pay little attention to anion values from the more conventional part of a soil test, but I definitely look at them on a Reams test — particularly the phosphate mentioned above, as well as nitrate nitrogen and the cation ammonia nitrogen.

Liquid calcium often helps to activate calcium in the soil and can give you a huge jump on your Reams test. I'll often try this before investing in calcitic lime. Sugar and vitamin B12 can do this, too. Molasses often helps to activate phosphorus. All of these can be mixed together. Organic matter and microbes help to release everything. Simply adding some compost may bring potassium up on a Reams test. Gypsum supplies calcium and sulfur.

If you're a serious food grower, get a soil biology test done and consult with the lab on how to improve your soil food web with specific composts, compost teas and microbial inoculants. Regardless, consider using any or all of these things anyway. Molasses and other sugars and biostimulants help stimulate existing biology.

Consider getting a refractometer and start measuring brix, not only of the food you grow, but of the food you buy. Measure your plants regularly during the height of the growing season and see which biostimulants have the most positive effect. Same goes for a conductivity meter to measure ERGS.

All of the limiting factors influence each other. For example, nutrient imbalances create poor living conditions for microbes. If calcium is below 60% and/or magnesium gets too high, it renders microbial inoculants, biostimulants and micronutrient sprays much less effective. On the other hand, a lack of organic matter and of a healthy soil food web make it difficult to change nutrient ratios, because while you may add the correct materials, the microbes need to do some of the work of rearranging them and the organic matter needs to be there to hold them. Just as plants, animals and microbes are interdependent in our garden, so are water, organic matter, biology, nutrients and energy.

Health Management Program

Every soil is different, but many of our soil management practices are similar across most soils, especially in the beginning. Later, specific micronutrients can be addressed. Here's a program I've developed over years of working both on my own garden and the gardens and lawns of clients. There's flexibility built into the program based on how far you want to go and on your soil conditions.

There's no such thing as a recipe that works on all gardens. I've tried instead to give you the procedures to find the solutions that will be best for your garden. That being said, I also want to give you some basic recipes so you can see where to start.

All of the measurements given are per 1,000 square feet.

Fall

If you're reading this in the summer, wait until fall to do these first tasks. If you're reading it in the winter, you can do these things in spring along with the "One Month Before Planting" section.

If your organic matter is low, add good compost that you've made or purchased. To build organic matter, I suggest at least three yards, which is about one inch over the whole area. If you don't have or don't want to pay for that much, that's okay. We've seen how less than ½ yard is plenty to bring in the biology and nutrients. If this is a vegetable garden, you may deeply till or double dig this into the soil the first year. Otherwise, you may lightly incorporate it into the top few inches of soil. On the lawn, rake it down into the grass. If you want, you can split this in half and apply half in spring and half in fall.

You'll also want to maintain a mulch layer in the garden throughout the year. Leaves are generally the best choice for this, but straw or even a small amount of wood chips would be helpful, too. Sheet mulching is another great method of starting a new bed that I often use.

Send a soil sample into a good soil lab that offers Reams testing and hopefully base saturation testing, too. This test is important, so it's not optional. When you get the results back, do what they say to the best of your ability. A soil test is the best way for most of us to know which of the mineral products to use, as we don't want to go adding minerals without knowing we need them.

The main products you'll be looking for are liquid calcium, calcitic lime, gypsum, and hard rock phosphate (or preferably soft rock phosphate). You may need other minerals, and you may consider calcium nitrate and MAP at 11-52-0. Then look at molasses and other biostimulants to help unlock soil nutrients.

One note I'll add to typical soil lab recommendations is to spread the applications out into two to four times throughout the year, if it's feasible. For example, if you need to add 40 pounds of calcitic lime, you could do 20 pounds in early spring and then again in late summer. Plants and microbes prefer continual access to a small amount of nutrients rather than everything at once. Not only that, but when you apply nutrients, they affect other nutrients. If you apply a whole whack of calcitic lime, it can bounce other nutrients such as potassium off the cation exchange sites.

Optional Task: Apply 50-500 pounds of rock dust, preferably paramagnetic dust, and incorporate it into the soil or compost pile.

Optional Task: Plant a cover crop to protect and improve the soil over winter. Consider a mixture of a legume and a grass.

One Month Before Planting

If you didn't do the soil test and follow their recommendations, spread five pounds of calcitic lime with a broadcast spreader or by hand if that's all you have. I feel confident recommending that without a soil test because it's rare to find a soil that wouldn't benefit from that small amount for some energy.

After that, preferably in the morning or evening, spray Phil's Foliar (see next table). This mixture could be allowed to sit for a few hours before spraying in order for the microbes to start breaking down the other ingredients. The amounts may be different for the brand of each product you buy, so be sure to check the label.

Phil's Foliar Recipe

⅓ cup EM or another microbial product

1 cup sea minerals or 1 cup liquid fish hydrolysate

4 tsp liquid kelp

⅓ cup molasses

4 gallons water

Optional Ingredients:

1 pint compost tea

½ teaspoon humic acids

½ tsp soil conditioner

¼ cup yucca extract

½ to 1 mg vitamin B Complex

⅔ cup liquid calcium

Specific micronutrients as needed

Seeding and Planting

When preparing to seed vegetables, I soak the seeds overnight in a mixture of one teaspoon of kelp or sea minerals per quart of water. The next morning I take them out of the water and sprinkle the seeds with a small amount of mycorrhizal fungi powder. I spread them out to dry slightly for a few hours to make sowing the seed easier. When possible, I do this during the second quarter, just before the full moon, saving root vegetables for the fourth quarter.

Spray Phil's Foliar recipe onto the soil after you seed plants, or directly onto the roots and foliage of transplants, sod, shrubs and trees as you plant them. Get mycorrhizal fungi onto the roots of all of these things while you plant them. For lawns and seeds, a powder can be purchased and sprayed. For transplants, shrubs and trees, it can even be rubbed directly on to the roots. Be sure to get the right kind of mycorrhizal fungi for your plants, which is easy to do. When in doubt, go for an endo/ecto mycorrhizal fungi blend.

Optional: A few days before planting, put out a growth-promoting nitrogen source at two pounds per 1,000 square feet, along with one cup of molasses or ½ cup of sugar to balance out the nitrogen. Depending on your soil's needs, products such as calcium nitrate, potassium nitrate or ammonium sulfate may be most appropriate. Even adding fish fertilizer would be good.

Throughout the Year

Spray Phil's Foliar recipe again every one to four weeks.

Optional: You can go back and forth each application between sea minerals and fish hydrolysate as the main micronutrient component of the spray, as they don't like to be together in the spray. I mostly stick with sea minerals. You can also occasionally substitute other microbial products for the EM and work with various other biostimulants.

Optional: To switch from growth to fruiting just before or early on in the initial reproductive stages of the plants, you can apply a spray to help fruit and seed set. Spray 4 tablespoons of apple cider vinegar and 2 tablespoons of ammonia in 2 quarts of water per 1,000 square feet. If you have it, you could instead spray 3 tablespoons liquid calcium mixed with 2-4 teaspoons boron, along with 1 cup liquid fish hydrolysate, 4 teaspoons kelp and 1-2 tablespoons of apple cider vinegar.

Other Optional Steps

Purchase a refractometer to measure the brix of the fruits and vegetables you're growing and check your progress over the next few years. Start making compost tea for spraying on your plants and soil, with either a purchased, tested brewer or a homemade brewer. Experiment with biodynamic preparations and other energizers, as well as radionics.

Case Studies

Case Study 1

This is the same test we looked at in the soil nutrient testing chapter (Chapter 5). Here are most important numbers:

Base Saturation Test

Nutrient	Unit	Ideal	Actual
K	%	2-5	2.2
Ca	%	60-70	36.6
Mg	%	10-20	11.6
Na	%	0.5-3	0.2

Reams Test

		Ideal	Actual	Notes
Nitrates		40	15	
Ammonia		40	6	
Phosphorus	1:1 P:K	200	61	1:4 P:K
Potassium		200	241	
Calcium	10:1 Ca:Mg	>2,000	451	2:1 Ca:Mg
Magnesium	14% Ca	280	219	
Sodium		<70	6	Very Low
ERGS		200	75	Very Low

This kind of soil is typical of what I've seen in several different geographic regions. The ratios may change, but the imbalances are common. Most nutrients are low. The calcium to magnesium ratio is far too narrow and the phosphorus to potassium ratio is not only too narrow, but the potassium is actually much higher than the phosphorus. ERGS is also low.

This soil has many problems that will take years to correct. The 3:1 calcium to magnesium ratio on the base saturation test closely coincides with the 2:1 ratio on the Reams test. These need to be widened. The soil could be lifeless because of chemical use, lack of water or other reasons. Nitrogen will also be low due to this narrow calcium to magnesium ratio.

Before supplementing nutrients, I would want to look at the soil and plants to see if their condition supports the data from the soil test. The soil is probably going to be compacted, lacking in air and devoid of life. Plants are probably not optimally healthy. Brix will be low. If this is all true, bringing in 40 pounds of calcitic lime and 20 pounds of gypsum will start moving the calcium to magnesium ratio up. These should be split into two to four applications. The gypsum helps bring air into the soil.

Some form of chemical nitrogen could be applied in the meantime at two pounds, or liquid fish if you want to stay organic. Either of these should be mixed with 1 cup of molasses or ½ cup of sugar. The phosphorus to potassium ratio is 1:4 when it should be 1:1, which is the same as saying the phosphate to potash ratio should be 2:1. I would add 5-10 pounds of soft rock phosphate and perhaps 2 pounds of MAP 11-52-0. Liquid calcium and molasses could be tried to bring up calcium and phosphorus.

None of these nutrients are going to be very effective, however, if the health and diversity of the soil food web isn't improved. That means applying sufficient water, organic matter, and perhaps microbial inoculants and biostimulants. All of these should help bring up the ERGS. I've given examples here of the fertilizers I most commonly use. If you work with a good soil lab, you don't need to get a diploma to figure out which fertilizers to use because the lab will guide you. I don't often recommend chemicals, but when the soil is this far gone, they can vastly reduce the time needed to make things right and get some reasonably healthy plants growing.

Case Study 2 — Heavy Clay

Here's an example of a heavy clay soil.

Base Saturation Test

Nutrient	Unit	Ideal	Actual
K	%	2-5	8
Ca	%	60-70	62.5
Mg	%	10-20	10.1
Na	%	0.5-3	3.8

Reams Test

		Ideal	Actual	Notes
Nitrates		40	70	
Ammonia		40	0	
Phosphorus	1:1 P:K	200	60	1:2.2 P:K
Potassium		100	130	
Calcium	10:1 Ca:Mg	>2,000	3,200	7.6:1 Ca:Mg
Magnesium	14% Ca	280	420	
Sodium		<70	100	Very High
ERGS		200	2,100	Very High

The base saturation is more in line for this soil than in the previous sample, but potassium and sodium are high. The Reams test shows a 7.6:1 calcium to magnesium ratio, with potassium and sodium also showing high. The phosphorus to potassium ratio should be 1:1 instead of 1:2. Phosphorus is often lower than potassium in damaged soils. Ammonia is 0, which is common, I think because the soil test doesn't measure the nitrogen in the organic matter.

The ERGS is way too high, indicating a salt problem — not just sodium, but other salts. Even though the calcium to magnesium ratio is good, this heavy clay is probably compacted with the current phosphate to potash ratio and the high ERGS reading. Salty fertilizers such as triple superphosphate and potassium chloride may have been used and should be discontinued. Rock phosphate can be brought in to increase phosphorus. The soil food web must be improved, too.

Gypsum is often used at 10-30 pounds to fluff the soil and bring more air in. A soil conditioner can also be used for this purpose, as well as biostimulants such as kelp, humic acids and some form of sugar to feed the soil biology. Compost could be tremendously helpful, and tilling may be necessary to bring air in, too.

Happy Growing

I hope I've been able to give you some good strategies in these pages and I urge you to continue to learn more. This chapter provides a good summary and recommendations for a garden health management program. I like to boil it down into the following six goals. We need to:

- Provide sufficient water to the entire soil and mulch, some of it possibly coming from cisterns and/or ponds.
- Increase the organic matter and humus content of our soil with compost, mulch, sheet mulch, cover crops and humates.
- Increase the diversity and health of the soil food web with compost, mycorrhizal fungi, compost tea, EM and other inoculants.
- Remineralize the soil with rock dusts and balance certain nutrient ratios with calcitic lime, rock phosphate and other fertilizers, based on a soil test and garden observations.
- Use biostimulants to further stimulate the system, especially sea minerals, kelp and fish fertilizers, humic acids and molasses.
- Ensure the soil has enough energy by measuring and adjusting ERGS, increasing paramagnetism and increasingly using biodynamics, energizers and radionics.

Bibliography

Andersen, Dr. Arden B. *The Anatomy Of Life & Energy In Agriculture*. Austin, TX: Acres U.S.A., 2004.

Andersen, Dr. Arden B. *Science In Agriculture*. Austin, TX: Acres U.S.A., 2000.

Astera, Michael and Agricola. *The Ideal Soil*. *www.SoilMinerals.com*, 2010.

Bartholomew, Mel. *Square Foot Gardening*. Emmaus, PA: Rodale Press, 2005.

Buhner, Stephen Harrod. *The Lost Language Of Plants*. White River Junction, VT: Chelsea Green Publishing Company, 2002.

Callahan, Philip S. *Paramagnetism, Rediscovering Nature's Secret Force Of Growth*. Austin, TX: Acres U.S.A., 1995.

Callahan, Philip S. *Tuning In To Nature*. Austin, TX: Acres U.S.A., 2001.

Chaboussou, Francis. *Healthy Crops: A New Agricultural Revolution*. Charlbury, England: Jon Carpenter Publishing, 2004.

Cocannouer, Joseph A. *Weeds Guardians Of The Soil*. Old Greenwich, CT: Devin-Adair Publishing Company, 1950.

Fryer, Lee and Dick Simmons. *Food Power From the Sea*. Austin, TX: Acres U.S.A., 2005.

Fukuoka, Masanobu. *The One-Straw Revolution*. New York, NY: New York Review Book, 1978.

Hamaker, John D. and Donald Weaver. *The Survival of Civilization*. Burlingame, CA: Hamaker-Weaver Publishers, 1982.

Hemenway, Toby. *Gaia's Garden: A Guide To Home-Scale Permaculture*. White River Junction, VT: Chelsea Green Publishing Company, 2000.

Hermary, Heide. *Working With Nature*. Cowichan Station, B.C.: Gaia College Inc., 2007.

Howard, Sir Albert. *An Agricultural Testament*. London, England: Oxford University Press, 1943.

Ingham, Dr. Elaine. *The Compost Tea Brewing Manual*, 5th Edition. Corvallis, OR: Soil Foodweb Inc., 2005.

Jeavons, John. *How to Grow More Vegetables Than You Ever Thought Possible on Less Land Than You Can Imagine*. New York, NY: Ten Speed Press, 2006.

Kervran, C. Louis. *Biological Transmutations*. Magalia, CA: Happiness Press, 1988.

Kinsey, Neal and Charles Walters. *Hands-On Agronomy*. Austin, TX: Acres U.S.A., 2006.

Krasil'nikov, N.A. *Soil Microorganisms And Higher Plants*. Moscow, USSR: Academy Of Sciences Of The USSR, 1958.

Lisle, Harvey. *The Enlivened Rock Powders*. Austin, TX: Acres U.S.A., 1994.

Lovel, Hugh. *A Biodynamic Farm*. Austin, TX: Acres U.S.A., 2000.

Lowenfels, Jeff and Wayne Lewis. *Teaming With Microbes*. Portland, Oregon: Timber Press, Inc., 2006.

Managing Cover Crops Profitably, 3rd Edition. Beltsville, MD: Sustainable Agriculture Network, 2007.

Martin, Deborah L. and Grace Gershuny, eds. *The Rodale Book Of Composting*. New York, NY: Rodale Press, Inc., 1992.

McCaman, Jay. *Weeds and Why they Grow*. Sand Lake, MI: Jay McCaman, 1989.

Mollison, Bill. *Permaculture: A Designers' Manual*. Tasmania, Australia: Tagari Publications, 1988.

Murray, Maynard. *Sea Energy Agriculture*. Austin, TX: Acres U.S.A., 2003.

Pfeiffer, Ehrenfried E. *Weeds And What They Tell*. Kimberton, PA: Biodynamic Farming and Gardening Association, Inc., 1970.

Rateaver, Bargyla and Gylver Rateaver. *The Organic Method Primer: The Basics*. San Diego, CA: Bargyla & Gylver Rateaver, 1994.

Shepherd, T.G. *2000: Visual Soil Assessment*. Volume 1. Field Guide for Cropping and Pastoral Grazing on Flat to Rolling Country. Palmerston North, New Zealand: VSA Publications, 2009.

Skow, Dan and Charles Walters. *Mainline Farming For Century 21*. Austin, TX: Acres U.S.A., 1995.

Smith, Jeffrey M. *Seeds Of Deception*. Fairfield, IA: Yes! Books, 2003.

Smith, Jeffrey M. *Genetic Roulette*, Fairfield, IA: Yes! Books, 2007.

Stamets, Paul. *Mycelium Running*, New York, NY: Ten Speed Press, 2005

Soil Biology Primer. Ankeny, IA: Soil and Water Conservation Society, 2000.

Tompkins, Peter and Christopher Bird. *Secrets Of The Soil*. Anchorage, AK: Earthpulse Press, 2002.

Tompkins, Peter and Christopher Bird. *The Secret Life Of Plants*. New York, NY: Harper Perennial, 2002.

Walters, Charles. *Eco-Farm, An Acres U.S.A. Primer*. Austin, TX: Acres U.S.A., 2003.

Walters, Charles. *Fertility From The Ocean Deep*. Austin, TX: Acres U.S.A., 2005.

Walters, Charles. *Weeds, Control Without Poisons*. Austin, TX: Acres U.S.A., 1999.

Wheeler, Philip A. and Ronald B. Ward. *The Non-Toxic Farming Handbook*. Austin, TX: Acres U.S.A., 1998.

Zimmer, Gary F. *The Biological Farmer: A Complete Guide to the Sustainable & Profitable Biological System of Farming*. Austin, TX: Acres U.S.A., 2000.

Resources

The Smiling Gardener Academy
Comprehensive online organic gardening course.
Website: *www.SmilingGardener.net*

Phil's Organic Gardening Website
Email: *phil@smilinggardener.com*
Website: *www.SmilingGardener.com*

Contact information for the resources mentioned in this book:

Acres U.S.A.
PO Box 301209, Austin, Texas 78703
Phone: 512-892-4400
Fax: 512-892-4448
Email: *info@acresusa.com*
Website: *www.acresusa.com*

Gaia College
2485 Koksilah Road, Cowichan Station,
British Columbia Canada V9L 6M7
Phone: 250-709-2229
Email: *info@gaiacollege.ca*
Website: *www.gaiacollege.ca*

Soil Foodweb Oregon
635 SW Western Boulevard, Corvallis, Oregon 97333
Phone: 541-752-5066
Fax: 541-752-5142
Email: *info@oregonfoodweb.com*
Website: *www.soilfoodweb.com*

Soil Testing Labs

Crop Services International
1718 Madison SE
Grand Rapids, MI 49507
Phone: 616-246-7933
Fax: 616-246-6039
Email: *DrDirt@cropservicesintl.com*
Website: *www.cropservicesintl.com*

International Ag Labs
800 W. Lake Avenue
PO Box 788
Fairmont, MN 56031
Phone: 507-235-6909
Fax: 507-235-9155
Email: *info@aglabs.com*
Website: *www.aglabs.com*

Kinsey Agricultural Services, Inc.
297 County Highway 357
Charleston, MO 63834
Phone: 573-683-3880
Fax: 573-683-6227
Email: *neal@kinseyag.com*
Website: *www.kinseyag.com*

Pike Agri-Lab Supplies, Inc   *Source for: Refractometer*
154 Claybrook Road
PO Box 67
Jay, ME 04239
Phone: 207-897-9267
Fax: 207-897-9268
Website: *www.pikeagri.com*

Products

Keep it Simple Compost Tea Brewer
12323 180th Ave NE
Redmond, WA 98052
Phone: 866-558-0990
Fax: 425-558-3695
Email: *kis@simplici-tea.com*
Website: *www.simplici-tea.com*

Remineralize the Earth
24 Hillsville Rd
North Brookfield, MA 01535
Phone: 978-257-2627
Email:*dan@realfoodcampaign.org*
Website: *www.remineralize.org*

SCD Probiotics
1627 Main Street, Suite 700
Kansas City, MO 64108
Phone: 913-541-9299
Fax: 816-876-2261
Email: *customerservice@scdprobiotics.com*
Website: *www.scdprobiotics.com*

Sea-Crop
Ambrosia Technology
PO Box 6,
Raymond, WA 98577
Phone: 360-942-5698
Email: *Info@sea-crop.com*
Website: *www.sea-crop.com*

Tainio Technology & Technique, Inc.
12102 S Andrus Road
Cheney, WA 99004
Phone: 509-747-5471
Fax: 509-747-8122
Email: *info@tainio.com*
Website: *www.tainio.com*

TeraGanix, Inc.
19371 US Highway 69 South
Alto, TX 75925
Phone: 866-369-3678
Fax: 817-394-1426
Email: *info@teraganix.com*
Website: *www.teraganix.com*

The Organic Gardener's Pantry
Victoria, British Columbia Canada
Phone: 250-216-3733
Email: *info@gardenerspantry.ca*
Website: *www.gardenerspantry.ca*

GoLdeN BaRReL BaKiNg PRoducTS (MoLaSSeS)
4960 HoRSeSHoE PiKe
HoNeY BRooK, PA 19344
(800) 327-4406
w³. GoldeN BaRReL.com

Index